NATIONALISM
THEORY AND PRINCIPLES

NATIONALISM
Theory and Principles

Abdul Mannan Bagulia

ANMOL PUBLICATIONS PVT. LTD.
NEW DELHI - 110 002 (INDIA)

ANMOL PUBLICATIONS PVT. LTD.
4374/4B, Ansari Road, Daryaganj
New Delhi - 110 002
Ph.: 23261597, 23278000
Visit us at: www.anmolpublications.com

Nationalism: Theory and Principles

First Published, 2006

ISBN 81-261-2560-8

PRINTED IN INDIA

Published by J.L. Kumar for Anmol Publications Pvt. Ltd., New Delhi - 110 002 and Printed at **Arora** Offset Press, Delhi.

Contents

Preface

The sense of belonging to a particular nation and being proud of its cultural heritage makes one a nationalist. Those nations and societies, which strove hard to preserve the nationalistic spirits emerged as strong and great nations. But the nations which were riddled with differences on regional, religious and ethnic lines could not emerge strong and great. It is not the administrative policies, but the people's large-heartedness and their sense of oneness as a nation and society, cutting across the boundaries of religious, regional and ethnic differences, which preserves and protects the unity and integrity of a nation. As a nation, rich with great civilization, all Indians have the right to be proud enough of its glorious cultural heritage. However, every matured Indian should see to it that self-respect does not border arrogance, jingoism and xenophobia.

The undersigned has made all attempts to incorporate in detail, all the components of the Indian Nationalism. The philosophies of Manu, Kautilya, Gandhi and views of Ambedkar on nationalism are elaborately and comprehensively dealt with, in order to present to the readers, all the developments and movements related to nationalism and its current relevance in an inimitable style. The present social scenario in India warrants such a work on a subject of great interest . Hence, this endevour is expected to be accepted widely.

—Editor

1

Philosophy of Manu

Introduction : The Smriti literature is an important source of the study of Hindu political institutions and thought. Amongst the Smriti literature, Manu Smriti occupies a predominant position. Manu expressed views on the origin of state, the role and qualities of kingship, Dandaṇiti and other important aspects of practical administration and diplomacy. Manu Smriti occupies a position of exceptional significance. It shall be desirable to know about his ideas on various political issues.

Nation's Origin

According to Manu Smriti, before people came in the civil state they were living in the state of nature. In that situation there was no harmony but disharmony; mutual differences, quarrels and distrust was the order of the day. The picture of the pre-civil state, as portrayed by Manu is nearly the one portrayed by Hobbes rather than that by Locke and Rousseau. A mythical version of Manu says that the creator, after seeing the disorder in civil state, decided to give them a king.

One of the duties of the king was to maintain law and order and to punish those who tried to encroach upon the rights of others. Thus according to Manu, state was not the product of evolution or growth but a sudden creation. The theory has given a touch of divinity to the concept of origin of state and has no economic basis.

Caste System

Manu believed that caste system was a part of our social fabric and that Hindu society has been much benefited by that. Caste system helps society in protecting social set-up, without which there will be disturbance and disharmony and also chaos. He therefore, believed that caste system was not an optional but an integral part of our political and social set-up.

Concept of Kingship

Manu believed in the divine theory of kingship. Since God created and gave kingship, it was essential that the people should give their unqualified support to the king. A king should not be considered only a human being and treated as such but he was a great deity in human form. The king combined in himself the qualities of Indra, Yama and Varuna. He performed all functions on earth only to keep the people confined to their respective spheres of activity and that too under instructions from God. The people have no right whatsoever to hate king or to disobey, disregard or defy his commands.

King's Qualities

A king must be a person, according to Manu, who has complete control over himself and over his senses. He should be in a position to satisfy his people about his actions so that they should feel that they were being governed and ruled with their consent rather than with the use of rod. He should also have the capacity to keep the people under his obedience which could only be possible through his intelligence and pleasing manners. Since his people are supposed to follow the examples set by him, it is essential that a king should be above *Kam, Krodh, Lobh* and *Moh* because under the influence of all these evils, the king not only forgets his personal welfare, but also collective welfare of the community, thereby rendering himself unfit for the high office to which he was elected.

King and Ministers

His ministers stood for absolute and uncontrolled or unchecked king to rule over the subjects without any fear of public revolt. The people had no right to question his authority in any form. But that was not the case. Hindu polity never believed in the theory of absolute authority of kingship and that is the reason why it has been said in Manu Smriti that a king without ministers was just trying to drive a chariot with one wheel alone. Such a chariot was bound not to go far.

Therefore, it was obligatory on the king to consult his ministers in all circumstances. Manu has, therefore, suggested that each king must have seven or eight ministers who should be consulted individually as well as collectively. Since ordinary business of life could not be transacted single handed. A king who tried to conduct state affairs all alone could not be successful in life.

Minister's Qualities

A king should be wise and careful in selecting his ministers. A good minister should be good warrior and capable enough to adjust the conflicting ideas. He should have the qualities of acting as an honest broker between the king and the subjects.

Selection Processes

Hereditary system was one method for the selection of a minister. Then another method was testing the ability of a person by the king himself. Still another method was that a king should ask his trusted friends and relatives to occupy ministerial posts. He has also suggested that persons belonging to noble class and caste should alone be given an opportunity to become ministers. A king should use his discretion in allocating portfolios and a ministers should only be given that portfolio which was likely to corrupt him least.

King's Administrative Performance

It was the duty of a king to protect subjects from external aggression and provide law and order. He was to see that state was free from thieves and robbers. He was required to protect private property and cheek inter-mixing of caste. A king should not only regulate trade but also to encourage traders and agriculturists.

Punishment Concept

For Manu *danda* was essential for the proper administration of state affairs. *Danda* helps the people in keeping them in their own sphere of activity. Relaxation in the use of danda was dangerous and the capable might not get an opportunity to come forward. It was the will of God to equip a king with authority of punishing subjects. Use of *danda however* should be impartial as partial use of *danda* was found to displease the subjects.

Taxation : Manu believed in the wage theory of taxation. For him right of protection and payment of revenues were directly linked with each other. He has also suggested percentage of revenue to be charged from each category of land. A considerable part *of* taxes should be spent on the welfare of the subjects.

On Justice and Judicial System : It was the foremost duty of king to see that judicial system was properly maintained. A king had no right to rule over his subjects, if he failed to give justice. The justice should be cheap and quick and its working should be reviewed. Review of judicial system was of primary importance. In his judicial system he has given special treatment to *Brahmins.* For him it will be fatal to separate justice from dharma. King should be impartial while pronouncing justice and if he tried to be partial he was bound to earn the wrath of God.

Inter-State Relations in Manu Smriti : According to Manu wars should be fought to preserve righteousness. For him, an enemy should never be underestimated. Every effort should be made to create factions in the ranks of the enemy. A king should try to get as many friends as possible.

Conclusion : Manu Smriti is one of the greatest contributions towards the ancient Indian political tradition. It reflects a mixture of ethics and religion with politics. Though a bit mythic the concepts give us a detailed account of administrative, socioeconomic and political aspects *of* a state. Though the *magnum* opus of Manu-that is, *Manu Smriti* has been scarcely criticized on various grounds by both Indian as well as Western scholars, is even being dubbed as a philosophical farrago, yet it has got its relevance even today.

2

Philosophy of Kautilya

He is also known as Chanakya (300 B.C) was the great Hindu statesman and philosopher who wrote a classic treatise on polity. *Arthashastra*, a compilation of almost everything that had been written in India up to his time on *artha* (property, economics, or material success).

He was born in the Brahmin caste and received his education at Taxila (now in Pakistan). He is known to have had a knowledge of medicine and astrology, and it is believed he was familiar with elements of Greek and Persian learning introduced into India by Zoroastrians. Some authorities believed that he was strongly influenced by a Zoroastrian or at least was strongly influenced by that religion. Kautilya became a counsellor and advisor to King Chandragupta of the Mauryan Empire of northern India but lived simply himself. He was instrumental in helping Chandragupta overthrow the power of Nanda dynasty at Pataliputra.

Kautilya's book came to be Chandra Gupta's guide. Each of its 15 sections deals with a phase of government, which Kautilya terms as "the science of punishment." He openly advises the development of an elaborate system reaching into all levels of society and encourages political and secret assassination. Lost for centuries, the book was discovered in 1905.

Arthashastra, the famous book; deals with a lot of administrative, socioeconomic and political aspects. Kautilya, apart from these, also excelled in other fields of activities. Let's now discuss those aspects which are categorized for a better understanding of his ideas and thoughts:

Aspects of Nation

Kautilya believed in seven elements of state (rajya) viz., *svamin* (the lord or sovereign); *amatya* (minister); *janapada* (territory as well as population); *durga* (fort); *kosha* (treasury); *bala* (army), and *rnitra* (ally).

To Kautilya the *svamin* could be one person or a number of persons. However the *svamin* of Kautilya is not a feudal chieftain but a veritable sovereign owing allegiance to none.

The second element of state is *amatya* (minister or any kind of high official). Kautilya says that the *amatya* must be native of the country and possess steadfast devotion towards the *svamin*.

Third element of state was *Janapada*, which has been interpreted differently by scholars. While some equate it with territory the others imply by it population. In fact the Sanskrit word *Janapada* is used in both these senses and one may assume that Kautilya implied by it territory as well as population.

Fourth element of state is *durga* or fort. Kautilya considered fort as a vital part of the empire and attached great importance to them for the defence of the empire. He refers to four kinds of forts-a water fort, a hill fort, a desert fort and a forest fort.

The *Kosha* or the treasury was the fifth element of state. Kautilya says that a good state should be big and variegated so that it may be capable of withstanding calamities for long and uninterrupted. Kautilya attached great importance to the growth of treasury and held that the following could help in augmentation *of* treasury—opulence of' industrial departments run by the state; abundance of harvest; prosperity of commerce and so forth.

The sixth element of state was *bala* or army. Kautilya defines six types of armies hereditary forces: hired troops; soldiers for fighting corporation; troops belonging to an ally; troops belonging to an enemy: and soldiers of wild tribes.

The last component of state is *Mitra* or ally. Kautilya envisaged two types of allies *(mitras) sahaja* and *kritrima. Sahaja mitra* consists of persons whose friendship was derived from the time of father and grand-father and were situated close to the territory of the immediately neighbouring enemy. The *kritrima* ally on the other hand was an acquired ally whose friendship was resorted for the protection of the wealth and life. Kautilya held that the ally of the first category was superior to the ally of the second category.

State and Kingship

Kautilya's *Arthashastra* throws a flood of light on Hindu polity and has developed the subject on scientific lines. *Arthashastra* has discussed executive, legislative and judicial functions of the state and has left no aspect of human life untouched. The treatise also discusses the origin of the state and kingship, constituent element of the state and organization of *spies.* Kautilya has tried to elevate the institution of kingship.

On Kingship : A prince should observe celibacy till 16th year of his age. He should have sense of discipline and receive lessons in war methods. He should also have self-control because such a person only could impart happiness to the subjects.

King : Working : It was expected from a king to be energetic and ready to serve people. He should divide his day in a way that no sphere of state activity was ignored.

King and His Council of Ministers : Kautilya has suggested that Government should have various departments, each headed by a Minister. A King must have his Council of Ministers which should be consulted from time to time, both individually as well as collectively. He has also, suggested that a Minister should be intelligent, bold, eloquent and possess sound physique. A king should have his *spies* to check the activities of his ambitious ministers. A Ministers should be put in-charge of department to which he is most suited but without personal interests and temptations.

State Activities : For Kautilya sphere of state activity was quite comprehensive. It should perform both civil and military functions. It should also encourage cultural activities. Those engaged in the spread of education and fine arts should be helped and encouraged to the maximum extent possible.

Finances of State : Kautilya wanted to see an overflowing treasury and desired that leniency should be shown while assessing taxes, but not in collecting them. All taxes should be properly accounted for. *Spies* should be used to check tax-evasion and none should be exempted from payment of due taxes.

Control Over Manufacturing : According to Kautilya state owned all mines and metals and should employ persons having knowledge of various metals. Mines producing metals of daily use were to be leased out. There was also to be superintendent to mints and examiner of coins to regulate currency. Superintendent of salt was required to see that salt was not adulterated.

Gold Control : Kautilya has suggested that the state should have control over gold and goldsmiths. Activities of the employees of this department were to be carefully watched. He was to check that counterfeit gold coins were not circulated in the market.

Control Over Commerce : Kautilya has suggested state to regulate commerce and industry. The superintendent of this department was required to check fluctuations and see that commodities were sold at most appropriate price. He was also to see that profits were most reasonable and those engaged in importing foreign goods were to be shown favours.

Control Over Forest Goods : The state was supposed to control forests and timbers and a superintendent was in charge of manufacturing goods out of forest timber.

Weights and Measures Control : State was required to see that ordinary consumer was not put to any disadvantageous position. Superintendent in charge was required to check under-weighing or under-measuring. He was also supposed to manufacture weights and measures and those not using them were to be punished.

Liquor and Wine Control : The state was supposed to control the sale and purchase of liquor. The people were not to be permitted to use liquor outside liquor shops. Spies were posted outside such shops to watch the activities of those who went there.

Kautilya and Government Servants : Since each state was supposed to have its employees. He suggested that these people should be adequately paid and kept satisfied. A low-paid or dissatisfied employee was bound to be corrupt and steal national wealth. He has suggested that those who brought more revenues should be given some incentive. In selecting service personnel, only administrative qualifications should matter.

Views About Employers-Employees Relations : According to him an employer should not tolerate a corrupt and dishonest employee. Honest and faithful employees should be encouraged.

Slavery : Kautilya has discussed in some detail rules regarding conduct and behaviour of slaves and masters. He has imposed certain obligations on masters so that slavery remained somewhat dignified institution. He has also suggested certain circumstances under which a slave could become a free man again. A master had no right to keep a person slave soon after he cleared all debts and discharged all obligations. A master who unnecessarily kept a person slave was to be punished. Equally the state has no right to unneccessarily keep a person under custody.

A Comparison with Aristotle's Views : Both Kautilya and Aristotle had quite opposite views on slavery. For Aristotle slave was animate possession of a master; for Kautilya a slave had his own rights and privileges. For Kautilya a slavery was not a hereditary institution whereas for Aristotle it was so for all purpose. As against Aristotle, Kautilya had discussed circumstances under which a master was bound to end his rights over his slave. Thus both near contemporaries discussed the problem from quite different angles.

Role of Ethics and Politics

For him state was above everything else and in some cases there was no harm in using underhand means in politics. For him politics was a scientific subject and it required wisdom to be a good politician. For Kautilya politics and ethics must go hand in hand, as according to him politics devoid of ethics was barren. State activities should concentrate on *dharma.* In order to promote *dharma* he suggested that the state should promote morality. *Purohit* was to be given a very prominent place and position so as to enable him to advice his monarch on the steps to be taken for promotion of morality and *dharma* as pronounced in *Dharma Sutras.*

He has suggested that in politics people with high moral character should be allowed to participate. For him ethics and politics were complementary and not contradictory to each other.

On Imperialism : In ancient India, Central Government was not required to interfere in local affairs and village administration was being run on the pattern of city states. Kautilya, however, favoured the idea of empire state and created allied problem of inter-state relation. Kautilya has, however, not favoured the policy of territorial annexation but that of effective control.

On War : Kautilya has expounded the theory of *Mandala* and has also discussed the circumstances under which war should be waged. He has suggested his king to be in a state of preparedness and ready to wage war.

For him offence was the best method of defence. He has suggested that king should be vigilant to see that neutrality of state was not being used to the advantage of enemy. War should be waged at the most appropriate and opportune time when enemy was weak. In war, spies should be used to create division among enemy ranks.

On Peace : King should decide when to conclude peace but he should be careful enough to see that by peace treaty, in the near future, enemy could be wiped out.

Kinds of Treaties : According to Kautilya, treaties were primarily of four kinds namely *(i) Atmamisha (ii) Purushunthara sandhi (iii) Addshiapurush* and *(iv) Upagraha.* He has also discussed characteristics of each treaty.

Kautilya and Machiavelli - A Comparative Study : It is, of course, true that both Kautilya and Machiavelli agreed with each other on certain points namely

(i) Both favoured the idea of powerful monarchy and as such believed that the king should pose to be powerful and strong.

(ii) Both agreed that neighbouring states could prove dangerous at any time and as such their activities should be carefully watched.

(iii) Both were of the opinion that the state should always be ready to wage war. Peace treaties should be honoured only by a weak state.

(iv) Kautilya and Machiavelli, both agreed that a king should follow a policy of expansion. They wanted to create a strong empire at the cost of then existing weak state.

(v) Both felt that in politics use of underhand means was not always immoral.

(vi) Both produced history as evidence in support of their arguments.

(vii) Both were practical administrators and have given preference to practice over theory.

Dissimilarity : Whereas both agree on certain points, they widely differ from each other on certain other points, namely

(a) Machiavelli wanted to have absolute monarchy whereas Kautilya wanted to put certain checks on his monarch.

(b) Kautilya wanted to combine ethics with politics as against Machiavelli who wanted to divorce both from each other.

(c) According to Ghoshal, Machiavelli wanted a strong Italy whereas Kautilya wanted to strengthen the rule of his king only.

(d) Kautilya has discussed in detail administrative set-up and machinery as against Machiavelli who has left much for those who were on the job.

(e) Machiavelli did not wish to give rights to the individuals and wanted to subordinate individual to the state whereas Kautilya extended individual's rights and privileges.

Though they differed from each other in certain respects, their greatest similarity was that both were patriots and for both of them love of nation was above everything else.

Discussion on Arthashastra

Some of our western thinkers have tried to challenge the originality of *Arthashastra* and the very existence of Kautilya. But as already discussed, their argument stands refuted. Kautilya had to be original because

(i) He was living in an empire state, as against city states.

(ii) Kautilya was a practical administrator and thus in his philosophy, theory and practice were bound to go hand in hand.

(iii) During his times personality of king was drawing more and more attention than it was hitherto drawing.

(iv) He wanted to have politically biased society as against socially prominent society existing at that time.

Arthashastra and its Originality : Kautilya's *Arthashastra* is original in many ways and respects.

(a) Arthashastra has tried to waive rigidity of caste system and wanted to shake the bonds of rigidity of this system.

(b) Kautilya was original in so far as statecraft was concerned. He has discussed in detail, activities of different departments and officers attached to them. He has also discussed for the first time, movements of armies and different kinds of treaties.

(c) He was original in so far as the organisation of the spy system and duties and responsibilities of spies were concerned.

(d) His originality is visible in so far independence of individual and authority of state are concerned. He has produced a very practical formula to solve this problem.

(e) He has made the science of polity quite scientific and that, to for the first time. He has very much broadened the scope of state activity

(f) Kautilya has given remarkable exposition to *Danda niti.* For the first time he suggested that those vested with power and authority should be put under effective checks and allowed to use minimum discretion.

(g) His *sapatanga* theory is still another original contribution to Hindu polity.

(h) Kautilya's secular outlook is his most significant original contribution. He made every effort to end priestly influence over the king.

Conclusion : Compared many to Machiavelli and with others to Aristotle and Plato, Kautilya is alternately condemned for his methods and trickery and praised for his sound political wisdom and knowledge of human nature. All the scholars agree that it was only because of Kautilya that the Mauryan Empire under ChandraGupta and later under Ashoka became a model of efficient government.

Arthashastra cannot be called as the summary of earlier works. That other thinkers have derived much from *Arthashastra* is sufficient to prove that the treatise is original and not a summary of previous works on the subject.

3

Philosophy of Gandhi

Gandhi was not a philosopher in the academic sense of the term. His ideas cannot be classed with any of the well-known schools of Indian philosophy. He was practical idealist so to speak. In advocating his philosophy of action, Gandhi always advised men to take into account the psychological fact of human nature. He had tremendous faith in the goodness of man. Like Rousseau he never considered man a born sinner.

According to him, in human being love cooperation and desire of general welfare always predominated over selfishness, violence and greed. To emphasize his point Gandhi used to give various instances from day-to-day experiences. His faith in the inherent goodness of human nature was the basis of his humanism. Because of the unconscious working of the law of love, the sum total of the energy of mankind was not to bring us down but to lift us up, he enthasized.

Gandhi began his life like an ordinary man. His earlier days were spent without anything extraordinary. But from the days of his childhood he could not understand why people maintained distinctions on the basis of castes and creeds. In his autobiography he has given the instance of an untouchable boy named Uka. He could never understand the instructions of his mother why it was sinful to touch Uka. Similarly, he could not understand why there was discrimination on the basis of colour.

The right of the Indians in South Africa moved him so much that he made up his mind to fight against all kinds of injustice. His personal insult and suffering at the hands of the whites changed the course of his ordinary life into one dedicated to the cause of the oppressed. His humanist philosophy is first noticeable in 1906, when he decided to fight against the segregation laws and Asiatic Registration Act in South Africa. From then onwards Gandhi worked with the motive of service to the needy even though his main centre of activity remained in India.

The equality of all men was the fundamental creed of Gandhi from the days of his boyhood. He did not hesitate to help the government of South Africa in the Boer War in organising the Indian Ambulance Corps which did praiseworthy work. With the desire of more humanitarian work Gandhi had made it a point, during his stay in South Africa, to work daily for a few hours in a small hospital helping the patients. It was in South Africa that he laid the foundation of his philosophy of life and made initial, experiments to test its practicability. When he returned to India it was not to start something new; it was merely to carry on work for the good of his countrymen.

Gandhi accepted the two Western criteria of human well-being-justice and liberty. But to these he gave an essentially Indian emphasis. By justice he meant devotion to the cause of the oppressed and the outcaste. He decided to fight against the British rule in India because it led to the degradation of the poor. Similarly, he considered it his duty to uplift the untouchables. By liberty, he meant realization of one's duties and complete dedication to perform them without any emphasis on the right. In all the spheres of his activity, his only emphasis was on the good of the people. In the words of F.R. Moraces, "Posterity, in assessing the place of Mahatma Gandhi, will rank him higher as a humanist than as a politician." For verification of this statement and proper assessment of Gandhi's position as a humanist it would be proper to discuss at some length his various ideas.

Gandhi was essentially a man of religion. He was not religious in the ordinary sense in which religion is understood in India. It was religion, based on truth and love or *nonviolence*. That is why religion for Gandhi became the basis of friendship among all mankind. He would quote *Dr. Iqbal "Majhab nahin sikhata apas mein bair rakhna* (religion does not teach to entertain mutual enmity), in order to explain the true essence of religion. He considered different religions as the different roads going towards the same destination on the basis of his non-experience and study of different religions he came to the conclusion that all religions were true and based on the same principles of truth and love. He emphasized repeatedly that religions were not for separating men from one another but rather for binding them. He was pained to see the conflict between different religions, he suffered personally to establish harmony and as a matter of fact laid down his life for the cause of religious unity.

Gandhi subscribed to the creed of equal regard for all faiths and creeds—*sarvadharma samanatva*. But he made it clear that equal regard did not meant that one should adopt the other's religion. It meant emphasizing the point of agreement and not the point of difference. He was a Hindu himself and admired it for its unique characteristics. But Hinduism to him was not limited to eating and not-eating, it did not consist of ritualism and dogmas. He considered Hinduism as the most tolerant creed because it succeeded in absorbing even creeds opposed to it like Buddhism. He said, "Hinduism is not an exclusive religion. In it, there is room for the worship of all the prophets of the world. It is not a missionary religion in the ordinary sense of the term. Hinduism tells everyone to worship

God according to his own faith or *dharma,* and so it lives at peace with all religions. He considered Hinduism not a mere religion but a way of life, relentless pursuit of Truth. It was his Hindu instinct which led him to understand the real spirit behind different religions.

According to Gandhi, the aim of religion was to lead man face to face with God. He considered God as identical to Truth. He tried to see God through the service of humanity, because he knew that God did not live in the some far off place in heaven but in the heart of every one of his creations. As God has created different faiths, there could be no question of our having only one religion. He said. "Man's ultimate aim is the realization of God, and all his activities, political and religious have to be guided by his ultimate aim of the vision of God.

The immediate service of all human beings becomes a necessary part of the endeavour simply because the only way to find God is to see him in his creation and be one with it. This can be clone by service of all." Gandhi further said, "If I could persuade myself that I should find Him in a Himalayan cave I would proceed there immediately. But I know that I cannot find him apart from humanity." Such humanitarian sentiments were the basis of all his religious activities, like daily prayer and religious discourses.

Gandhi's faith in God was like that of an Advaitin. But at the same time he called himself an *anekantavadin* or 'believer in the relativity of Reality.' His support to different notions of reality helped him in correctly judging different religions. It was this balanced religious approach which led him to take the whole world in the embrace of his love. He said, "My *Anekantvad* is the result of the twin doctrine of *Satya* and *Ahimsa." Satya* or truth and *ahimsa* or non-violence (born of love) are the two principles which could help was no higher way of worshipping God than serving the poor and identifying himself with them. He chose to travel in third-class compartments and wear merely loin cloth reminding himself that he belonged to the lower order of mankind where humanity and love were found to be the richest.

To Gandhi the nearest approach to Truth or God, was through love of mankind. As it has been earlier pointed out, he took love in the sense of non-violence. It was on this understanding that Gandhi tried to explain that differences in religions were only in their methods of approach to God. Everyone of us must identify oneself with other human beings because God is within us. Truth and love are the instruments which bind us to one another and to God. As a Hindu, Gandhi did not believe in the orthodox view of God and had no faith in idol worship. He said, "God to be God must rule the heart and transform it. Fie must express himself in even the smallest act of his votary."

Gandhi laid emphasis on the three cardinal virtues of a really religious person: first truth as a divine quality; second, non-violence or ahimsa and third *brahmacharya*. He considered ahimsa as the supreme religious duty in accordance with the teachings of the Mahabharata-'*ahimsa param dharmah*'. Ahimsa is the basis of true religion. He used to stress this point in his post-prayer addresses and often quoted the sage and poet Tulsidas in this connection. Thus, religion for Gandhi did not consist of worshipping God or reading a religious book: it consisted of entire human activity. Religious life meant identification with mankind. Like the ancient rishis or sages, Gandhi regarded religion as self-realization, as the striving of the human personality to express itself in service, suffering and sacrifice. He did not know any religion apart from this.

Gandhi had a perfectly rational attitude towards religion. Religion being a practical discipline must help in solving day-to-day problems. Fie said, "I reject any religious doctrine that does not appeal to reason and is in conflict with morality." The moment we lose the moral basis, we cease to be religious. Religion cannot override morality. All kinds of selfishness and narrow-mindedness are immoral. Thus, religion demands genuine consideration for all faiths. Through his teaching and recitations from the different faiths in his prayer meetings, Gandhi tried his best to give a broad basis for religious outlook of man. This may be considered as Gandhi's greatest contribution to religion and thereby to the ideal of universal brotherhood.

Gandhi was a humanist because his transcendental love of humanity recognized no limitations of race, or barriers of country. During his last clays he had to bear the tremendous strain of communal tension in the country. He undertook fasts. On October 3, 1947, in his post-prayer address he said that if his message of love could not affect the people, it would be best God took him away. From this one can imagine how deeply pained he was knowing the conflict between men of different religions.

It was a tragedy that he became a victim of religious hatred for which he fought and suffered throughout his life. Paying tribute to him on his seventy-eight birthday, Sarojini Naidu said that as a religious man he shared the quality with the few great leaders of the world who founded great religions. He brought hope to the hopeless, courage to those who were afraid. He shared with Christ the, gospel of love and with the great Mohammad the gospel of brotherhood of man, equality of man and oneness of man.

Through the religious principles of truth and love, Gandhi wanted to create a social order devoid of classes and castes. He, described himself as a "social revolutionist" At the age of twelve, he came to understand that the concept of untouchability was against the real spirit of Hindu religion and was a sin. During his stay in South Africa, he found distinctions on the basis of colour. Gandhi made a thorough study of the Hindu scriptures and came to the conclusion that regarding certain people as untouchables was not only against reason but also against the real spirit of Hindu religion. He considered untouchability as something against the instinct of mercy, pity and love. A religion believing in the worship of the cow could not possibly recommend boycott of human beings, the suppressed classes. In the eyes of God, all creatures are equal. God had endowed all human beings impartially with the same shape and the same natural desires. Thereafter, there could never be a religious sanction to look down upon any human being as inferior to us.

On his return from South Africa in 1915, Gandhi realized that mere political freedom was of no use to Indians. He felt that various social diseases were eating the very vitals of the nations. It was this idea which led Gandhi to start a social revolution in the country. According to him, Hinduism always insisted on the brotherhood not only of all mankind but of all that lives. There will never be peace on earth and goodwill among men unless we strive to establish equality between man and man. He said, "I believe that if untouchability is really rooted out, it will not only purge Hinduism of a terrible blot but its repercussions will be worldwide. My fight against untouchability is a fight against the impure of humanity."

Gandhi claimed to be a sanatani Hindu. On this basis he said, he failed to find even a single instance in which untouchability had the sanction of the Hindu scriptures. He went to the extent of declaring that had there been approval of untouchability in Hinduism, he would have renounced it. He held that religion to be worthy of the name could not be inconsistent with the fundamental truths of ethics. He felt that no real social reform in India was possible if a sizeable number of people remained isolated and oppressed. He elevated the position of the untouchables by calling them Harijan-men of God. He insisted on their participation in all religious and social activities. He used to move among them and eat with them. He admitted that like many other evils untouchability was one which had been handed over to us from generations. At the same time, he considered it the sacred duty of every Hindu to eradicate it. He said, "The Hindu religion is replete with illustrations of great men lifting their unfortunate brethren from their miseries. Will not the modern Hindus copy their own great men, and once for all rub out the blot of untouchability that so defiles Hinduism?"

Gandhi's humanistic treatment of the whole problem of untouchability led him to fight for their religious, economic and political rights. He refused to take them as a separate class apart from the Hindus. On this issue his argument was simple when he said, "God did not create men with the badge of superiority or of inferiority, and no scripture which labels a human being as inferior or untouchable because of his or her birth can command our allegiance. It is a denial of God and Truth which is God." Gandhi was of the opinion that no social reform was possible unless each one of the individuals was mentally transformed and economically uplifted. With myriads of oppressed and neglected individuals nothing could be achieved.

The condition of Indian society is now fairly changed because Gandhi set the ideal of equality irrespective of caste and creed in the manifesto of the Congress Party much before it came to power.

Like untouchability, Gandhi was also against the system of castes as it was practised in India. But he did not consider caste system as altogether sinful like untouchability. The latter he considered as weeds and the former as a crop. Destroying the caste system would mean destroying the crop for the weeds. He regarded men and women equally as brothers and sisters, treating them as equals in every act of life. He believed in the ancient Hindu system of 'Varnashrama Dharma' the four classes, but strictly, in its Vedic sense. Division into castes should not restrict social intercourse for it was meant to define only duties. Explaining the age old humanistic basis of the *Varnashrama* Dharma, Gandhi emphasized that Varna was based on worth and was connected with a man's mission on this earth, his station in society. *Varnashrama* determined a firm basis for ideal social organization. According to it, man was never condemned to remain in one caste, he could elevate himself to higher caste by actions. Man could even lose his *varna* by failing to perform duties meant for him.

Gandhi considered all men as children of one human family, like branches of the same tree. He refuted social distinctions on the basis of castes. Speaking at Palni, Chennai on February 4, 1946, Gandhi said, "The Bhangi is or should be on a par with the Brahmin in all social relations. There is no reason why he should not, other things being equal occupy the chair which Maulana Abdul Kalam Azad occupies with distinction." In his interview with Nirmal Kumar Bose on December 14, 1934, Gandhi tries to explain his views on the issue of castes. He said every man was born with certain limitations. The law of Varna was deduced on the observation of those limitations. It defined spheres of action for different people. The law itself admitted no distinctions of high or low, and at the same time was a guarantee to each the fruits of his labour. The law was misused and degraded by interested people. "But," he said, "my conviction is that an ideal social order will only be evolved when the implications of this law are fully understood and given effect to."

Gandhi was rational and practical besides being a humanist. He had faith in the inherent equality of all men. On the basis of this conviction Gandhi aimed at establishing an ideal society where men of different castes could meet and live as brothers. He supported the idea of inter-caste dining and marriage for removing social barriers. He himself practised this in his life. In his ashram at Wardha, Harijan boys were freely admitted and lived together with the non-Harijans. He also solemnised many inter-caste marriages; one of them was the marriage of his son Devdas with the daughter of Sri Rajagopalachari who was a Brahmin. Gandhi also advised Harijans to purify their life and work for the good of the society. Thus, he kept the ideal of *sarvodaya-uplift* of all, before Indians.

As a staunch devotee of truth and justice, Gandhi laid special emphasis on the necessity of recognising women as equal to men. He reminded men of the teaching of the ancient Indian seers who honoured women. The natural differences determine only the different duties and not superiority or inferiority. He called upon women to shed the age old mentality of slaves and help men in the process of human evolution. He considered women as "the incarnation of ahimsa". He believed that a woman could help a great deal in purifying the life of a man by giving to man her infinite love and infinite capacity to suffer. He made efforts to eradicate evil customs like illiteracy, child marriage and widowhood. He thought that mankind as a whole could not make any progress in the real sense if women, an important part of it, remained oppressed and neglected.

In his vision of bringing social revolution in India, Gandhi did not intend to use any force. He wanted to abolish untouchability, conflict among different castes and other social evils by changing the hearts of the people. He wanted to make everyone realize his duties and capacity for serving society. On March 7, 1942, Gandhi wrote in the *Harijan:* "The present inequalities are surely due to the peoples' ignorance. With a growing knowledge of their natural strength, inequalities must disappear. If the revolution is brought about by violence, the position will be reversed but not altered for the better. With non-violence, that is, conversion, the new era, which people hope for must be born." His non-violence, approach towards social reconstruction made him a distinct and unique kind of social reformer and ushered in a new era of humanism.

Gandhi considered communalism as the worst social evil in India. Communalism meant to hint fight between people of different faiths for their respective supremacy. He was secular in his outlook. With his broad religious attitude there could be no room for such a conflict. In the fight for human decency, for a world without wars, Gandhi was the front rank soldier. His message was the answer to the cry of exasperated mankind. The All-India Muslim League in the name of rights for the Muslims in India branded Hindus as its enemies.

This led to the growth of suspicion among the Hindus and Muslims resulting in open fights on many an occasion. He emphasized that India could not survive if Hindus and Muslims fought against each other. He asked people to adopt a rational and human approach towards the whole problem so that permanent peace could be brought about.

In order to help both the Hindus and Muslims to live peacefully together. Gandhi emphasized the ideal of a secular state to the Congress Party. On hearing the news of communal clashes on the eve of partition of India, Gandhi undertook the most taxing tour of Noakhali in East Bengal and Bihar for establishing peace. In reply to a friend's question during September. 1947, Gandhi advised Hindus to befriend Muslims, to share their joys and sorrows and to help them in distress. He was so much pained by the communal clashes that he decided to sacrifice his life for the cause of communal peace. Declaring his fast into death on January 12. 1948, Gandhi said, "The fast will end when and if I am satisfied that there is a reunion of hearts of all communities brought about without any outside pressure, but from a awakened sense of duty."

The communal riots did not make Gandhi a pessimist. He had great faith inhumanity. His faith stood the test. He wrote to Amrit Kaur on August 29, 1947, "You must not lose faith in humanity. Humanity is an ocean. If the few drops of the ocean are dirty, the ocean does not become dirty." His fast a few days before his death had an immediate effect on both the communities and they mutually agreed to make a joint promise to maintain peace.

According to Gandhi, India as a nation must have the capacity for assimilation. The real spirit of nationality cannot interfere with one another's religion. Gandhi reminded Indians that they were one nation with different religions. So the only duty was to work in unity for the good of the nation as a whole. He said, one religion and one nationality could not be synonymous. He laid stress on mutual understanding and mutual tolerance among not only the Hindus and Muslims but also among men of all faiths.

Political freedom for India was Gandhi's main ideal during his struggle against the British rulers. He felt that without freedom nothing was possible. In his fight for India's freedom he had a wider humanistic goal. His attitude of a saint in tackling all human problems continued even in the sphere of his political activity. As Professor Hiren Mukerjee says, "Throughout his career, which for fifty years was more public than that of almost any other public figure, there could be seen a sort of co-existence in his composition of the saint and the politician." Gandhi considered freedom of self-expression as the birth right of human beings, and for that matter, Indians. His aim was to liberate ordinary human beings from external restrictions so that they could develop fully. He had faith that tree India could help the world could help humanity groaning under the weight of effete traditions and conflicting interests. He cherished the dream of free India as the model of civilized living where men could live with goodwill towards one another.

Gandhi's whole life was directed towards the welfare of mankind. He considered politics as worthless if it could not become an integral part of the life of human beings. For this reason he based politics on religious principles of truth and non-violence. In his opinion, politics could not be separated from religion since both meant the same ideal, that is, service of mankind. Both the political leader and religious devotee must work for the good of humanity. It is said that in this way he spiritualized politics, for politics devoid of religion kills the soul. He was a politician turned religious.

Having tremendous faith in the principles of non-violence, Gandhi applied it in fighting against political suppression. It was in South Africa that for the first time this weapon was used for saving the political rights of the Asiatics living there. He coined the term *satyagraha* (soul-force) through which non-violence was to be applied in politics. This meant personal suffering in order to convert the evil-doer. This involved the humanist belief that suffering has a direct instrumental value. Through non-cooperation, civil disobedience and personal suffering he tried to achieve everything he cherished. Because of his self-sacrifice and immense soul-force, some of the British government representatives themselves, became his disciples and friends.

Gandhi was a democrat. Writing in the *Harijan,* he said that true democracy must be the ruler of the people in its real sense. The transfer of power from the Britishers was not the ends but the means for improving the condition of ail men and women. In his address to All India Congress Committee on August 8, 1942, he said, "The Congress does not believe in the domination of any group or any community. It believes in democracy which includes in its orbit Muslims, Hindus, Christians-everyone of the communities inhabiting this vast country." Democracy meant complete decentralisation of political powers. It must begin from the bottom and not from above; this is why Gandhi laid emphasis on the *Panchayati Raj.* Such a democracy is possible only through non-violence. Democracy sustained by violence cannot protect the weak." "My notion of democracy", he said, is that under it the weakest should have the same opportunity." Democracy must provide social justice to all.

The ideal of self-rule or *Swaraj,* as Gandhi termed it, meant the Kingdom of God or *Ramarajya.* The aim of such government should be to recognize the equality in birth and consequently the right of equal opportunity, Moreover, a born democrat must be a disciplinarian. Democracy does not mean freedom to everyone for doing everything. Mutual tolerance must be considered as a golden rule for a true democratic order. *Ramarajya* conceives of a society in which all its members get equal opportunity to express themselves and in which none suffers under forced opinion. Gandhi said, "The *Swaraj* of my dream is the poor man's *Swaraj.* The necessaries of life should be enjoyed by you in common with those enjoyed by the primes and the monied people."

"The Swaraj of my dream recognizes no race or religious distinction." He liked it to be *purna swaraj* so that everyone is well protected." Gandhi was not a narrow nationalist, India under Swaraj must serve the whole world. He said, "India nationalism is not exclusive, nor aggressive, nor destructive. It is health giving, religious and therefore humanitarian. India must learn to live before she can aspire to die for humanity."

For Gandhi freedom was not merely a political fact but a social reality. As a politician he never tolerated or compromised with injustice wrong, tyranny and authoritarianism. He was a patriot but his patriotism was the same as humanity. He was a patriot because he was humanitarian. He even said India must die if in her death, the world was to live.

Mere political freedom, for Gandhi, meant nothing, without economic freedom, that is enough opportunities for economic growth. Freedom is a mockery if millions go about naked and starving. For this the only human approach, according to Gandhi, was to provide work for the workless. He stressed on the basic economic theory and he worked throughout his life to free Indians from the degradation of poverty. On the occasion of his first trial, in 1922, Gandhi said, "Little do town dwellers know how the semi-starved masses of India are slowly sinking into lifelessness. No sophistry, no jugglery on figures can explain away the evidence that the skeletons in many villages present to the naked eye." He warned that such a crime against humanity would have to be answered for one day.

According to Gandhi, the main ideal of any economic programme must be human happiness combined with full mental and moral growth. The wealth of a nation is its people who produce it. Therefore, if economic policy does not provide each according to his need, it is of no value. One of the economic imperative, for Gandhi, was immediate engagement of the entire population in productive work of any kind. He advised complete decentralisation of the productive process. This led to the evolution of constructive programme based on *'Swadeshi'* and *'Khaddar'*.

Through the practice of *Swadeshi* and *Khaddar*, Gandhi evolved a practical remedy for crushing poverty of the millions of village people who lived in India on the border line of starvation. His vows of *Swadeshi* and *Khaddar* went deep into his conception of human progress. *Swadeshi* would mean self-dependence and *Khaddar*, work for the million idle manpower of the country. He asked people to accept *Swadeshi* as a religious duty. *Swadeshi* must permeate economic as well as religion and politics. In religion it would mean belief in the ancient religious scriptures; in politics, faith in the indigenous political institutions such as the *Panchayats;* in economic, development of India's resources and methods through cottage industry.

In advocating the production and use of *Khadi*, Gandhi had a humanitarian motive. He wanted to transform the society from the apparent directions. *Khadi* was to become a unifying force. Through the increasing use of *Khadi*, Gandhiji felt, Indians would understand the dignity of labour. Moreover, manufacture and use of *Khadi* meant more and more self-dependence and use of leisure time for productive purposes.

Gandhi is often criticized for opposing the modern means of production. He considered growing industrialism as a curse for mankind, because it meant exploitation of the weak by the strong. He did not consider modern devices of production as indispensable for the permanent welfare of the human race. By spreading the movement of *Khadi*, Gandhi aimed to check exploitation, concentration of wealth in the hands of a few and unhealthy competition. He said, "I don't believe that industrialisation is necessary in any case for any country. It is much less so for India. Indeed I believe that independent India can only discharge her duty towards a groaning world by adopting a simple but ennobled life, by developing her thousands of cottages and living at peace with the world." He retired from the Congress in 1934 in order to dedicate himself to the cause of *daridranarayan,* the poor man, who represent God.

It would be a misrepresentation of Gandhi if it is said that he was against mechanised industry. His antipathy to industrialisation was impelled by the same humanistic urge. He regarded machinery as anti-social for it was meant to replace human labour, and thus, increased unemployment. His supreme consideration was man. In the words of Yusuf Meherally, his protest against the machine was essentially a protest against the enslavement of humanity in the name of technological progress. Writing in a *Young India,* Gandhi said. "1 would favour the use of most elaborate machinery if thereby India's pauperism and resulting idleness be avoided." He welcomed any improvement in the spinning wheel and other cottage machinery.

The object in opposing the craze for machinery was to save the villages of India and thereby India as a nation. Industrialisation on a mass scale, he thought, would lead to passive or active exploitation of the villagers. "If we are to humanise society and bring moral significance to acts and relationships we should work for a decentralised village economy where machinery could be employed so long it does not disturb much the fundamental frame-work of society and the freedom of human spirit." Thus Dr. S. Radhakrishnan explains the significance of Gandhi's approach to the problem in the following manner:

"Gandhi was a socialist in his economic theory. He was in favour of state control over all useful industries so that they work for the benefit of humanity instead of profit motive. Under socialism he believed all are supposed to get their share of the national income and thus no question of exploitation arises. He often used to say that all land belonged to God. For him socialism stood for the ideal of social transformation by purification of means, through the spirit of love and human unity. He was against all forms of exploitation and wanted a general moral disapproval of it. The individual exploiter must be approached with love and for bearance. Once exploiters were convinced and they shed selfishness, everything would become easy."

Gandhi, however, did not approve socialism of the Western type which gives no importance to the reformation of the individual. It binds the individual to the organised social order. Society cannot be reformed without reforming the individual and improving his lot. While both, Gandhi's socialism and the Western one, maintain a social programme for the growth and development of society and aim at bringing happiness to mankind by ending all kinds of class conflicts and equal distribution of wealth, their methods differ. Western socialism wants to realise its aims by dispossessing the rich of wealth by force.

Gandhi wanted to change the heart of the rich and make him shake off his tendency to exploit. He said, "I believe that men are capable of developing their will to an extent that will reduce exploitation to the minimum. I look upon an increase in the power of the state with the greatest fear because, although while apparently doing by minimising exploitation, it does the greatest harm to mankind by destroying individuality which lies at the root of all progress." The greatest stress is laid on the purity of means for social transformation. Writing in the *Harijan,* Gandhi said, "Socialism is as pure as crystal. It, therefore, requires crystal like means to achieve it. Impure means result in an impure end." The emphasis is on not using men as means but as an end. This was directly the outcome of his humanistic approach to problems.

Gandhi was not a socialist if, socialism means complete collectivism and abolition of private property. As a socialist he had sympathy and solidarity with the exploited masses, with a passion and striving for social justice, with economic arrangement conducive to the free development of human personality, with a peaceful international society. He considered non-violence as a virtue held by mankind. The importance is given to the interpersonal and international relationship along with respect for the dignity of the individual and worth of human personality. The aim is to establish a classless society by changing the hearts of the people. Humanism was the basic principle of his economic theory.

Gandhi advocates the method of non-violence for solving all human problems, whether religious or social, whether political or economic. It meant not offending anybody, not harbouring an uncharitable thought, even against one who behaved as an enemy, it meant helping an evil-doer. Non-violence in its active form meant goodwill towards all life. In his interview at Utmanjai (Peshawar) on October 20, 1938, Gandhi said, "The basic principle on which the practice of non-violence rests is that, what holds good in respect of ourself equally applies to the whole universe. All mankind in essence is alike. What is, therefore, possible for me is possible for everybody." The principle of non-violences is based on the belief that man's supreme happiness consisted in the realisation of his oneness with the rest of the creation. The practical application of nonviolence in fife is Satyagraha or soul-force.

The principle of non-violence is not new, only its importance is stressed in relation to the human species. Democratic order cannot be saved without non-violence. True democracy means village industries, primary education through crafts, removal of untouchability, communal harmony, prohibition and non-violent organisation of labour. Gandhi remained firm on this principle because he was sure that in human relationship truth could not be realized by any other means. Non-violence means humanistic attitude towards life. He said, "Non-violence is the greatest force at the disposal of mankind. It is the mightiest weapon of destruction devised by ingenuity of man. Destruction is not the law of the humans. Man lives freely by his readiness to dies, if it need be at the hands of his brother, never by killing him. Every murder or other injury, no matter for what cause, committed or inflicted on another is a crime against humanity."

Gandhi's religion was the religion of humanity based on the conviction that every man has in him the spark of love. He was never tired of saying that truth and non-violence could lead to the establishment of a world without hatred, wars and all kinds of conflicts. He asserted that as long as organised violence and race for ornaments persisted in the world there could be no humanism. "The path of non-violence advocated by Gandhi rises above all artificial barriers of caste, creed, religion and nationality, and yet raises the dignity of man in spheres of life."

The spiritual discipline which Gandhi suggested can be adopted by all individuals, all communities and all nations the world over. In the world of gloom it can become the hope of mankind. Gandhi has a wider aim in preaching his philosophy of love. He frankly said, "My mission is not merely brotherhood of Indian humanity. My mission is not merely freedom of India. But through realization of freedom of India, I hope to realize and carry on the mission of the brotherhood of man." He claimed no status but that of a servant of India, and in serving India he tried to serve humanity at large.

Gandhi was a nationalist in order to be a true internationalist. In his press interview in Yarvada jail on September 20, 1932, he said that it was not possible to be a internationalist without being a nationalist. Indian nationalism must organise itself for the benefit and service of humanity. In India's freedom, he sought the benefit of the entire human race. For ideal international relationship he suggested a drastic transformation and reconstruction of the political and socio-economic structure of the nations. This was to give broad institutional and socio-economic basis to the world peace. He advised non-violent nations to organise themselves into a world federational league. He laid down principles for ideal international organisation, such as, nonviolence, freedom from colonialism, equal representation of all nations, general disarmament and a small international police force to keep order in the absence of universal belief in non-violence.

Gandhi truly belonged to all time and all mankind. He recalled the Indian tradition of not mere tolerance but of profound respect for all faiths. His life as a whole was a teaching to the successive generations. The qualities of his character like simplicity, the quest for truth, gentleness shall continue to be cherished by mankind for ever. The value of individual self-reformation is a constantly recurring theme in Gandhi's thought, and it is necessary to stress that no social theory worth the name can or does belittle its importance.

Dr. Rajendra Prasad has compared the life of Gandhi with the river Ganges which serves all who seek to make use of her. "If we want peace and happiness and to live as human beings we must follow the path chalked out by Gandhiji for in it lies our own good and that of the world." He used all his energy for the uplift of humanity. Gandhi belonged not to India but the whole world, he belonged not only to our generation but to posterity as well. Future generations will remember him as one of the greatest spiritual forces of all times. On January 20, 1948, when a misguided youth threw a bomb at a prayer meeting in the Birla House compound, he remained unmoved and asked the police officer not to harass him in any way. "Gandhi presented to the world all that is noblest in the spirit of man. He illumined human dignity by faith in the eternal significance of man's effort. He belongs to the type that redeems the human race."

It is regretful that India has paid only lip sympathy to the ideals of the Mahatma Gandhi during the last so many years of independence. Indian society is badly divided into castes and the ideal of social equality is yet to be realised in practice. The Gandhian method of non-violence and Satyagraha has better appreciation outside India. It is a common feature now-a-days for the public to destroy national property for getting their demands fulfilled. Similarly, for the national government *lathi-charge* and firing are as convenient means of dealing with the public demands as they were considered during the British Government. The disintegrated elements are most powerful these days. The rapid industrialization has vitiated the economic atmosphere of the country resulting in the rapid growth of unemployment and misery among the educated youth of the country. There is corruption and nepotism in the political circles and domination by vested interests. It is devoid of those values for which Gandhi lived and died. The country is in need of a leader like Gandhi to fight against those forces which have enslaved the society internally. Unless the social conscience of the nation is aroused Gandhian ideals and values would continue to be Utopia.

The Gandhianism

Gandhian Political Ideologies : Gandhism political philosophy has ushered in a new era in the history of political thought. It made the world believe that even the greatest political problems could be solved only by personal sacrifices and making the opponent realise the excesses and mistakes committed by him. Under it personal sacrifice in the right direction was far more effective a weapon than any other method for fighting against the opponent. For Gandhiji, non-violence or ahimsa was the most suitable reply for violence and force. For him, non-violence was a creed as well a faith.

Gandhiji wanted to establish an ideal society in which Panchayati Raj based on real democratic principles will flourish. He felt that democracy could not come from above but must start from down below and go upward. In Gandhism, religion has a definite place and Gandhiji did not wish to separate religion from politics. In his own words, "It is the permanent element and human nature which counts no cost too great in order to find full expression and which leaves the soul beyond restless until it has found itself known its maker and appreciated the true correspondence between maker and himself."

In his economic ideals, he was a socialist but of a different nature. He did not believe that force should be used to snatch superfluous wealth from the rich for distribution among the poor but he appealed to the capitalists that they themselves should give their wealth to the community and the poor so that it could be put to proper He followed the ideals of persuading the enemy, rather than hating them. For him it was not the man but the institution which was bad and as such the former and not the latter should be hated. Gandhism believes in the use of pure Swadeshi rather than Videshi. He believed in the policy on non-cooperation, civil resistance, strikes, gain on fast and even migrating to another country as weapons against the opponent for obliging him to accept the legitimate demands of the oppressed.

Gandhism is not communism minus violence as some of the thinkers make us believe. Both, of course, believe in a classless society and also believe that capital is a theft but they do not go beyond that. The Marxists believe in the use of force whereas in Gandhism force has no place. Similarly in Marxism end justifies the means whereas Gandhism believes that right means should be used to get lasting ends.

Gandhiji's Life

Mohan Das Karam Chand Gandhi was born on 2nd October 1869 at Porebunder in Kathiawar. His father was Dewan of the State and mother, a devoted religious lady. He was married at the early age of 12. He was a shy and mediocre student but very obedient and punctual. He could impress his teachers by his shyness and obedience. It was at the age of 19 that he was sent to England with a vow neither to touch wine nor woman nor eat meat there. It was, of course, a very difficult task not suited to his temperament and, therefore, decided to remain an Indian gentleman. Under the influence of his religious mother he spent quite a lot of his time in studying Bhagwat Gita and many other religious books. Gandhiji's life career can broadly be divided into three stages namely.

1. Before his return to India from South Africa;
2. From 1921 to 1947; and
3. From 15th August, 1947 to 30th January, 1948.

During the first period of his career he practised the ideals which he wished to follow in his subsequent life. Till then he was not quite well-known to Indian multitudes. He had then not come to the fore-front to mould the thought and imagination of the people. During the second period of his life career he put into actual practice what he had so far been practising. By this time due to his work in South Africa he had earned great reputation and Indian masses were most willing to extend their hand of co-operation to him. It was during this period that he dominated the whole political life of India.

It was his one-man guidance which was most valuable and most willingly responded to by the multitudes in India. It was also during this period that he successfully guided India to the path of freedom and achieved that with minimum of bloodshed. He forced one of the most powerful colonial and imperial powers in the world to leave the soil of India with no ill-will or bitter feelings.

During the third phase of his life Mahatma Gandhi straggled to end that hatred which the partition of the country had brought with it between the two manor Indian communities, namely the Hindus and the Muslims. As usual he preached the noble cause of Hindus-Muslim unity and was assassinated while fighting for this ideal cause. His death was lamented all over the world and glowing tributes were paid to him after he was no more to guide India in her future development.

First Phase of Gandhiji's Life : On his return from England Mahatma Gandhi started his practice at Rajkot but subsequently he shifted to Bombay. It appears that Nature had destined him for a very noble cause and soon an opportunity came when for a professional work he had to go to South Africa on behalf of a Muslim firm. Though he had no intention of stay there and had planned to come back soon after his business commitment was over yet due to the pitiable conditions of Indians of all communities there, he had to prolong his stay even after he had finished his commitment there. He saw with great dissatisfaction the discriminatory treatment being meted out to Indians. He decided to struggle for legal equality for his countrymen.

But before he could give a call to his people he himself practised the method of Satyagraha, inner purification and self-discipline. He had to labour hard for successfully implementing this new weapon on a foreign soil but credit goes to him for successfully practising them in his future struggle.

He called upon the Indians there to disobey all discriminatory laws. He asked the people to disregard Asiatic Registration Act which required all Asiatics to give their thumb impression and to register themselves. He even led a deputation to England but found that only Satyagraha could solve the problem. Thousands were sent to jails and Gandhiji was the leader of all this movement. Ultimately his determination won and justice prevailed over injustice. All discriminatory laws were repealed and Gandhiji was successful in his noble mission.

Second Phase of Gandhiji's Life : In 1914 Gandhiji returned to India with all honour that he had won during his 20 years stay in south-Africa and decided to guide Indian political life. It goes to his wisdom that he did not immediately plunge into Indian politics and was rightly advised to listen more and speakless. After fully assessing the situation in India he decided to enter Indian politics. First of all he was a very strong supporter of the British sense of justice and said, "I discovered that the British Empire had certain ideals with which I have fallen in love and one of those ideals is that every subject of this British Empire has the freest scope for his energies and honour and whatever he thinks is due to his conscience. And 1 have found that it is possible for him to be governed least under the British Empire. He even supported the cause of

Indians contributing their maximum in men, money and material in British army in the First World War.

He, however, justified his action that an enemy in danger and difficulty should not be embarrassed in any way. He had so much love for British sense of justice that in their support in the First World War he organised an ambulance corps in London. In 1918 he wrote to the Viceroy, "If I could make my countrymen retrace their steps, I would make them withdraw all Congress resolutions and not whisper Home Rule or responsible Government during the pendency of the war. I would make India hand over all her able bodies sons as a sacrifice to the empire at this critical moment; and I know that India by this very act, would become the most favoured partner and racial distinctions would become a thing of the past."

It was, however, in 1920 that his confidence in British sense of justice was rudely shaken and he became a non-co-operator. After the close of the war when India was expecting better treatment and greater share in the running of the administration, the country was given the Rowlatt Act followed by a massacre at Jallianwala Bagh and the constitutionally fighting country was given the most unsatisfactory reforms known as Montague-Chelmsford Reforms. Above all, the Muslims of India had also been betrayed and the integrity of Khilafat in Europe was not maintained. He himself has written that, "Event that have happened during the past month have confirmed me in the opinion that the imperial Government have acted in the khilafat matter in an unscrupulous, immoral and unjust manner, and have been moving from wrong to-wrong in order to defend their immorality. I can retain neither respect nor affection for such a Government.

Your Excellency's light hearted treatment of official crime, your exhorbation of Sir Michael O. Dwyer, Mr. Montague's despatch and above all the shameful ignorance of Punjab events and the callous disregard of the feelings of the Indians betrayed by the House of Lords, have filled my greatest misgivings regarding the future of the empire, have estranged me completely from the present Government and have disabled me from rendering, as I have hitherto whole heartedly rendered, my total co-operation."

After having completely lost his faith in British impartiality Gandhiji entered Indian politics with his full vigour and strength. He was determined to win India's freedom through his weapon of non-violence and passive resistance which he had successfully practised in South Africa. He also felt that Hindu-Muslim unity was most essential for Indian freedom and decided to struggle for it as well. In 1924 a special meeting of the Congress was organised in which Gandhi ji said, "Non-violence is the first article of my faith and it is the last article of my faith but I had to make my choice ; I had either to submit to a system which I considered has done irreparable harm to my country, or incur the risk of the mad fury of my people bursting forth when they understood the truth from my lips." Gandhiji, however, had to give up his experiment when Chauri Chaura incident took place in U.P. where a few constables were burnt alive and this shocked his faith in the people. In this way, Gandhiji's first attempt to lead the nation to freedom through non-violence was not a success to the expected extent.

Gradually, Gandhiji took the country with him towards independence and he dominated the whole Indian political life. He was put behind the bars but nothing deterred him from his decided path. In 1931 he went to London as the sole representative of Indian National Congress but he found that the conference was in no mood to give freedom to India. He also found that disruptive elements were knowingly being introduced on the conference table with certain motives to slow the progress', of India's winning freedom. In 1942 Gandhiji started his famous Quit India movement which opened the eyes of the Britishers and made the rulers realize that India was now not going to tolerate any injustice. Gandhiji was the main moving force behind the Congress when subsequent negotiations with the British delegations, including the Cripps Mission Plan, Wavell Plan, Cabinet Mission Plan or the Mountbatten Mission Plan were put forth before India. It was his efforts and under his guidance that Indian National Congress could successfully negotiate with one of the world's greatest imperialist powers.

Gandhiji was, however, much shocked to learn that the Hindus and the Muslims were fighting with each other on political issues. He could easily see that a great sacrifice was required to introduce harmony and end communal fury and hatre between the two communities which the political leaders had implanted in the minds of the people during all these years. The hatred which expressed itself in Noakhali where there was a slaughter of Hindus and events in Bihar where there was some reaction against the Muslims, shocked Gandhiji. He went at both the places and decided to go on fast until the people of both the communities decided to discard communal hatred as a political weapon. Similarly on September 7, 1947 there were riots in Delhi and Gandhiji had to adopt the same method. The response was very encouraging.

Third Phase of Mahatma Gandhiji's Life : It is unfortunate that the father of the nation, who so much sacrificed for, guided so ably the nation, could not reap the fruits of independence. He could hardly breathe for a few months in free India when his end came. He started with the very basis assumption that the Hindus and the Muslims must live together as brethren for the prosperity of India. He, therefore, demanded that all mosques which had been converted into temples or where people had begun to reside after migration from Pakistan should be returned to the Muslims. He also pleaded that a sum of Rs. 55 crones, due to Pakistan, should be given to that country. It is unfortunate that some of the orthodox Hindus could not understand the lofty ideal behind Gandhiji's idea and on 30th January, 1948 when he was going to attend a prayer meeting, an orthodox Hindu, Nathu Ram God say, shot him dead.

Gandhiji's death shocked many. He was, perhaps, the first non-official citizen of a country whose death was mourned even by U.N.O. High tributes were paid to him on his death and he is still remembered and will always be remembered for the ideals which he preached. In the words of Naginder Nath Gupta, "There were willing hearts in India waiting for his call and they at once realised the nature of struggle that lay ahead of them. Since then the struggle of national freedom in India has grown ever wider and today it comprehends the entire nation, it has been a glorious record, which is being added day after day, of sacrifice and suffering of women that vied with men in offering themselves as sacrifices at the altar of liberty and that was only due to Mahatma Gandhiji." According to Sir Stafford Cripps, "There has been no greater spiritual leader in the world in our own times than Mahatma Gandhi." Acharya Kripalani said about Gandhiji, "Mahatma is more right when he is wrong than we are when we are right."

Dr. Rajendra Prasad said, "Mahatma Gandhi's movement operated both horizontally and vertically. He took up causes which were not entirely political but which touched very intimately the life of large masses of people." Dr. Stanley Jones said about Mahatma Gandhiji, "He is stronger in death than he was in life. Millions around in the world are now interested in the Mahatma and his ideas - millions who would have only given him a passing glance had he not died for his ideals-martyr for the things for which he lived." Leon Blum, a French socialist, wrote about him, "I never saw Gandhi, I do not know his language, I never set foot in his country and yet I feel the same sorrow as if I had lost some one near and dear. The whole world has been plunged into mourning by the death of this extraordinary man." According to Lord Halifax, "I suppose there could be few men in all history who by their personal character and examples have so deeply influenced the thought of their generation."

Before we actually discuss the basic principles of Gandhian philosophy, it is interesting to discuss whether there is any separate 'ism' as Gandhism. Normally by 'ism' we understand a set philosophy given and preached through a set of literature readily available to the masses. We also believe that these basic ideas have been brought close together and adjusted in such a fashion that these do not contradict each other. If this is the sole test of a 'separate `ism', perhaps few might like to say that Gandhism does not exist at all. The critics will try to plead that Gandhiji in many of his movements the course of action was not always predetermined.

In fact, in Gandhism one is bound to find that it was an experiment which was being carried out constantly and as such his whole philosophy was on an experimental basis only this, but like an ,ism' Gandhian philosophy cannot be fully appreciated on the basis of theory but one is obliged to have practical knowledge of the Gandhian way of life. Not only this but like a philosopher Gandhiji did not coin or originate new ideas. Even Gandhiji himself used to say that "I am not giving any new `ism'." In his own words, "There is no such thing as Gandhism and I do not claim to have originated any new principle or doctrine. I have simply tried in my own way to apply the eternal truths to our daily life and problems.

The things I have formed and conclusions I have arrived at, are not final. I may change them homely. I have nothing to teach to the world. Truth and non-violence are as old as hills. All I have done is to try experiments in both on as vast a scale as I could do. In doing so I have sometimes erred and learnt by my errors ; well, of my philosophy, if it might be called by that pretentious name is done in what I have said, you will not call it Gandhism ; there is no ism about it."

But all that does not appear to be very convincing to say that Gandhism was not an 'ism' at all. Subsequent study will reveal that Gandhiji had certain basic principles of his philosophy which had no contradictions but were consistent. The ideas of noncooperation and non-violence were coined by him. Similarly he gave a new technique of fighting against the powerful nations. It was his basic idea which was given for the first time that a true and non-violent individual has nothing to fear even from a mighty empire based on violence, force and having all government authority under its control. He tried to see that these basic principles were consistently followed. His philosophy has come to stay and is being preached and made available to the modern generation in a very systematic form. It shall, therefore, be much safe to say that there is a separate Gandhism. If Gandhiji himself said that there was no separate Gandhism that was only due to his greatness.

Philosophy of Ghandhi

Gandhiji came on the scene of India and soon caught the imagination of the masses. His philosophy was very simple. He drew his philosophy from different sources. For Gandhiji most important source of inspiration was Bhagwat Gita. He found solution to every problem in Gita. He learnt from Gita that one should act for getting the results.

Gita in actual life, thus made him a man of action. From Gita he also picked up the philosophy or self-control, which he followed throughout his life. Again it was Gita that gave him the philosophy that truth was infallible and gives everyone courage and strength, even against the most powerful enemy. It is truth which gives man even mindedness and a balanced thinking and relieves from worries and pressures of life. It makes life ideal and happy.

From Buddhism and Jainism, Gandhiji picked up the philosophy of non-violence. He was also influenced by Rukin's 'Unto this Last.' It was from here that he learnt that only such economy was good which looked after the welfare of all. Then he learnt that all had equal right to earn their livelihood and life of a worker is both worth living and enjoying.

On Gandhiji influence of Tolstoy was in no way less. In was from him that he learnt that tyrannical government should be refused to be obeyed. He expounded the philosophy of non-resistance on this very basis.

In this way, Gandhian philosophy drew its inspiration not from one but from many sources and when it came out in practical shape from Gandhiji, it was a sound composite philosophy, which stood the test of time even against the mightiest empire of the world, in India's freedom struggle.

Gandhiji was a practical thinker and as such it has rightly been said about him that he was a great Karmayogi. It was his faith that theory should follow the practice and this he applied while discussing the future of his state. He left very much to the practice and as such he only gave broad outlines of the society which he wanted to have at any future date.

Views of Gandhiji on Nation

Gandhiji firmly believed that the present state was unwanted because it was a highly centralized organization. Not only this, he even condemned the state because it was based on force and as such believed that every thing should be achieved only by forceful methods. For him the state has many evils and was deeply rooted in violence. Since it is based on force and is centralized it is bound to crush individual freedom. Gandhiji felt that the modern state was becoming an end in itself but it was forgetting that an individual was an end while state was only means to an end. He attached greatest significance to individual than to the state.

Opposition Centralised Authority : Gandhiji felt that in the present set-up state authority had been centralized and the power passed on a few individuals and there was every danger that such power might be misused. As early as in 1931 he wrote, "To me political power is not an end but one of the means enabling the people to better their condition in every department of life. Political power means capacity to regulate national life through national representatives. If national life become so perfect as to become self-regulated, no representation is necessary.

There is then a state of enlightened anarchy. In such a state every one is his own ruler. He rules himself in such a manner that he is never a hindrance to his neighbour." He also felt that a stage must come when the authority of the state small not be wanted and it will change its very character and then instead of centralization it will pass on to decentralization. That decentralized state will be the real democracy based on most democratic principles. To quote him again, "I look upon an increase in the power of the state with greatest fear, because although while apparently doing good by minimising exploitation, it does the greatest harm to mankind by destroying individuality which lies at the root of all progress. We know of so many cases where men have adopted trusteeship but nowhere has the state really lived for the power. The state represents violence in a concentrated and organized form."

4

Ambedkar's Views

Bhimrao Ramjee Ambedkar (1891-December 7, 1956), was one of the great jurists, lawyers and political leaders of modern India. As a post-graduate student, he had done advanced studies in the field of economics. He was a student at the Columbia University in the City of New York and at London School of Economics. He also studied economist at Bonn. His works on the Indian Rupee as well as on Provincial Finance and Currency are notable.

Role in Constitution

As one of the prime architects of the text of the Indian constitution and as an outspoken militant champion of the aspirations and claims to equality of the so-called untouchable, Ambedkar has won undying recognition. He had experienced the agonies, anguishes, frustrations and humiliations of being born in the Mahar cast, which is an untouchable Maharashtrian community. His books on Indian sociology touching upon the problems of the *shudras,* the Untouchables, etc. breathe a note of deep realism and are also characterised by bitter denunciations of the old law givers, some of whom like Manu, poured forth words of contempt and bitterness against the suppressed sections of the Hindu society.

Ambedkar's Socio-political Ideas : As a sociological historian, Ambedkar did not accept the hypothesis of an Aryan invasion of India. The majority of Western and Indian scholars, however, tend towards accepting the hypothesis of Aryan invasion. "I do realize that in the ancient Vedic and Sanskrit literature there is no explicit mention of an invasion of north-west India by foreigners round about the second millennium B.C. Nevertheless, on philosophical grounds, the views of the western scholars appear more appealing to me". Ambedkar had forcefully put forward the views that the Sudras were not dark-skinned aboriginals enslaved or subordinated by the Aryan invaders but they too were Aryans who belonged to the Kshatriya solar dynasty.

The subordinate status of the Sudras was brought about by a bloody battle between Sudras, the Shudra king, and vasistha. Due to social vicissitudes and changes of fortune, they became degraded from their kshatriya status. The vedic king Sudras, son of Divodasa Atithigva, is regarded by Ambedkar as a Sudras on the basis of Mahabharata, *Santiparva* (Chapter LX)." The technique to bring this about was denying the *yajnopavita* to them. The Dasas and Dasyus, far from being savages were civilized and in fact were more powerful than the Aryans." But the Sudras were totally different from these Dasas and Dasyus. The Purusha Sukta, the Vedic charter for the subordinate status of the *Shudras is* regarded by Ambedkar as a "later interpolation."

Fight for Equality

According to Ambedkar, the Hindu scheme of social structure based on the four varnas or *Chaturvarna* breeds inequality and has been the parent of the caste-system and untouchability which are merely forms of inequality. They demanded a radical social solution. The India's constitution which has provided for complete equality before law and the equal protection of laws to all citizens, under Article 14, and in Article 17, not only has abolished untouchability of laws to all citizens, under Article 17, but has made its practice, in any form, an offence punishable under law.

Ambedkar was realistic in pointing out that the Indian bureaucracy which shared the prejudices of the Hindus against the untouchables was responsible for the woes of the untouchables. Hence, there is realism in his view that, in order to make public services responsive to the needs of the untouchables, there should be more members of the Untouchable community in the higher executive.

5

Growth of Nationalism

Indian Nationalism

(Indian Nationalism : Dadabhai Naoroji, Tilak, Savarkar, Gandhi, Jayaprakash Narain, Nehru, Subhash Bose, Ambedkar, Ram Manohar Lohia.)

Origin of Nationalism

Most of our Indian historians have spared no pains to establish that our struggle for freedom continued even during the darkest period of our slavery. They believed that the death of Harsha brought disintegration in Indian Empire and Muslim traditions dominated the Hindu civilization but the basic concepts of Hindu civilization namely those of joint family system, Panchayati Raj or village autonomy and even caste system continued to be the basis of our civilization. Hence for them India nationalism was a deep-rooted institution and it always inspired the Indian masses.

Growth of Nationalism

Indian political thought developed in the background of Indian National struggle or in other words our struggle for nationalism was against British colonialism. It is, therefore, most imperative to study the nature of our struggle for national freedom. Briefly speaking Indian struggle for freedom started even before Hume founded Indian National Congress. We find that as early as in nineties of 18th century Raja Ram Mohan Roy came to forefront but even before him persons like Surendra Nath Banerjee and others had set the ball rolling though not with great momentum. There was also Hindu nationalism and Muslim nationalism and if we agree with, Wahabi Movement was the first Muslim war of independence. But real and earnest national struggle started as the people began to come under the fold of Indian National Congress and gradually this organization began to assume the role of a popular organization.

Extremist Movement : The Congress was originally under the influence of moderates who believed in making petitions and prayers to the rulers for getting more and more political rights. Most of these moderates were of the opinion that India could develop and prosper only under British rule and in fact, for them, this rule was a great blessing. It was gradually, however, that the extremists began to come to the front and began to dominate our political life and platform. Under the inspiring guidance of Lal, Bal and Pal, the extremist influence in the Congress was unshakable.

First World War aroused great hopes in the minds of Indians who felt that their cooperation in war effort shall be properly rewarded but instead the nation got Jallianwala Bagh tragedy and most unsatisfactory constitutional reforms embodied in the Government of India Act, 1919. There was great dissatisfaction and frustration among the people of India. In 1920, Mahatma Gandhi started his non-cooperation movement which was well responded but he had to give up, due to many unhappy events including the Chauri Chaura incidents.

In 1922 under the Presidentship of Pandit Jawaharlal Nehru, the nation resolved to have full freedom and to make the British leave our country. In 1931, there was famous Gandhi-Irwin Pact and subsequent Round Table Conferences to solve constitutional deadlocks and to give the people of India constitutional progress.

In 1935, India got famous Government of India Act, 1935, under which India became a federation of Indian provinces and princely States. The proposed federation was to come into being under certain conditions which did not mature with the result that central set as envisaged in the Act could not be put into operation.

Attempt to solve problem. Then there followed a regular struggle for national freedom. During the Second World War India made it amply clear that her cooperation in war efforts was subject to the condition that some political rights will be extended to us immediately and that a clear picture about India's political fate after the war was over, should be agreed at this state. By this time our political thinkers like Mahatma Gandhi, Jawaharlal Nehru, Subhash Chandra Bose, Maulana Abdul Kalam Azad and many others had dominated our political life and gave clear political ideas. Philosophy of non-violence, non-cooperation, Swadeshi and Boycott were the main weapons of our struggle. One after the other proposals for solving our constitutional deadlock were put forth by the rulers and these enlightened political thinkers gave appropriate reaction. In this struggle were both the moderates as well as the extremist and due to their combined and collective efforts nation got its independence in 1947.

This brief survey will make it very clear that for fighting against one of the most powerful colonial powers of the world, India had political thinkers of a high standard and standing.

Causes of Nationalism

1. *British Rule :* For centuries India could not see political unity with the result that the people of India lost the very image of a strong and united India. Practically after the death of Aurangzeb India was divided and disintegrated among various tiny states and one province thought the other as enemy and so was the

case with the communities. But it was under the British regime that whole of British India was united. The people of India now began to get the image of united India. The rulers were in no mood to permanently settle in India and made her their home and this further stregthened bonds of unity amongst the Indians.

2. *Improved Transport and Communication Facilities:* Throughout Mughal supremacy, India could not get a quick and well connected system of communication and transportation. The Britishers in their own interest, and in order to promote their trade interests developed quick means of transportation and communication with the result that Indian masses came in close contacts with each other. Our national leaders could express their ideas and convey their viewpoint very easily. In addition to this, shortening of distance made people of India realise that their country was one and they were not far away from each other. Not only this but the masses came very close to each other and this promoted unity and strengthened feeling of nationalism.
3. *Economic Policy of Britishers :* The Britishers came as traders with the object of improving their economic conditions. Therefore, gradually they followed the policy of sacrificing our economic interest and preserved their own. There was a regular drain on our economic resources with the result that whereas our economic conditions deteriorated, theirs immensely improved. Not only this, but due to this economic policy, here was unemployment in our country and masses on the whole suffered. Our handicrafts were practically ignored and those who sat behind the spinning wheel and hands which held needles came on the road. On the contrary, economic condition of the people of England greatly improved. There was increased employment in England and unemployment in India. In other words, the people of England enjoyed at the

miseries of vast multitude of India. As it has been said that the most unfortunate aspect of the problem was that the Finance Minister of India looked after more the interests of Britishers rather than those of Indians and all this was bound to reverse in its reaction. But our great disappointment was that the Britishers did not care to improve our economic conditions and followed a free trade policy which was only advantageous to well advanced nations of the world rather than the poorly developed industrial countries like India.

4. *Rural Attitude* : The attitude of the Britishers was also one of the leading factors for Indian discontentment. The Britishers always tried to establish their supremacy and stressed that they had come to rule and govern India. They felt that culturally, economically and socially we were backward. We were not allowed to travel in first class railway compartment. Even the Indian Princes were asked to unlace the shoes of British hunters. They were not allowed to act as jurors. Not only this, but life of a British gentleman was considered far more valuable than that of many Indians. The Britishers worked under the notion that the Indians knew only fear. In the words of Sir Theodore Morrison the Britishers worked under certain notions namely, "The first was that the life of one European was worth those of many Indians. The second was that the only thing that an oriental understands was fear. The third was that England had been forced to lose many lives and spend many millions to hold India and did she not merit some more substantial recompense than the privilege of governing India in a spirit of wisdom and unselfishness." This attitude became more revengeful after the rising of 1857. Even those British officers who did not suffer from superiority complex began to develop a rough complex attitude of superiority but superiority with a revenge. It is evident from the fact that most of the

Viceroys in India did not care for our feelings and sentiments. We find the Lord Lytton arranged Delhi Darbar when there was a serious famine in south. Similarly the same Governor General waged Second Afghan War when the nation was passing through economic crisis. Against all sentiments he passed his most condemned Vernacular Press Act in 1878. This attitude of the Britishers was very sharply reacted to by all sections of public opinion who moulded their philosophy to respond to this attitude.

5. *Educational Policy of Britishers* : The Indians were accustomed to study their religious books and as such before the coming of the Britishers who had no knowledge about literatures contained in other languages. As the English became the lingua franca and many of the Indian youths gradually studied English with care they were very much influenced by that. Not only this, but Indian youth had an opportunity to go to England and live there. Thus, the people of India could get what was contained in English literature. Fortunately it was a literature which contained much about liberalism, which pleaded rights for the people and which gave them the spirit of struggle with which the people of England fought against their monarchs in order to get their rights. They also had an opportunity to see the British political institutions at work and found that whereas the people of England demand rights and liberty for themselves, they deny same to the people of India. This was an eye awakening for us and we also demanded similar rights for ourselves.

6. *Other European Contract* : Gradually we came in contact with other Western countries and studied their national, social and political movements. They found that there was a wave of liberal reforms in many of European countries and felt that the people of those countries were struggling hard to get their rights from their

Governments. Perhaps there was no Western country in fifties of 18th century which was not fomenting liberalism. Indians also could not remain uninfluenced by all this.

7. *Controversy on Ilbert Bill :* It was during the regime of Lord Ripon. who was otherwise a sympathiser of India, that the most important Ilbert Bill controversy arose. No doubt the Britishers who were in very superior position, won their point but at a great cost. It was thereafter that we lost faith in British sense of justice and impartiality. Deep faith which had been rooted after centuries, was rudely shaken and as Surendra Nath Banerjee remarked, "No self-respecting Indian could sit idle under the fierce light of that revelation." It was a call to the high patriotic duty to those who understood its significance.

8. *Revivalist Movement :* With the passage of time India's past glory was revived and the Indians came to know about their heritage. In 1803, a teacher at Fort William College wrote a history of India which depicted poor knowledge of Britishers about India's past but gradually persons like Sir William Johns, and Alexander Cunnigham and Max Muller gave a glorious and vivid account of India's past cultural heritage. In the Indian society persons like Ranade, R.G. Bhandarkar, Rajindarkar, Rajindra Lal Mitra and Har Prasad Sastri who revived Indian glory and aroused national feelings among our people. Not only this but our religious and social reformers like Raja Ram Mohan Roy, Ishwar Chandra Vidyasagar, Swami Dayanand Saraswati, Rama Krishna Paramhans and Vivekanand claimed that our native rule in its worst form was far better than the best rule of a foreign Government.

9. *Role Played by Indian Press :* The Indian Press also helped a lot in consolidating our national movement. Papers like Amrit Bazar Patrika, The Hindi, The Kesri, and

> The Bengalee did a lot in bringing such information to the notice and knowledge of masses, which was practically unknown or unrevealed at that time.

It was under these circumstances that with the formation of the Indian National Congress, our national movement was consolidated. It was during this period that persons like Raja Ram Mohan Roy, Dadabhai Naoroji and Surendra Nath Banerjee and Gopal Krishan Gokhale gave their liberal policies and ideas. The task before them was not only political but they were also required to consolidate our social and economic conditions in a most suitable and practicable manner. Though Indian National Congress cannot claim that national movement started with it yet no one will deny that the formation of this organization opened a new chapter in the history of our national struggle. As the time passed Lokmanya Bal Gangadhar Tilak came to the front with his extremist ideals and preached that the liberal policy could do no good to nation. He had many supporters in the Congress organization itself particularly in the youth of India which was greatly dissatisfied with the 'Go Slow' policy of the rulers and appeasement policy of moderate national leaders. There was split in Congress at Surat in 1907 which was mostly due to the policies of Lord Curzon and the situation created by the partition of Bengal in 1905. The extremists in themselves were divided and there were revolutionaries who found themselves unadjustable even with the extremists. It was under these circumstances that Lokmanya Tilak and Lala Lajpat Rai gave their political ideas demanding Swaraj; which they said was their birth right.

During First World War Mahatma Gandhi who had then come from south Africa, vigorously pleaded that Indians should fully cooperate and put all their resources at the disposal of the British Government. He had then full faith in British sense of justice and impartiality. But as the war came to a close and the Britishers emerged victorious. The Indians had pinned high hopes in the British Parliament but on the contrary, even the faiths of Mahatma Gandhi was shaken when the

Government announced the reforms of 1919 and the events leading to ghastly tragedy of Jallianwala Bagh. It was in this atmosphere that Mahatma Gandhi gave his political ideas and put forth before the Indian masses his policy of non-cooperation, non-violence and Satyagraha.

In our national struggle another phase came when it was seen that the Britishers were not coming to terms and there was need and necessity of putting some extra force and pressure on the British Government for getting our justified demands met. In order to mature this thinking there came the policy of Netaji Subhash Chandra Bose who fought for Indian freedom on a foreign soil.

Inspiration from the West : In the foregoing paragraphs we have made an attempt that English education and policy of the British Government largely helped in awakening and bringing the people of India close to each other. There can be no denial today that in our nationalism we get much inspiration from the West. Their struggle against their monarch for demanding right inspired the people of India. Similarly the desire of the British people to establish their cultural and spiritual supremacy made the Indians study about their cultural heritage. The work of Asiatic Society of Bengal founded in 1784 by Sir Jones and the work done in the society by persons of eminence like Sir Charles Wilkies and H.T. Colebrook proved a source of great inspiration for the Indians. It is, thus, safe to conclude that the Indians drew much of inspiration from the West than from within India for developing their spirit of nationalism and also national struggle.

Indian Renaissance : It was under these circumstances that India renaissance was born with Raja Ram Mohan Roy as its chief exponent and pioneer. An attempt was made to revive rich Indian cultural heritage and Indian spirituality in its true sense and brought before the people of the world. The people of India should tell the universe as to what was best in them. They should be told that Indian culture is an integral whole. Not only this but the people should be made to understand as to what is true dharma or religion in its true sense. It was with this object in view that many of the Indians and foreigners took pains to accomplish this difficult but noble task.

This was very much helped by the impact of Western system of education and learning. Another factor which contributed in this direction was an attempt by many people like Guru Nanak Dev, Kabir, Chaitanya Maha Prabhu, Tulsidas and the followers of Brahma Samaj, Swami Dayanand, founder of Arya Samaj and persons like Raja Ram Mohan Roy, R.L. Mitra, Har Prasad Sastri, R.G. Bhandarkar and R. Dutt who tried to establish that Indian culture was the most glorious and shining with which even the most advanced countries of the world could not compete. Not only this, but in this revival were the people like and Ram Krishna Paramhansa Vivekananda who at the Parliament of Religions at Chicago in 1893 gave a very vivid description of Indian culture and true Hindu religion. In southern India, a spirit of renaissance which was spiritual and religious in character, was inspired by Subba Rao Puntulu. Rangaiah Naidu and G. Subramaniya Aiyyar and in Bengal, Tagore. J.,C. Bose and P.C. Roy were the persons who inspired the people. Prarthana Samaj, Arya Samaj and similar other institutions took up this task very seriously and in right earnest. It included persons like Mahadev Govind Ranade who was born and developed in Indian culture and civilisation.

Dadabhai Naoroji

Born in a Parsi priestly family in Bombay, Dadabhai Naoroji was the first Indian lecturer at Elphinstone Institute. In 1856 he proceeded to England to manage the business interests of Cama & Co., and later he became a partner of this concern. During the first twelve years of his stay in London, he vigorously applied himself to the task of educating Englishmen, in and out of the Parliament, on all matters affecting India. He founded the East India Association in 1867 for this purpose.

Returning to India in 1869, he kept himself busy in public

life. In 1876 he accepted the Dewanship of the Baroda State but left it on account of his differences with the British Resident.

Naoroji started the Rasi Goftar, and founded about thirty institutions, designed to promoted the political and social advancement of the country. In 1885 he was nominated to the Bombay Legislative Council and in 1892 he became the first Indian to be elected to the House of Commons—where he fervently pleaded the cause of his country.

Naoroji, popularly known as the "Grand Old Man of India" was thrice chosen President of the Indian National Congress in 1886, 1892 and 1906. He led a simple but heroic life devoutly dedicated to the services of his country. Naoroji was also the author of scholarly books on the political and socio-economic aspects of India.

Dadabhai was a unique figure in Indian public life for nearly half a century. He was one of the finest products of western education in India. He was a pathfinder and original thinker in several fields. Although in the field of social and economic philosophy he was not as deep learned and original as Bentham, Adam Smith or T.H. Green, in the Indian context, where there was not as yet any systematic thinking on problems of production, wealth, capital, national income, political obligation, etc., it was a bold theoretical endeavour on the part of Dadabhai Naoroji to have produced that classic on Indian economic philosophy, Poverty and Un-British Rule in India. In spite of repetitions and the absence of an all governing theoretical structure, this book which contains the speeches, statements and letters of Dadabhai Naoroji for over thirty years, is marked by the earnestness of a man who had won great esteem and prestige because of his steadfast unwearied endeavors in the cause of the economic emancipation of India.

Economic Philosophy **:** Dadabhai built up the theory of the economic foundations of Indian nationalism. He pointed out that Indian economy was subjected to heavy "Drain". The drain of India's resources resulted in the colossal exploitation of country. The growing "immiserization" of the country was a heart rending phenomenon. Thus "Dadabhai became an eye opener to Indians to the appalling story of their grim poverty. He made then conscious of the calamitous consequence of economic drain, famines, pestilences and starvation to which they were subjected. Dadabhai's "Poverty and Un-British rule in India", wherein he expounds the "drain" theory, is a classical book in the field of Indian economics and Indian nationalism. Dadabhai was the pathfinder in the application of the statistical methods of problems of Indian finance. He attempted to reveal the economic ruin of India not on the basis of hypothesis and assumptions but tried to base, his propositions on solid fact. He applied an objective methodology also to the discussion of the other practical, political and economic problems of India.

Dadabhai deplored the "unnatural" financial and economic policy of the British rulers because India had been saddled with a huge public debt which was imposed as a political burden on the country by the constraint of a foreign imperialism and was also encumbered with the economic burdens of a heavy administrative agency both in England and in India. Thus, the inhabitants of the country were deprived of their "natural right" and their means of subsistence. This intermittent process of the exhaustion of the "very life blood of the country" was a painful and heart rending phenomenon. Hence, the only way for the promotion of the economic prosperity of the country was to check the ruinous drain. Dadabhai wrote "...That not till this disastrous drain was duly checked, and not till the people of India were restored to their natural rights in their own country, was there any hope for the material amelioration."

Dadabhai was pained to see the grim spectacle of India's exploitation. The dark and terrible spectra of disease, half feeding or starvation was the shape in which life presented itself to millions in India who had been subjected to the salt tax, excessive revenue exaction and terrible famines. Thus, millions of the people were forced to extreme economic misery and a deliberate policy of prevention of the stimulation of industry of India. The promotion of works of public utility and the carrying on of public administration for public good. Dadabhai looked to this Proclamation as a Magna Carta for Indians.

It was the demand both of ethics and constitutional laws that England should govern India for India's good. This implied that the rampant misery, drain, distress and destruction in the country had to be ended. It was the responsibility of the British democracy to bring about a better state of things and reduce the political and economical suffering of India. It would serve no useful purpose merely to repeat the slogan that England had brought to India law, order and peace. The only true and lasting method to make British rule a 'blessing' in India and a 'benefit and glory' to England was "by allowing India her own administration under their superior controlling and guiding hand." Dadabhai had the boldness to proclaim in the British House of Commons that there could be no healthy and true finance in India until the "evil of foreign domination" was reduced to reasonable dimensions because the "evil of the foreign rule" involved the triple loss of wealth, wisdom and work. It led to disproportionate financial extortion, it resulted in the diminution of administrative experience in the country because the foreign personnel left India after retirement. It also meant the employment of Indians to the extent that all prize posts were monopolized by the British. Without adequate employment of Indians in the public services, their resourcefulness, initiative and capacity for the performance of significant duties could not be developed and hence Dadabhai opposed the exclusion of Indians from the higher services.

Imperialism generates administrative evil and financial deprivation. The thoughtless drain of India's wealth in the past had been a terrible misfortune. Its continuance was bound to be a deliberate plunder and destruction, and would immensely damages the life blood of the people. The deplorable miseries had to be ended, otherwise the country would be reduced to a worsening state. Furthermore, this process of economic drain and exploitation carried on by the engine of political constraint would ruin the moral fibre of the British administrators. A despotism corrupts the holders of political power by damaging and deadening their moral sensibilities . The despot used to habits of pride, haughtiness and domination in his relations with the colonial inhabitants would incorporate a socially defiant elements in the British body politic after his return to the home country. Dadabhai, thus, showed great political insight in pointing out the moral evils of despotic imperialism.

Dadabhai pleaded that political power should be rooted in the affection, will and feelings of the people. But the British policies of two fold restraint—"gagging and disarming"—showed that the British power was not based on the "loyalty of the people". Hence, Dadabhai urged that the foundations of political authority had to be laid in the contentment of the people and popular contentment could be fostered only by people's confidence.

Political Views : In the early stages of his career Dadabhai had genuine faith in the blessings of British rule. He had sincerely hoped that the British would treat India as a sacred charge entrusted to them. To make the British people and legislators aware of the Indian point of view he contested and won after hard struggle a seat in the British Parliament. In his presidential speech at the Indian National Congress in 1886, he had proclaimed "loyalty to the backbone" of Indians.

Hence he advised Indians to cultivate the judicious harmony of loyalty to Britain and patriotism towards their own country. But due to a series of disappointments Dadabhai came to the conclusion that without the acquisition of the right of self-government India could not stop its destruction. Plato had said that an oligarchical city is not one city—it is two cities in one, the city of the rich and the city of the poor. Dadabhai spoke in a similar fashion when he said that there are two Indians—an India of the few rich and the exploiters and the India of the vast exploited millions. He pleaded that England should not allow the horrible process of economic polarization to be perpetuated. The myth of India's fabulous wealth was an unfounded delusion. The objective fact was that India was slowly sinking deeper into the abyss of extreme poverty. In the context of crippling poverty, she had been saddled with a very costly civil and military administration.

Political Ideas : The concept of the moral foundations of political authority has been advocated by all the Indian protagonists of liberalism. Justice, generosity and humanity alone constitute the golden links which hold political structures together. Only the identity of will and aspirations among citizens can provide longevity to a political system. Dadabhai said: "You can build up an empire by arms or by ephemeral brute physical force, but you can preserve it by the eternal moral forces only. Brute force will, some time or another, break down; righteousness alone is everlasting." The union of heart, feelings and sentiments constitutes the real basis of political power. It is a common view to recognize force as the basis of authority but a deeper probe reveals the inadequacy of this conception.

Dadabhai was candid enough to recognize some of the benefits of British rule to India accruing from the "advanced humanitarian civilization of Britain," and the introduction of western education, trained administrative personnel and mechanical technology like the railways, but he also frankly spoke against the evil qualities of the then prevailing system of government. He warned that a despotic and autocratic government could not continue as the "evil system of government" was leading to bankruptcy and ruin. It was a "cruel farce" and needed radical change. If the British rule continued to be "a heavy yoke of the stranger and the despot" it was "doomed to perish". The infamy of despotism and tyranny could not be perpetuated. Dadabhai, however, trusted that narrow-minded injustice was not a part of the character of the English nation.

Dadabhai believed in the civilization role of the British rule in India. He hoped that soon England would realize that the inglorious policy of mounting economic greed was not only short-sighted but it contained germs of peril even for the ruling country. He wanted to end the heavy drain of India's economic resources. Once the drain was ended, a situation could be created for the long continuance of the British empire in India.

The fulfilment of India's political hopes depended on the renaissance of the moral consciousness in England. Dadabhai desired and expected that England would honestly, honourably, conscientiously and faithfull fulfil the promises and pledges that she had made to India. The connection between India and England had to be established on the basis of righteousness, justice and liberality. India's problems would be solved if these pledge were fulfilled. He earnestly wanted the implementation of the declaration contained in the Charter Act of 1833 and the Proclamation of 1858. He hoped that England would vindicate her sense of justice, generosity and freedom. He had earnestly trusted that Great Britain would produce a statesmanship the would redeem the pledges made by British rulers of the past and would thus fulfil Britain's mission to humanity. The Proclamation of 1858 had announced that the Government of India would maintain the four principles of religious toleration, liberty, career open to talents and equality before the law. It also emphasized not attain national greatness.

In the Congress presidential speech at Calcutta in 1906 Dadabhai stressed three important rights of the Indian people. The first was the right to the increasing appointment of Indians in the public services and the placing of the departmental administration in their hands. The second was the right to increasing representation of Indians so that India may have legislative assemblies on the model of the self-governing colonies. The third was the right to just financial relations between India and Great Britain. Dadabhai had great hopes that in his lifetime the British rulers, would take steps to institute honourable self-government for India. He advised Indians to persevere in the path of agitation through petitions, and meetings. Agitation is the moral alternative to resort to brute force. He frankly stated that the basic principles of the British administration in India are unsound and hence wanted the Congress to agitate against them. He realized, however, that self-government was the only lasting remedy for India.

On theoretical grounds he had, for many long years, been a free trader like Cobden, but in the unnatural economic confusion, cloudiness and misery prevailing in India, Dadabhai advocated Swadeshi. He, however, still had faith in the "revival" of the true old spirit and instinct of liberty in the minds and hearts of English statesmen. Like Burke, he retained faith in the ancient and inbred integrity of the British people. He hoped that India would be a loyal partner and co-operator and not the dependency of England. He still asked the Indian people not to become desperate but to keep in mind one significant English word "persevere".

During the First World War, Dadabhai Naoroji appealed to his countrymen to stand by the side of the British. It was unfortunate that only two months before the Announcement of Montague on August 20, 1917, about responsible government, this veteran fighter for India's rights passed away.

Dadabhai Naoroji was a phenomenon in modern Indian history. He was a great political guru and leader. He was an economist who had a deep grasp of the problems of public finance, foreign trade and national income. He was also a social and political thinker of great eminence. Although he may not rank with Ricardo, Mill and Marx, as a pure economic theoretician, his overwhelming personality and lofty moral character brought popularity to his ideas on contemporary Indian economics and politics. Thus, his concept of "drain" to his ideas on contemporary Indian economics thinking as the concepts of "exploitation" and "class-struggle" are in the Marxist and socialist circles.

Dadabhai Naoroji had a moral approach to political action. His personal life was marked by transcendent purity and he brought to his political activities the same kind of moral favour. His devotion to the cause of India was deep and earnest and he pursued political activities in a dedicated spirit of personal abnegation. He was the embodiment of a pure and perfect patriotism. He pursued the path of political agitation because he regarded that as the most potent technic for India's social and economic rehabilitation and progress. In self-government alone, he felt lay India's hope, strength and destiny. His endeavour for the uplift of the country influenced Gokhale. Thus, through the purified earnestness of his life and activities, this patriarch of Indian nationalism strengthened the concept of moralization of politics.

Bal Gangadhar Tilak

Lokmanya Bal Gangadhar Tilak, the Hercules of Indian nationalism, was among those thinkers and leaders of the early twentieth century who won appreciation from all people due to his love for the country, simplicity and scholarship. His political opponents saw him with jealousy due to his courage to face failure and defeats. The story of his life and work, is the history of western India during the forty years from 1880 to 1920. It is also the history of the birth and growth of Indian nationalism. The greatest tribute of Lokmanya Tilak was paid by his life long political opponent Gokhale who is reported to have said that born a hundred and twenty years before Tilak would have carved out a kingdom for himself. He gave a new turn to Indian political thinking and forced the Indian National Congress to adopt a radical programme of fighting for freedom of the country. Thus, Tilak made a unique contribution to the national movement for freedom of the country.

Religious Thoughts : Tilak was a Hindu and he took pride in his religion. He had great reverence for the Hindu scriptures. He was of the definite view that the fall of the Hindus was not due to the Hindu religion. He held Lord Krishna in high esteem. This is amply proved by his Commentary on the Gita—called Gita Rahasya. He was not opposed to all religious ceremonies or rituals and he wanted them to be changed to suit the changed circumstances. He was not a reactionary in matters of religion.

The view of Tilak was that Hindu religion provided a moral and social tie and united the people. He called upon the people to revive that union. To quote him, "A Hindu of this place is as *much* a Hindu as the one from Madras or Bombay. The study of the Gita, Ramayana and Mahabharata produces the same idea throughout the country. If we lay stress on it forgetting all the ordinary differences that exist between different sects, then by the grade of Providence we shall long be able to consolidate all the different sects into a mighty Hindu nation." He believed that science was no substitute for the sacred Hindu religion.

In his Commentary on the Gita, Tilak expounded the doctrine of Karma Yoga, "The Religion of Action". His view was that our forefathers never intended that the goal of life should be mediation alone. No person can expect God to protect him if he sits with folded arms and throws his burden on others. God does not help the indolent. Proper action alone is the road to salvation. That man is truly learned who is also the doer. Gita-Rahasya is a more important work of nationalist literature than of philosophy. Tilak gave his countrymen a stirring and vigorous call to selfless action. To quote Sir Radhakrishna, "It was Mr. Tilak's robust patriotism that predisposed his mind to this activist view."

Education System : The view of Tilak was that the Western system of education in India was ruinous to the future health and well being of the nation. The younger generations were being educated away not only from their families and the great majority of the Indian people but also away from the value system of India's civilization. The Government supported Western education which uprooted the youth from their ties with the past and made them Indians only in name. Moreover, Western education was available only to a few persons who could afford to go to Western schools and the great bulk of the people of India were left untouched by any kind of formal education. What was necessary was the introduction of national education in the country.

The plan of national education involved the establishment of schools throughout the country dedicated to giving young India a truly national educational background. The useful lessons of western education were not to be ignored but were to be supplemented with the lessons of India's own great culture. Tilak wanted the Congress to support with all its asset the establishment of schools and colleges throughout the country to provide inexpensive and wholesome education emphasizing the new spirit of self-reliance which young people could not expect to receive in the institutions supported by the Government.

Tilak condemned the existing system of English education on the ground that it neglected religious education. He emphasized the importance of religious education for the building of character in these words: "Secular education only is not enough to build up a character. Religious education is necessary because the study of high principles keeps us away from evil pursuits."

Extreme Love for Country : Tilak put great emphasis on love for the country. History and tradition, religion and philosophy, action and unity were made meaningful in the concept of love of the country. To quote Tilak, "God and our country are not different. In short, our country is one form of God". The love of nation, like the love of God, has to transcend narrow provincialism, communalism and sectarianism. It has to be the first cause for both action and unity.

A Political Weapon : Tilak was one of the first to realize that boycott which originally started with the refusal of the people to purchase goods manufactured in England could be expanded to the point of jeopardizing the foundation of the hold of British administrative machinery in India. In a speech at Poona in 1902, Tilak said, "You must realize that you are yourselves the useful lubricants which enable the gigantic machinery to work so smoothly. Though downtrodden and neglected, you must be conscious of your power of making the administration impossible if you, but choose to make it so. It is you who manage the rail-road and the telegraph; it is you who make settlements and collect revenues; it is in fact you who do everything for the administration though in a subordinate capacity. You must consider whether you cannot turn your hand to better use for your nation than drudging on in this fashion."

Boycott became a very important political weapon but its effective use demanded courage and a large measure of self-sacrifice. This fact was emphasized by Tilak in a speech at Calcutta. "If you have not the power of active resistance, have you not the power of self-denial and self-abstinence in such a way as not to assist this foreign Government to rule-over you? This is boycott and this is what is meant when we say that boycott is a political weapon."

Tilak declared that the Moderates could not deliver the goods and the people should look up to the Extremists for the liberation of their country. The repetition of resolutions full of prayers to the Government could not bring any results. The remedy was not petitions but boycott. To quote him, "We are not armed and there is no necessity for arms either. We have a strong weapon, a political weapon in boycott. The whole of this administration which is carried on by a handful of Englishmen with our assistance. We are in subordinate service. We are clerks and willing instruments of our own oppression in the hands of an alien Government and the Government is ruling over us not by its innate strength but by keeping us in ignorance and blindness to the perception of this fact. Every Englishman known that they are a mere handful in this country and it is the business of everyone of them to fool you into believing that you are weak and they are strong. What the new Party wants to do is to realize the fact that your future rests entirely in your hands."

Swadeshi : Like the other Extremists, Tilak also advocated Swadeshi. Tilak wrote, "The object is to bring about the spread of Swadeshi things, visible and invisible, to bring about the gradual disappearance of visible foreign things and to bring about the gradual disappearance of foreign ideas also." Again, "Like the bodies, our mind also should become Swadeshi. Swadeshi thought should always reign in our hearts." Swadeshi was the first assertion of the spirit of independence. The Indians were asked to become self-reliant and independent in all thing and thereby earn all the rights and privileges of free men. The Swadeshi movement was a movement of national regeneration. Swadeshi was a practical application of the love of the country. To quote Tilak, "To recognize the land of the Aryas as mother earth is the Swadeshi movement." It was an economic, political and spiritual weapon.

Demand of Swaraj : Swaraj played an important part in the political philosophy of the Indian value system. It referred both to the self-rule of the individual and the self-rule of the political community. Swaraj was a part of both the philosophy of life and the philosophy of politics. To quote Tilak, "The idea of Swaraj is an old one." For the individual, Swaraj means the exercise of his freedom lawfully. It means the choice of cosmos over chaos and the regulation of all actions morally in accordance with the Swadharma of the individual. Unless there is Swaraj, the individual cannot live in his true nature. He cannot attain and fulfil the purpose of life. Likewise, Swaraj is meaningful in the classical philosophy of politics for the political community. It means the lawful exercise of freedom by the community. Unless there is Swaraj, the right ordering of the community can never be attained. Men cannot live in their true nature and the purpose of life and creation cannot be fulfilled. The political community exists only to preserve and promote the Dharma and without Swaraj that is not possible. Therefore, Swaraj is necessary for both the individual and the community. Without Swaraj, life is not worthwhile. Tilak maintained that "Our life and our Dharma are in vain in the absence of Swaraj."

The view of Tilak was that the evils of the nineteenth and twentieth centuries in India were largely the result of the weakening of the Indian social order on account of its long struggle to preserve the Dharma in the absence of Swaraj. The only lasting remedy for the social evils is the re-establishment of Swaraj or self-rule. Life has no moral purpose unless there is Swaraj to protect and promote the Dharma.

Tilak defined Swaraj in these words : "People's rule instead of that of bureaucracy is Swaraj." This was the essence of his argument that the social reformers wanted to have the support of British bureaucracy to enforce the measures of social reform. His own view was that unless the people supported the reforms, the reforms were not only meaningless but also undemocratic and without moral significance. There must be popular control over the power of Government. Swaraj must be democratic.

Tilak believed that all progress, all hope for national advancement, rested on Swaraj. No issue had precedence over Swaraj. In his public speeches Tilak often said, "If we do not get Swarajya, there will be no industrial progress; if we do not get Swarajya, there will be no possibility of having any kind of education useful to the national, either primary or higher. If we do get Swarajya it is not merely to advance female education or to secure industrial reform or social reform. All these are parts of Swarajya. Power is wanted first." Swarajya was a moral imperative, for "there is no question which is not dependent upon Swarajya." Again, "We demand Swarajya, as it is the foundation and not the height of our future prosperity."

Tilak was not interested in securing Government posts for deserving Indian. He repeatedly said, "To get posts for big salaries is not the meaning of Swarajya". Swarajya meant a total change in political theory. To quote Tilak, "It is true that what we seek may seem like a revolution in the sense that it means a complete change in the theory of the Government of India as now put forward by the bureaucracy." Tilak always insisted, "Swarajya is the foundation."

In one of his meetings, Tilak declared. 'We are at present clamoring for Swaraj and therefore the Shivaji festival is the most fitting one for us to celebrate. If Shivaji was able to establish Swarajya two centuries ago, we too may expect to achieve it some day. Swarajya belongs to us by birth-right. The Moderates can be compared to Shivaji's father Shahji who always used to advise his son not to take up arms against the mighty Muhammadan monarchs of the Deccan. But Shivaji, who can be compared to the Extremists of the present day, gave a new turn to events. We are masters of our fortunes and can govern them if we only make up our minds to do so. Swarajya is not far off from us. It will come to us the moment we learn to stand on our legs." His slogan at the meeting was: "Swaraj is my birth right. I will have it."

Passive Resistance : Tilak was a practical political leader and a realist. He foresaw that violence would be wasteful and ultimately ineffectual. To quote Tilak, "We say prepare your forces, organize your power and then go to work so that they cannot refuse you what you demand. We are not armed and there is not necessity for arms either." Being a realist, Tilak recognized that "the military strength of the Government is enormous and a single machine gun showering hundreds of bullets per minute will quite suffice for our largest public meetings." Action must be direct but it must be passive as well. To quote Tilak, As our fight is going to be constitutional and legal, our death also must, as of necessity be constitutional and legal. We have not to use any violence."

Philosophy of Defiance : Tilak taught the people of India the philosophy of defiance. If the Government was not prepared to concede willingly, any methods could be employed to make the Government do what the people wanted it to do. He was convinced that no power in the world could withhold from the people their right to independence. The people looked upon Tilak as "the man who is to expel the British from India." Tilak did not make a fetish of non-violence. To risk life for the cause of one's country is the greatest sacrifice one can make.

Tilak wanted genuine reform in society and not simple imitation of Western life and manners. He believed that such reform must come from the people and not from a foreign

Government. He struggled to reawaken India to her past and base her future greatness on her past glories. Knowing fully well that real progress can only be made by a self-governing people, knowing the moral progress can only be made through moral and democratic decisions, knowing that Swaraj or self-rule was the pre-requisite of real social, political, economic, cultural and spiritual progress. Tilak began to think in terms of achievement of Swaraj. The social reformers were prepared to criticize almost everything Indian, to imitate the West in the name of improvement and rely upon the power of a foreign Government to bring about this improvement. They were convinced that only by social reform could they earn political reform and social reform must precede political reform.

The view of Tilak was that political reform must precede social reform. It is only popular Self-Government that is moral Government. It is only a moral Government that can create moral social changes. Hence, self-rule is necessary and the first object to be pursued must be political reform and not social reform.

Was Tilak a Realist? : He recognized that it was not simply the forms and practices of society which had to be changed. The evils in social practices were the direct result of the spirit of orthodoxy which filled the forms of social order and resisted change. That spirit was the result of a hundred years of foreign overlordship, defeat, instability, defensiveness and inflexibility. Tilak believed that effective reform must ultimately depend upon a reawakening of the true spirit of Indian people. Instead of criticizing social forms as the great evils. Tilak started his battle against the spirit of orthodoxy which was locked up in forms, rituals and customs that had survived their usefulness. The orthodox spirit had served its purpose because it had transmitted classical values to a new generation which could understand them and bring about the necessary rebirth an re-application of those values. The degraded aspects of the spirit of orthodoxy were lethargy, indolence, inaction and exclusiveness. They had fed on disunity and divisiveness born of defensiveness and rigidity. From that had arisen casteism in all its worsts manifestation, defeatism and fatalism, the loss of the ideal of harmonious social cooperation of courage and self-respect. The spirit of atrophied orthodoxy had religious justification.

Tilak believed that there must be a change in the heart of the people and not as the reformers believed, a change in the form of institutions. He tried to reach the people in order to change their hearts N.G. Kelkar writes about Tilak, "Though his paper, The Kesari he exercised an impossible influence over the masses and it is this influence that is mainly responsible for the infusion of a new spirit among the people." Tilak taught both from the class room and the public platform his new message of awakening India.

He tried to reach the people through the employment of national festivals. He popularized two great festivals: The Ganapati festival and the Shivaji festival. Ganapati is the Hindu deity of learning and propitiousness. The object of the Shivaji festival was to revive the memory and glory of Shivaji, the liberator of Maharashtra and the restorer of Swaraj through his battle with the' Mughal Empire. He emphasized the dynamic spirit of shivaji. He wrote, "It is the spirit which actuated Shivaji in his doings that is held forth as the proper ideal to be kept constantly in view of the rising generation." Tilak worked ceaselessly to reach the people and educate them through the festivals. Throughout Maharashtra, he spread his message among the people through religion and history, the association in the popular mind with gods and heroes and an appreciation of the heritage of the past as a guide to the future. He became the spokesman of the tradition directed masses of India and also the defender and awakener of India's philosophy of life. He taught first the Dharma of action. He reminded the people that India could not become a great nation through negativism and indolence but through a dynamic willingness to meet the problems of the day and solve them morally. He reminded the people that God did not protect those who kept setting with folded arms. God did not help the indolent. No society could survive, let alone prosper, if the people refused to assert themselves actively. Action alone must be the guiding principle. The people must have an energetic and self-reliant approach to life. Self-respect is the necessary foundation for effective action and eventual self-rule. To inculcate the spirit of activism, Tilak constantly appealed to the greatness of the religious faith of the people and the lessons of the history of India.

Jayprakash Narayan

Propounder of Total Revolution philosophy, Loknayak as he was popularly known, Jayprakash Narayan was a great freedom fighter, prominent socialist leader, author of several books and trusted lieutenant of Vinoba Bhave's Bhoodan Movement. He was born on 11th October, 1902 at Sitabdiara village near Patna. While he was in college he participated in the Non-Cooperation Movement in 1921. He did his M.A from Ohio University.

He actively participated in the" Civil Disobedience Movement, and Quit India Movement. He formed the All India Socialist Party. After independence he refrained himself from power-politics and joined Bhoodan Movement. He again came into limelight during emergency in 1975 and became instrumental in the formation of the Janta Party Government in 1977. He died in 1979.

Jawaharlal Nehru

In the history of modern thought. Jawaharlal Nehru's name figures with prominence. After Gandhiji, he was the only leader who could influence the Indian masses through his ideas and charming personality to the extent that people could not think of an alternative to him for leadership of the country for nearly two decades after independence. It is out of scope for us to deal with his multifarious personality and philosophy in some detail. We will have to confine our discussion to his philosophy on socialism and the ideals of peace and secularism.

When Nehru returned from England in 1912, after completion of his education, there was no political turmoil in the country. Even then he became a member of the U.P. Congress Committee in 1913. His first meeting with Gandhiji in 1916 could not produce great impact on him. For this reason he joined the Home Rule League founded by Lokmanya Tilak and Annie Beasant in 1917. In 1919 Gandhiji asked the Viceroy of India to withdraw the Rowlatt Act. But the government refused to accept the demand. Consequently Gandhiji launched the Satyagraha movement. Jawaharlal could not keep away and joined the movement. During 1919-1920, Nehru came under the influence of Gandhian philosophy and left his legal practice to join national movement. In the years to follow he so much influenced the social, political and economic thinking of the country before and after independence that history of modern Indian thought cannot be considered complete without reference to his philosophy.

Early Days of Life : As a student in England Nehru was influenced by the ideas of George Bernard Shaw, Bertrand Russell and Keynes. Expressing his sentiments during those days he said, "I was a patriot and wanted India to become free". Between 1922-23, he developed interest in social and economic problems while he was deeply influenced by rational attitude combined with Marxism, the western humanism and liberalism of these countries. As president of All India Congress at Lahore he declared his faith in socialism. He said "India achieved great success in the construction of a stable society. But she lagged behind in an important matter. No solution could be found to the problem of disparity. India deliberately ignored the problem as a result of which millions of people lead a miserable life. They have no chance of progress." Nehru expressed similar views in his autobiography. "Our ultimate goal can be nothing but opportunities. Such an organised and planned society will establish a classless society in which all the people will get economic justice with equal cultural and economic development of mankind. In such a society there will be encouragement for cooperation, selfless service, love, sympathy and good work. In the end, such a system could be established in the whole world. Any obstacle in the way of achieving this goal will have to be removed by peaceful methods or force."

For the construction of Indian society on the basis of equality, social justice and security, Nehru tried to evolve a social philosophy. In order to achieve the goal of classless society, he emphasized the need for total transformation of social life through democratic methods. He was of the view that the process of the rich becoming richer and the poor becoming poorer has to be stopped by planned method so that the poor can rise above their condition whenever opportunity arises. But in Nehruji's political philosophy there was only revolutionary thinking instead of revolutionary action. This was the basic difference between him and the other socialists. He did not think revolutionary action was necessary for changing the social and economic structure of society.

Nehru and Communism : Nehru was greatly impressed by the efforts of the Soviet Union to bring about total change in the social life by planned methods after the revolution. Even then he could not accept the practical form of communism. In fact there is self-contradiction in communism implying to denial of individual freedom, indifference towards humanitarianism, contempt for moral and spiritual aspect of life. Communism has deprived human experience of values and ideals. Due to its relation with violence, communism has encouraged bad tendency in man. Classless society is a noble ideal but violent methods cannot be supported for its realisation. Nehru considered violence as wholly unscientific, irrational and uncivilized methodology. He said, "Socialism ultimately is not only a way of life but also a scientific point of view about social and economic problems. If we implement socialism in a backward and undeveloped country, it will not eliminate backwardness altogether. In fact we will be left with only a poor and backward society." It is only by planned methods that we can take the nation slowly and gradually towards socialism.

Nehru's Dream : With full faith in principles of socialism, Nehru stressed the need for social and economic changes for evolving a socialistic society. In the third decade of this century he said, "I have gradually accepted the point view of scientific socialism and now I can claim myself as a socialist in the real sense of the term." In his message on the occasion of All India Socialist Conference, 1936, he said, "Political freedom is implied in socialism because without it there cannot be social and economic freedom." After 1934 he continuously talked of socialism as the only remedy of poverty, unemployment and other social problems. On May 19, 1936, Nehru said at Bombay, "We have to construct a new social system in which all are assured of equal opportunities for development, in which there will be no exploitation, in which there will not only be political democracy but also economic democracy in the form of economic equality."

In 1934 when some Marxist leaders of the Congress Party formed a separate Socialist party, Nehru extended his full support to it up to the end. He attached great importance to the views of Jayaprakash Narayan, Acharya Narendra Dev and Acharya Kripalani. In 1938 he wrote, "I am certainly a socialist, I have faith in the socialist thinking and methodology. I am not a communist because I am against the tendency of communists to consider the communist doctrine as sacred. I also do not like somebody telling me how I should think and how I should act." It was this attitude which led him to invite the socialists in 1953 for cooperation.

For nearly seventeen years after independence Nehru remained solely responsible for determining social, political and economic policies of the country. During this period he always talked about the scientific socialism and worked for construction of really socialist society. For him, socialism was a philosophy of life. He laid special emphasis on four important conditions for solving the problem of India through socialism, raising the standard of life of the general masses, providing them better means of life, proving them opportunities for physical, cultural and spiritual development, and ending of economic disparity gradually by non-violent means. An impartial assessment of Nehru's socialism we notice a few very important features which kept him away from other socialists of the country. The first and foremost feature is that he wanted to bring about social and economic change through gradual and non-violent methods. Due to religious and cultural heritage of India combined with a long period of foreign domination, the process of gradual change remained stationary to a great extent. As a result of it, economic disparity continued even with best intentions of the government. Nehru laid the basis of planned development according to the Russian pattern but even after two Five Year Plans during his lifetime, the basic problems of poverty and unemployment remained unsolved.

The second important point to note is that at the time of achieving independence, India was divided into castes and sub-castes with complete control of capitalism over the economic system of the country. For social and economic transformation of the country it was necessary to end both these systems. The Constitution made provision for ending caste system through laws but nothing was done to destroy capitalism. As against this the capitalist class took under its influence the country's politics using all possible means. In this way it became nearly impossible to bring about economic change according to the socialist principles. Thus, Nehru could not put into practice his socialist philosophy. Ultimately, he had to accept private sector and public sector working together for socialist pattern of society. But due to bureaucracy and widespread corruption, public sector industries could not succeed much. Only private sector could extend its field.

What Nehru talked about Nationalisation? : The third important point is that Nehru talked about nationalisation of industries and socialisation of the entire economic system before independence. After assuming power he removed this from the list of priorities. Socialism is a practical philosophy and for achieving this ideal what is required is extreme reformative measures. Marx said very clearly that the capitalist class would not voluntarily withdraw its influence over the society and all the privileges of enjoyment. This is perfectly right and has been proved during all these years after independence. The socialist leaders had only one complaint against Nehru, that he attached too much importance to slow and gradual change and did not take effective steps to improve the lot of the poor people. For giving more importance to socialist thinking against socialist practice he could not realise the ideals of socialism inspite of being a great socialist thinker.

Nehru : A True Secular Indian : Socialism and secularism are two inseparable concepts. In democratic socialism there is no place for religious politics. Whatever Nehru did in favour of developing secular thinking in the country that is his most significant contribution to the modern Indian thought. Inheriting progressive ideas from his father, Pt. Nehru was of the view that India should solve her political problems within the framework of federal structure consisting of multi-religious, multi-lingual and multi-caste societies. He had no attraction for religion and during the freedom movement he always denounced communalism. In 1932, when Gandhiji started his fast on the issue of separate electorate, Nehru was greatly annoyed. Humanity was his temple and service of the general masses was his religion. Once he said, "These days the greatest temple, mosque or Gurudwara is the place where man is engaged in the welfare activity."

Evolution of secular tradition in this country is Nehru's greatest contribution. When India got freedom there were five crore Muslims with majority population of Hindus. For the development of an ideal democratic state, religion was an important factor. There was a serious problem of organising the nation with her different religions, languages and cultures. For solving this problem, Nehru gave practical shape to the secular policy of the Congress. He was in favour of developing modern scientific culture with industrial civilization of our time. He asked people to behave with each other as human beings and not as Hindu, Muslims, etc.

Nehru and India's Foreign Relations : After independence it was necessary to develop a relation of friendship with all countries of the world. This was the only way of growing strong and powerful. Nehru also felt that India must play an important role in international politics through her efforts for establishing peace and harmony among various nations. This thinking led him to develop the policy of non-alignment. He thought that with her policy of non-alignment India would be able to influence the big powers of the world and consequently help in decreasing the possibilities of another world war.

With India's freedom many other nations of Asia and Africa also became free from foreign domination. These countries, due to their limited resources, could easily turn towards the communist or the American block for political and economic security. But there was danger to their independent existence in such a state of interdependence. In order to stop this process and in order to strengthen freedom of Asian and African countries, Nehru entered into negotiation with these countries and formed a powerful group of non-aligned powers manifested in their seventh conference held in 1983 at New Delhi under the presidentship of Mrs. Indira Gandhi. Through the foreign policy of non-alignment, Nehru helped the newly independent countries to follow a new path. On September 19, 1956, Nehru said in America, "We think that by mutual exchange of views and trade together with mutual relations with all countries of the world, we can learn something and develop faith in each other. For this reason we are trying to have friendship with all nations of the world inspite of differences in our policies and structures. We think that in this way we will not only serve our country but help in contributing to peace and cooperation in the world."

Nehru was great nationalist. But he was against the tendency of isolation. Peaceful co-existence for him was the practical form of non-alignment. He was of the view that millions of people living in non-aligned countries would work as a great moral force in holding the big powers from entering into conflict. He considered Panchsheel as the only guarantee for the future of mankind. His policies were criticized in some quarters after the Chinese aggression in 1962. But firm in his conviction Nehru said, "If China breaks the Panchsheel it is bad to her only. It is the only way of international behaviour. It was right, it is right, and it shall continue to be right in the future also."

Maker of India : Among the builders of modern India he occupies a unique place both as a thinker and practical guide. Unlike most of the other leaders he not only helped the country in breaking her chains of slavery but also actively contributed in giving a new direction for leading a life of freedom, peace and dignity. He set in motion the process of planned development with the ultimate goal of complete social and economic transformation or the society. It is quite easy to find fault and human weakness, to criticize even saints and prophets. But any impartial judgement will acknowledge the great contribution of Jawaharlal Nehru to the development of modern India. Political integration of India after independence was a gigantic task in view of nearly six hundred small and big princely states, a number of languages, cultures and interests. Nehru was the only leader who could feel the pulse of the country and understand the problems before her. It was his real greatness that all the states were integrated into the union of India without any trouble, without any violence. In this task he had the able support from Sardar Partel. Not only this he laid the firm foundation of the largest democracy in the world and created democratic consciousness in the masses. The great political maturity which India, with her over sixty per cent illiterate masses, has exhibited over the past thirty years is only due to the democratic consciousness.

Jawaharlal Nehru has created urge in the masses for a better life, raised their hopes and expectations, charted a course for them and set before them a goal and vision. Considering India's size and its strategic situation, this galvanizing of the Indian masses will long be a live force affecting and influencing the course of human history. He set in motion forces long-term social, economic and political changes. The crusade against communalism, casteism besides process of planned development had an obvious purpose. He was spearheading the struggle for national liberation with a vision of a new Indian society. As a philosopher, guide and the very spirit of India's revolution, the rich legacy of Nehru is the democratic tradition he has left. Inspite of his socialist convictions and revolutionary mould, Nehru attached great importance to the individual. He wrote, "I suppose I am temperamentally and by training an individualist and intellectually a socialist....I am attached to socialism because it will release innumerable individuals from economic and cultural bondage."

A man like Nehru is born once in a thousand years. According to Norman Cousins, "Nehru was not one man but a procession of men. He was a philosopher, a writer, a historian, a political thinker, all harmoniously blended in one. He was a philosopher historian who best rode upon this earth and guided the destinies of a vast continent for over forty years, giving a new hope to the millions of people in whose eyes he found only misery and unhappiness; and there he stands with Lincoln and Lenin and with them he belongs to the ages.

Subhash Chandra Bose

Born in Cuttack, a religious and rebellious Subhash Chandra distinguished himself as a student, went to England and stood fourth in order of merit in the I.C.S. examination. Disturbed at the Jallianwala Bagh massacre and encouraged by Gandhiji's plan for non-cooperation, Subhash resigned in 1921 from the service while on probation. Thereafter he began a turbulent political career when he returned to India and joined the *Deshabandhu* as his principal lieutenant. Serving as the chief executive officer of Calcutta Corporation he was put under detention for three years in the Mandalay jail on the ground of his alleged association with violent activities. On his release on medical ground Subhash became the president of the Bengal Provincial Congress and pleaded for India's complete, independence in opposition to the Nehru Committee's advocacy for Dominion Status. Acting as the G.O.C. of volunteers at the Calcutta Congress session in 1928, Subhas Chandra became well known as a radical leader of the young and "the new". He was in the thick of Salt Satyagraha, resenting the Gandhi-Irwin Pact of 1931.

Once again the authorities decided to detain an aggressive Subhash and released him when his health deteriorated. Banished to Europe he returned despite a ban on his entry and was detained till 1937. Soon he was unanimously elected the Congress president at Haripura and he set up in October 1938 a National Planning Committee. At Tripuri Subhash Chandra was re-elected president by defeating Gandhiji's candidate Dr. Pattabhi Sitaramayya.

Following political differences and the curtailment of his powers, Subhash resigned from Presidentship in 1939. Subsequently he formed the Forward Bloc coinciding with the outbreak of the second World War and organised the Anti-Compromise Conference at Ramgarh. Arrested in connection with the Holwell monument agitation, Subhash had gone through a period of introspection in jail and was convinced that the assistance from Britain's enemies should be sought for India's independence. The result was his dramatic disappearance from Calcutta soon after his release and his founding of the Indian Liberation Army in Germany by recruiting Indian prisoners of war. In 1943 Subhash Chandra—now known as Netaji—moved to East Asia, re-organised the Azad Hind Fauj (Indian National Army) as its supreme commander and proclaimed a free provisional government with the Andamans and Nicobar as its' territory.

In January 1944 the I.N.A. marched towards the homeland with delirious battle cries of "Chalo Delhi" and "Jai Hind", crossed the Burma Frontier and reached Kohima and Imphal. The campaign had to be withdrawn with the collapse of Japan in the war. But the saga of heroism of Netaji and his men, when revealed, unified and inspired the country against the British Raj.

B.R. Ambedkar

Bhimrao Ramjee Ambedkar (1891—December 7, 1956), was one of the great jurists, lawyers and political leaders of modern India. As a post-graduate student, he had done advanced studies in the field of economics. He was a student at the Columbia University in the City of New York and at London School of Economics. He also studied economics at Bonn. His works on the Indian Rupee as well as on Provincial Finance and Currency are notable. As one of the prime architects of the text of the Indian constitutions and as outspoken militant champion of the aspirations and claims to equality of the so-called Untouchables, Ambedkar has won undying recognition. He had experienced the agonies, anguishes, frustrations and humiliations of being born in the mahar caste, which is an untouchable Maharashtrian community. His books on Indian sociology touching upon the problems of the Sudras, the untouchables, etc., breathe a note of deep realism and are also characterised by bitter denunciations of the old lawgivers, some of whom like Manu, poured forth words of contempt and bitterness against the suppressed sections of the Hindu society.

Ambedkar and His Political Ideas : As a sociological historian, Ambedkar did not accept the hypothesis of an Aryan invasion of India. A.C. Das, Dr. Sampurnananda, and the Arya Samajist scholars repudiate the hypothesis of an invasion of India by a Central Asiatic or European, Indo-European speaking or Aryan, speaking people. The majority of western and Indian scholars, however, tend towards accepting the hypothesis of Aryan invasion. "I do realize that in the ancient Vedic and Sanskrit literature there is no explicit mention of an invasion of north-west India by foreigners round about the second millennium B.C. Nevertheless, on philosophical grounds, the views of the western scholars appear more appealing to me". Ambedkar has forcefully put forward the views that the Shudras were not dark-skinned aboriginals enslaved or subordinated by the Aryan invaders but they too were Aryans who belonged to the kshatriya solar dynasty.

The subordinate status of the Shudras was brought about by a bloody battle between Shudras, the King, and Vasistha. Due to social vicissitudes and changes of fortune, they became degraded from their kshatriya status. The vedic king Sudas, son of Divodasa Atithigva, is degraded by Ambedkar as a Sudras on the basis of *Mahabharata, Shantiparva* (Chapter LX). The Brahmins were responsible for the degradation of the Shudras. The technique to bring this about was denying the *yajnopavita* to them. The Dasas and Dasyus, far from being savages were civilized and "in fact were more powerful than the Aryans." But the Shudras were totally different from these Dasas and Dasyus. The Purusha Sukta, the Vedic charter for the subordinate status of the Shudras is regarded by Ambedkar as a "later interpolation".

According to Ambedkar, the Hindu scheme of social structure based on the four *Varnas* or *Chaturvarna* breeds inequality and has been the parent of the caste-system and untouchability which are merely forms of inequality. He felt that the problems of the untouchables could not be solved by mere tinkerings and palliatives. They demanded a radical social solution. The Indian constitution which has provided for complete equality before law and the equal protection of laws to all citizens, under Article 14, and in Article 17, not only has abolished untouchability but has made its practice, in any from, an offence punishable under law, has gone a very long way in giving a constitutional and legal foundation for the redemption of the sorrows and troubles of the untouchables.

Ambedkar criticized Gandhi's role in the second round table conference. He challenged his claims to represent the untouchables and charged him with entering into a "mean deal" with Muslims in order to get rejected the demand of the untouchables for separate electorate. Ambedkar was realistic in pointing out that the Indian bureaucracy which shared the prejudices of the hindus against the untouchables was responsible for the owes of the untouchables. Hence, there is realism in his view that, in order to made public services responsive to the needs of the untouchables, there should be more members of the untouchables community in the higher executive.

It appears that, possibly, Ambedkar was not satisfied with the constitutional provisions for the untouchables in the Indian constitution. During the days of the round table conference, he had sponsored a demand for a separate electorate for the untouchables. His conversion to Buddhism shows that he contemplated a future of the untouchables somewhat in separation from the broad stream of the Hindu society. Gandhi did not want to disrupt the organic structure of the Hindu society. But Ambedkar wanted the separation of the untouchables from the Hindu society. It may, however, be noted that the approach of Buddhism of social problems was only half revolutionary because it was also half conservative. Buddhism seeks to liberalise the structure of the caste, indirectly, by ignoring the caste considerations in the Sangha as well as in the lay community. But it did not make a protracted and a radical attempt to root out caste itself.

Ambedkar had supported the demand for Pakistan if the Muslims were bent upon having it. He felt that if there was no other alternative, Pakistan had to be accepted. He stated, "No partition but the abolition of the Muslim League and the formation of a amixed party of Hindus and Muslims is the only effective way of burying the ghost Hindu Raj." He realistically pointed out that Pakistan would liberate both the hindus and Muslims from the fear of enslavement and encroachment.

Dr. Ambedkar was a social prophet of the untouchables. He denounced the monstrous iniquities and outrageous calumnies which Brahmanical Hinduism has heaped upon the untouchables and the bitterness of his fury against Hinduism is apparent in his works. There is no doubt that he was a patriot and would not be opposed to national integration. Nobody can be opposed to his view that for the untouchables, the liberation from the degrading humiliations imposed by Hinduism was a matter of more urgent necessity than even the political liberation from the alien British rule.

Whatever might have been the origin of the system, it has been the most unjust social order in actual practice. Hence, Ambedkar deserves the credit for having made Hindus aware of the great tension-generating social problems which must be tackled, otherwise, they may eventually bring about the doom not only of the Hindu society but of the total Indian political system as well. In order to clothe the fabric of modern political system with legitimacy, it is essential that people who have been suppressed for centuries are given their legal rights and become equal citizens in all spheres of life. In the history of modern Indian political thought, Ambedkar will have a significant place because through his scholarly writings, speeches, leadership and constructive work, he made significant the awareness of the political, economic and social problems of the vast Untouchable community whose members may be now more than eight crores.

Ram Manohar Lohia

Born at Faizabad in U.P., Lohia obtained his Doctorate from Berlin University, Germany, and developed a strong aversion for violence after witnessing the growth of militarism there. This attitude later led him to join Gandhiji's camp. Meanwhile he grew into a Socialist and had close contact with the Socialist leaders of different countries. In 1934 he became a founder-member of the Congress Socialist Party and edited its journal, *'The Congress Socialist'*. In 1936, at the instance of Nehru, he took over the Foreign Department in the Congress and was instrumental in organising and developing fraternal relations with the progressive forces in various countries. He also established a separate branch to look after the interests of Indians overseas.

Aa a member of the A.I.C.C. he was imprisoned and subjected to severe torture several times. He played an inspiring and leading role during the Quit India movement and remained engaged in underground activities. In free India, Lohia founded the Socialist Party which was later merged with the K.M.P.P., and renamed as P.S.P. Later he formed the Socialist Party of India assumed the name S.S.P., after its merger with P.S.P.

6

National Movement

Mass Movements launched against the Government by the nationalist organization, the Indian National Congress, under the leadership of Gandhiji characterized the political occurrences in India from the year 1919 onwards. The Gujarati ,press was associated with these movements and this led to a further change in its nature-a phase that continued upto 1947 as will be seen in this chapter.

Mahatma Gandhi on Scene

Gandhiji returned to India from South Africa on 9th January, 1915. He decided to stay permanently at Ahmedabad and set up an Ashram at Kocharab, a suburb of Ahmedabad, on 25th May, 1915. From there he used to move about all over in the country, and during the course of his travels he went to Bihar, there he learned of the working conditions in the indigo plantations. He took up the issue on behalf of the plantation labourers.

Meanwhile his acquaintance with the Gujarati leaders and organizations was increasing and he was invited to preside over the second Gujarat Educational Conference held at Broach during October that year. Again, in November he was invited to preside over the Gujarat Political Conference held at Godhra. By that time he had been elected as the president of the Gujarat Sabha, a political organization, functioning in Ahmedabad since the 1880's. Soon after that he was called upon to intervene in a dispute between the mill-agents and the textile workers in Ahmedabad. The workers had been advised to go on a strike and subsequently Gandhiji had undertaken a symbolic fast in March 1918, to resolve the deadlock. Immediately after this he was invited to attend to the grievances of the peasants in the Kheda District. The peasants there were reluctant to pay their revenue dues as famine-like conditions were prevailing in that area. Gandhiji took up the matter by organizing the peasants and secured relief for them from the Government.

In February 1919, the Government intended to pass two bills known as the Rowlatt Bills. One of them, meant to be introduced in the Council, provided for a change in the penal law by stipulating a court of three High Court Judges to try cases which were characterized as of a revolutionary nature. The other one was a temporary measure intended to deal with the situation arising from the expiry of the Defence of India Act which was operation as a war-time measure. Under this the possession of a document deemed to be seditious in the nature and the intention to publish or to circulate such a document was made punishable with imprisonment. These measures intended to be passed by the Government had created widespread comments in the press. Meetings were held as a mark of protest against the bills. Gandhiji declared his opposition to the Rowlatt Bills by calling them an unmistakable symptom of a deep-seated disease in the governing body. Pursuant to his stand in opposing the bills; he started collecting signatures for a pledge which headed the Satyagraha Pledge the purpose of which was to show resentment against the Rowlatt Bills. He also constituted a Satyagraha Sabha in Bombay and created a band of persons to break the existing prohibitory orders by selling prescribed literature and by publishing an unregistered newspaper called the Satyagraha.

Gandhiji intended to proceed to the Punjab for attending protest meetings. He was prevented from doing so on 10th, April, 1919, and was removed to Bombay on 11th April. On the 13th firing was resorted to on crowds which had gathered at the place called the Jallianwala Bagh in Amritsar in the Punjab. It is reported that several hundred persons lost their lives as a result of this firing. The news of Gandhiji's internment led to disturbances and Government declared martial law in Ahmedabad on 12th April. Disturbances were reported from other places in Gujarat such a Nadiad, Anand and Viramgam where loss of life and property took place Gandhiji declared his disapproval of the disturbances. He also declared his resentment at the Government actions and, called upon the latter to set up an inquiry.

Gandhiji persisted in his demand for an inquiry into, what he termed as the 'Punjab wrongs'. He made an issue out of this and joined it with a movement known as the Khilafat Movement.

A special session of the Indian National Congress was convened at Calcutta in the first week of September 1920. Gandhiji moved a resolution on Non-cooperation as a means to remedy the Khilafat and the Punjab wrongs and to attain Swaraj. That resolution was passed by a majority of 1855 votes against 873. In December that year at the 35th session of the Congress held at Nagpur, Gandhiji moved for an alteration in the creed of that organization. It became then, 'the attainment of Swaraj by peaceful means'. When the 36th session of the Congress met at Ahmedabad during December 1921, Gandhiji was declared to be the 'executive authority' of the movement that was contemplated by this organization in a resolution adopted unanimously.

Gandhiji used to write sometimes for the English daily, the Bombay Chronicle which was started by Sir Pherozshah Mehta and was edited by Mr. B.G. Horniman. He also occasionally contributed to the English monthly Young India with which Mr. Jamnadas Dwarkadas. Mr. Umar Shobhani and Mr. Shankerlal Banker were associated Articles by Gandhiji were published in the Hindustan of Mr. Ranchhoddas Bhavan Lotwala as well as in the Gujarati monthly Navajivan and Satya edited by Mr. Indulal Yagnik. After Gandhiji had settled in Gujarat and after his participation in different public activities, he felt the need of a Gujarati journal to publish his views elaborately and extensively. He put the proposal before Mr. Shankerlal Banker and Mr. Indulal Yagnik. Both were associated with the Navajivan and Satya. They took up Gandhiji's proposal and decided to convert their monthly into a weekly. It was decided to publish the proposed weekly, under a new name Navajivan from Ahmedabad under the editorship of Gandhiji.

The first issue of the Navajivan came out on 9th September, 1919. Gandhiji as the editor said, 'There is no dearth of journals in Gujarat at present. But, being a Gujarati by birth and a Gujarati in deed, I aspire to be absorbed into the life of Gujarat, for I can serve the country only by doing so. This will be the first occasion when I shall be known publicly in Gujarat as an editor. I wish that the Navajivan should reach the huts of the farmers and the weavers (because) I am going to write in their language; I am going to pray that the Navajivan be read by the women folk as well". Gandhiji had announced in the same issue that it was the solemn resolve of all associated with the Navajivan to say whatever they felt, no matter what restrictions Government had enacted for the press. He also declared that the Navajivan would not contain any advertisement.

The Navajivan in its issues during December that year took up the Khilafat and the Punjab issues in view of the 34th session of the Indian National Congress due to meet at Amritsar (Punjab), and after the session concluded gave details in its issues during January 1920 about the resolutions adopted with the text of the speeches made thereon. Gandhiji wrote in successive issues about the demands made by the Congress organization and explained their implications.

The weekly frequently gave information about the tours

undertaken by Gandhiji, and published in detail the speeches made by him from place to place. In addition to that the weekly used to include articles on Swadeshi, Khadi, Spinning, Satyagraha, and Cow-protection. Gandhiji used to request those who were literate to read the Navajivan aloud before those who were not capable of reading; he also expressed his satisfaction that the Navajivan was read so extensively by the people of Gujarat.

Again, in November and December 1920 the weekly contained articles written by Gandhiji, each one of the explaining the Non-cooperation movement that was contemplated. These aimed at clarifying Gandhiji's stand on the movement and the programmes suggested by him. Its issue dated 22nd December, 1920 was full of information about the 35th session of the Indian National Congress due to meet at Nagpur that year. When the Congress was in session, arrangements were made to procure telegraphically the news about the business transacted, at Nagpur.

The Navajivan during January 1921 was full of details about the resolutions made and the speeches delivered at the Nagpur session. When that body held its 36th session at Ahmedabad during December 1921, a whole issue of the Navajivan was devoted to news about it with full texts of the speeches of the participants in; the discussions of the resolutions moved and adopted. It appears from some notices appearing in the Navajivan during, those days that arrangements were made to sell single copies or the weekly through hawkers in the city of Ahmedabad and that as these copies were soon exhausted reprints had to be issued to meet the demand.

Gandhiji was running an English weekly the Young India at that time. Some articles written for that journal were published in Gujarati in the weekly Navajivan Gandhiji had written an article Tampering with Loyalty in September 1921. That article was published in the Gujarati weekly Navajivan dated 2nd October, 1921, under the caption; 'Rajdroha' (Rajdroha means sedition in Gujarati). Again Gandhiji had written an English article, 'The Puzzle and its Solution' in the Young India in December 1921. That was published in Gujarati in the Navajivan dated 15th December 1921, under the heading 'Viceroy in Munzvan" (The Dilemma before the Viceroy). A third article appeared in the Young India during February, 1922, under the title 'Shaking of the Manes'.

It appeared in the Navajivan dated 26th February 1922, as 'Hoonkar, (Roaring of the Lion). The Government which was watching these writings of Gandhiji decided to launch prosecutions against him as the editor and against Mr. Shankerlal Banker, the publisher of the Young India, for what the Government termed 'seditions' writings, subsequently, Gandhiji and Banker were arrested, in the second week of March 1922. They were charged with contravening section 124-A. of the Indian Penal Code, were convicted and sentenced. Gandhiji was released in 1924 on health grounds.

Since the Nagpur Session of the Indian National Congress in December 1920, news had been current in the country that a Civil Disobedience movement would be launched as a mark of protest against, the policies of the Government. Gandhiji himself had declared this in July of that year and had been suggesting it by saying, 'We are approaching a crisis'. He visited Bombay towards the end of October 1921. While speaking before some members of the Congress there, Gandhiji declared that he would shortly launch such a movement in the Bardoli area of the Surat District. He declared further that the movement would be guided by him. When preparations for the movement were being made, the Prince of Wales landed in Bombay.

The Prince's reception was officially boycotted by the Congress and people had been advised to observe a hartal, as a mark of protest against the Prince's arrival. During the organization of the hartal, classes ensued between some Congress volunteers and Parsi and Christian shopkeepers who refused to join the anti-Prince demonstrations. In such an atmosphere Gandhiji declared a postponement of his proposed

'Civil Disobedience movement'. At the end of 1921, however, widespread arrests were made in the country.

Those arrested included Mr. C. R. Das, the president elected of the Indian National Congress to be held in December that year at Ahmedabad, Mr. Motilal Nehru, Mr. C. Rajagopalachari and Mr. Jawaharlal Nehru. The Gujarati press which had been giving news about these arrests was dropping hints that Gandhiji might be arrested at any movement. Meanwhile the 36th session of the Indian National Congress met at Ahmedabad. The session adopted a resolution approving the bunching of a Non-cooperation movement and vesting Gandhiji with the 'exclusive authority' for the conduct of that movement.

The Gujarati press published elaborate accounts of the whole session. The Navajivan wrote welcoming the movement. The Gujarati said, "The Congress session at Ahmedabad was unique-was indicative indeed of a personal triumph for Gandhiji. It added we can say that now the Indian National Congress and Gandhi have become interchangeable terms; the Congress means Gandhi and Gandhi means the aim of independence of the Congress. Some papers termed Gandhiji, the sole authority to conduct the movement, the 'Betaj Badshah' an uncrowned king.

Meanwhile, the revenue authorities of Surat District published what they termed an 'Explanation' on 18th January, 1922, addressed to the people of Bardoli and 'advised' them not to join any campaign for non-payment of revenue dues. This was published in full and criticized by Gandhiji in the Navajivan dated 29th January, 1922. Soon after that the conference of the peasants and local workers met at Bardoli and decided to launch a Civil Disobedience movement. Gandhiji addressed an 'open letter' to the Viceroy on 1st. February, 1922, explaining his stand on the Bardoli issues and, declaring what he termed the inevitability of the movement.

The Gujarati press started giving the day-to-day happenings on the front page in big type. Gandhiji's letter especially was featured by the press very prominently. Almost all the dailies picked up one sentence or the other of the letter and quoted it in the head-lines. The Gujarati, featuring the letter said, 'the Gujarati press has plunged itself headlong into this jung (fight).' The Bombay Samachar pledged its support to the movement; the Hindustan, exhorting the people 'to support the movement', found fault with the Government for 'their policy'. The Bombay Samachar, publishing the news about the progress of the movement, commended the firmness of the people. Comments were published by the Sanj Vartman, the Prajabandhu, the Prajamitra and Parsi, the Gujarat Mitra etc.

The Viceroy sent his reply to Gandhiji's letter and Gandhiji sent his rejoinder on 7th February, 1922. Hardly had that reached the Viceroy when the morning papers the next day gave news about disturbances at Chauri Chora village in Gorakhpur District of the United Provinces (the present Uttar Pradesh). It was reported that some 22 police constables seeking refuge in a police chowky had been burnt alive by crowds on 5th February, 1922. Gandhiji declared that he could not allow violence to be associated with his movement and hence he ordered suspension of the Civil Disobedience movement. Gandhiji clarified his contentions in the Navajivan dated 19th and 26th February, 1922. He said, 'It was not possible to continue the movement in view of the shock that I had sustained on account of what had happened at Chauri Chora'. It appears from the biographies of some of the Congress leaders that Gandhiji's decision caused widespread criticism both from the people and the press in the different parts of India.

However, the reactions of the Gujarati press as a whole were favourable to Gandhiji's stand and were, 'Gandhiji deserves congratulations on his bold action in calling off the movement', 'Gandhiji's step is indicative of the righteousness of the struggle of the Indian people: of the backing that we get from our religious teachings'. Similar comments continued to appear till the end of February that year. At times these comments included elaborate refutation of the arguments advanced in some sections of the Indian praise which did not agree with Gandhiji's act.

No sooner did these controversies subside than Gandhiji was convicted for writing allegedly seditious articles. The trial was reported verbatim by almost all the dailies and weeklies in Gujarati. The Bombay Samachar devoted a full page to the statement made by Gandhiji during the trial. Other journals which reported the judgement said that the section on sedition (section 124A I.P.C.) had been misused by the Bombay Government and that with Gandhiji in jail, the Government, had exposed itself to violence.

The press, which was keeping pace with the rapid succession of events, was expanding rapidly. From 74,900 copies per issue in circulation in 1918 it reached a total of 1,23,690 copies per issue in circulation by 1922.

As regards its contents at that time, the dailies contained, news among other things, about the political happenings in the country. When the leaders of the Indian National Congress were arrested during October-December 1921, the dailies published prominently the news about the arrests from every part of the country and commented in their editorials on the policy of the Government. The weeklies used to publish the weekly round-up of the news under different headings such as Deshman that raheli dharpakdo (the arrests being made in the country) or Kon kon pakadayun (who has been arrested). In some instances the weeklies published the latest information about some arrests or the latest statement of some political leader, if such information or statements were procured just, in time. The dailies used to procure the news through the news agency and through their respective reporters or correspondents. The weeklies included the speeches or statements of the political leaders, but in greater detail than the dailies. The weeklies contained, again, exhaustive comments on the political happenings in the country.

One more feature of the weeklies in this respect was the publication of special articles pertaining to political issues in, the country. From the monthlies that are available it appears that some of them which were devoted exclusively to politics contained a monthly review of the political scene as well as special articles on current topics. Some of the monthlies which were general interest magazines (as they put it), or which were literary journals, also gave the month's news and comments on the political events in the country. They all referred to the views of Gandhiji in their comments. So did the caste periodicals, their special feature being the publication of poems eulogizing Gandhiji and the national cause. But, though the main preoccupation of the Gujarati press was politics, the dailies, weeklies and the monthlies all contained stories, poems, tit-bits, literary criticism and above all advertisements in the varying amounts. Also, almost the whole of the Gujarati press; followed the practice of bringing out special numbers on certain, occasions, and most of the journals also continued the practice, of gifting away novels to their subscribers. Indeed an overdose of the political pill has to be coated with other palatable matter tool.

Mahatma Gandhi, as an Editor : Gandhiji was released from detention on 5th February, 1924, after he, had undergone a surgical operation. He assumed the editorial responsibility of the Navajivan and the Young India in the first week of April that year. He continued to review the political situation in the country and to spread his views through these journals. The Gujarati press was coming more and more under his influence. This is evidenced not only by the increasing space devoted by it to Gandhiji's views and activities, but also by the reports of the two conferences that Gujarati Journalists held (December 1925 and December 1927 both in Ahmedabad) it was declared that the 'press corps in Gujarat were under the total influence of Gandhiji and that, the call of the nation has become the life and blood of the Gujarati press'.

At the beginning of the year 1928, the Government of

Bombay proposed to raise the laud revenue assessment in the Bardoli area of the Surat District by 22 per cent. The landholders of that area disapproved of this increase; they approached Gandhiji and told him their grievances. Gandhiji agreed to help organize a no-tax campaign in that area. He addressed an appeal to the peasants of Bardoli on 5th February, 1928, in which he said that the name of the Bardoli connotes Swaraj and vice versa. He advised the peasants 'to show their strength in the civil resistance movement' and named Vallabhbhai Patel as their 'Sardar' (leader) for the conduct of the movement.

The Navajivan had been reporting the progress of the movement, and Gandhiji devoted one whole issue of his weekly to Bardoli matters. He published in it the full text of the 'letters exchanged between Vallabhbhai Patel and the Governor of Bombay. The Gujarati press had already started reporting news about the activities in Bardoli. The Bombay Samachar, commenting upon the issue, blamed the Bombay Government for what it termed as 'an unjust levy'. The Sanj Vartaman quoted the arguments of Vallabhbhai; the Gujarat Mitra said that 'Bardoli was agog with activities'. The Jame Jamshed exhorted the people of Bardoli to 'keep up their pledge', the 'Sanj Vartman reiterated Gandhiji's advice to the Satyagrahis of Bardoli. The Gujarat said that the demand of the people of Bardoli was just and hence 'victory will undoubtedly come to the people'. Some papers advised the Bombay Government to act judiciously and wisely; some emphasised the demand of the Satyagrahis to set up an inquiry into the matters.

The Government made arrangements to confiscate the properties of those who did not pay their revenue dues. They had deployed a special police force for the purpose, Government had also set up a publicity bureau to publish hand-outs from time to time. In these hand outs Government gave its own version of the revenue assessment issue. The Congress workers had also set up their information office from which they issued daily Patrikas (leaflets). These they distributed all over the District and sent some to the newspapers in Surat, Broach, Bombay, and Ahmedabad. It is reported that more than 10,000 leaflets were distributed every day.

The Government started taking action against those who did not pay up their revenue as per the Government assessment. By May 1928, the number of confiscations of property had increased and many peasants' properties were taken over by the Government. Vallabhbhai then addressed an appeal to the people to raise funds for rendering monetary assistance to, the Bardoli Satyagrahis. Gandhiji reiterated that appeal; through the Navajivan. He said, 'The present Satyagraha is a Yogna—a sacrifice which needs offerings'. He called upon the people to donate to what he termed the 'Satyagraha Fund'. This appeal was published and supported by journals through out Gujarat. The Prajabandhu and the Navajivan opened a 'Bardoli Satyagraha Fund' and started collecting contributions. They also devoted special columns to the publication of the periodical collections received for the fund. It was reported by these journals that Rs. 1,99,857 had been collected by June 1928 and that the figure surpassed four lakhs of rupees by August that year.

After some negotiations the Government agreed to set up an inquiry into the revenue assessments and the Satyagraha was called off in August 1928. The announcement was carried by all the Gujarati dailies and weeklies and was praised profusely with comments. The Pratay said, 'The victory is great as well as memorable'. Other journals such as the Deshbhakta, the Nootan Gujarat, the Sanj Vartman and the Gujarati paid tributes to the Satyagrahis, the Government and to Vallabhbhai, who, they all said, 'emerged as a true Sardar (leader) of the people of Gujarat'. Gandhiji had brought out one whole issue of the Navajivan called the/ 'Bardoli Ank-the Bardoli Special Number' in which he paid tributes to the people of Gujarat for the support that they had given to the movement. The Sanj Vartman, the Bombay Samachar and the Gujarati published photographs depicting the different stages during the Bardoli Satyagraha movement.

The 44th session of the Indian National Congress which met at Lahore during the last week of December 1929, resolved to change the creed of the Congress organization by construing the word 'Swaraj' in article one of that body constitution to mean 'complete independence-Puma Swaraj'. That resolution had authorized the All India Congress Committee to 'launch upon a programme of Civil Disobedience including non-payment of taxes'. This became a starting point of a series of events culminating in a mass-movement against the Government.

When the Congress session met at Lahore the Gujarati dailies and weeklies were full of reports about it. Then followed comments on the resolutions and speeches made there. The number of editorials on the main. Independence, resolution of the Congress was more than that pertaining to any other subject. The main topic of discussion was the interpretation of the term Swaraj with reference to dominion status. Commenting upon this in the Navajivan dated 5th January, 1930. Gandhiji had explained that the word Swaraj meant 'absence of dependence of India on anyone in any matter'. The Bombay Samachar there upon published the following words in bold type on its front page in its issue dated 9th January, 1930, 'Congress tharavthi bhadki uthelu Britain' (Britain has been alarmed due to the Independence resolution of the Congress). Gandhiji wrote again on the Independence resolution in the Navajivan dated 12th January. In that issue he also reported his speech before students of the Ashram in which he said.

I do not know what form the Civil Disobedience movement, will take I am desperately in search of some effective, formula however.

The subsequent issues of some of the dailies were full of hints that Gandhiji might be arrested at any' time. Some of the press headings were Gandhijini dharpakadna vagata bhankara Gandhijini dharpakad thavani vaki (both meaning that Gandhijis arrest was imminent).

Gandhiji then wrote to the Government and put out a list

of 'demands' (these were even including repeal of the salt tax) which, in an article, he characterised as the soul of independence and a test of true Swaraj. Quoting these words the Bombay Samachar and the Gujarati wrote editorials on 16th February, 1930, and the Gujaratmitra and Darpan on the 18th while the Prajabandhu had been writing similarly since the 13th of that month. The gist of all words picked from the weekly Gujarati dated 16th February, 1930. The responsibility for the current unrest lies entirely with the British Government. But people would not put off their contemplated movement in spite of the steel frame of the bureaucracy.

Gandhiji then wrote in the Navajivan dated 23rd of that month, saying, 'If I am arrested, people must continue the programme of Civil Disobedience'. He wrote again on 2nd March in the same journal saying that he proposed to break the salt 'law' in contravention of the Governmental restrictions.

He then sent a letter to the viceroy explaining his stand on the current issues and published the full text of his communication in the Navajivan dated 9th March. He also announced that on the 12th March he would begin to track on foot a distance of 241 miles from Ahmedabad to Dandi in the Surat District where he proposed to collect natural salt in contravention of the prohibitory; regulations with a view to putting Civil Disobedience into action.

Gandhiji's letter was published by the Gujarati dailies and weeklies with big headings along with editorial comments some of the headings were Gandhijini Viceroys hradaydravak appeal (A heart moving appeal by Gandhiji to the Viceroy), Gandhijinu sarkarne akhrinamu' (Gandhiji's ultimatum to the Government). While the editorial comments were, 'still there is time for the Government to act judiciously': 'the present movement is a Mukti Sangram for Bharat (freedom fight for India) in which Gujarat must make its offerings': Gujarat will not lag behind this time.

Gandhiji started as scheduled on the 12th March with a batch of 78 Satyagrahis. The Bombay Samachar splashed the news on the front page in bigger type. 'Tapasvi Rama Panchavati chhodi Lanka leva vicharechhe- The ascetic Rama abandoning his hermit abode in Panchavati sets out to take Lanka'. So did all the Gujarati journals. Describing the situation the late Mr. Nandalal Bodiwala, founder editor of the Ahmedabad daily Sandesh, and other newspapermen said that ever since the news was in the air that a Civil Disobedience movement was going to be launched people had been, as it were, addicted to reading the day-to-day political happenings and press comments. Hence, almost all the Gujarati dailies had sent their correspondents to cover the news about Gandhiji's march, as did some English dailies and foreign journals. Bodiwala said that he had brought out special supplements in a bigger size to publish the news about the distance traversed by the marchers, about the manner in which people received the marchers in their respective villages and especially about the utterances made by Gandhiji from time to time.

He said that the demand for news had increased so much in Gandhiji that not only dailies but weeklies and fortnightlies even had to issue special supplements. He himself had to bring out four and at times six supplements a day. So had the Khedarartman (Kheda District) and the Pratap (Surat District) to do. Popular identification with the movement and their expectations from the press were such that any journal not supporting the movement would meet with public condemnation. For instance, of all the Gujarati journals in Bombay. Mr. Ranchhoddas Bhavan Lotwala's journals were writing against the Civil Disobedience movement and were characterising it as a 'mind' step. It is reported that some people in Bombay had called a meeting to express their disapproval of Lotwala's journals and subsequently the latter suffered a loss.

Gandhiji reached Dandi on 5th April, 1930. He want to the seashore the next day and picked up natural salt declaring that 'everyone was free to prepare and sell salt no matter what the Government did', and that 'people throughout the country should break the salt law and should be willing to court arrest if that be the consequence'. The newspapers which gave news of Gandhiji's defiance of the salt law also published news about similar acts of defiance from almost all parts of the country. The Navajivan which had been publishing the news, about Gandhiji's march and the reports of his speeches since he set out on 12th March, gave information in greatèr detail about the arrests and lathi charges throughout the country. It was issuing supplements for this purpose. In one of them was published on the front page in bold type a message from Gandhiji saying: 'I congratulate Gujarat: I want still more from the people'.

Gandhiji then proceeded to Dharasana where the Government salt depot was situated. But he was interrupted and was arrested on 4th May, 1930. That led to a number of demonstrations and arrests in the country. The comments in the Gujarati press from 5th May, 1930, onwards can be summarised as 'Mahatmaji has contributed his mite: it is up to the people now to show their strength; a fund should be raised to help continue the Satyagraha; people should stick to their pledge; non violence as preached by Gandhiji should not be abandoned'.

While the nature of the news and comment appearing in the Gujarati press regarding the nationalist movement was as has been described, the growth that it had attained by the middle of 1930 was as indicated below.

There were 91 Gujarati journals and dailies, 71 weeklies and 9 fortnightlies with an aggregate of 2,08125 copies per issue in circulation by that time. Data about the monthlies in circulation during 1930 are not available as in figure of 36,500 copies per issue, while the weeklies had touched a total of 1,62,875 and the fortnightlies that of 8,750 copies per issue in circulation by that time. The Gujarati dailies were published now not only from Bombay, but in addition from Surat, Nadiad, and Ahmedabad and were very critical of the Government.

When the press comments and reports reached such a stage the Government promulgated an ordinance, Ordinance of 1930, under Section 72 of the Government of India Act of 1919. That ordinance revived the Indian Press Act of 1910 which had been repealed in 1922. Under the ordinance, which according to the Government was meant to 'Provide for the better control of the Press', magistrates were empowered at their discretion to demand securities of not less than Rs. 500 from any person keeping a printing press. It may be recalled that keepers of printing presses were required to make a declaration under Section 4 of the Press and Registration of Books Act. 1867. From the publishers, who were required to make a declaration under section 5 of the 1867 Press Act, Magistrates were also empowered under the ordinance to demand securities. Powers to declare such securities forfeited were conferred upon the magistrates when it appeared to the local Governments that any matter published was likely to have a tendency, directly or indirectly, whether by inference, suggestion, allusion, metaphor, implication or otherwise, to do certain things which would bring the Government into hatred or contempt. When the ordinance became operative the Prajabandhu of Ahmedabad suspended publication, as the editors put it, 'before securities were demanded'. The Navajivan also closed down officially but efforts were made to continue publication of a sheet or two of cyclostyled copies of the journal.

During this period, a Round Table Conference had been convened in London by the British Government of discuss Indian problems. Subsequently, negotiations took place between ,Gandhiji and the Government, and the Government issued orders to release Gandhiji and the other Congress leaders by the last week of January 1931. The Prajabandhu had recommended publication from 16th November, 1930, and 50 too had the Navajivan by the middle of March next year. Gandhiji went to London to attend the Round Table Conference on 29th August, 1931. The news about the proceedings at that conference was supplied to the press by Reuter's news agency, and the Sanj Vartman sent its own correspondent to cover the news from London.

The press during those days was full of-news about the conference proceedings and of comments which exceeded in space which was allotted to the news from London. Gandhiji returned to India by the end of December 1931. He was arrested again on 4th January, 1932. By now the Indian Press Emergency Powers Act of 1931 was already in operation. The people raided the office of the Navajivan on 14th January, 1932. The Prajabandhu which had started publication from 16th November, 1930, closed down again on 10th January, 1932. However, the management of that weekly made arrangements to issue a single-sheet daily newspaper called the Gujarat Samachar from 16th January. 1932. The then editor, Mr. Indravadan Thakur states that the management did so to supply the reading public with the latest news about current politics, hence, the daily contained only news and no editorials. It may be noted here that the circulation of the new dailies in Ahmedabad (the Sandesh and the Gujarat Samachar) increased rapidly as did that of the Bombay Samachar in Bombay. To cope up with the demand the Bombay Samachar had to be published on a newly purchased rotary printing machine.

The mass-movement culminated in the release of Gandhiji and the other Congress leaders. Before these events be recorded a reference to the Gujarati press as it stood by the end of the year 1932 should be made here.

There were in all 207 Gujarati journals of varied periodicity including II dailies, one bi-weekly, 68 weeklies, four fortnightlies, 102 monthlies, six bi-monthlies, 13 quarterlies, one half-yearly and an annual in circulation at that time. These were published from 26 different places. Taking the contents of the Gujarati journals at that time, it seems that they contained mostly political news. But next to that they also contained articles of literary, commercial and religious interest. By this time, besides, a more clear-cut specialization of the interests had been effected in the Gujarati press. There were 57 periodicals which published mainly news and other matters referred to above. Besides this there were 36 Gujarati journals addressed to different sectarian interests (Hindu-l2, Jain-8, Muslim-5, Parsi-10 and one journal meant exclusively for the Indian Christians).

There were 22 Gujarati journals meant for different castes. Again, there were four journals meant for labourers, two for the Harijan-uplift movement, five for women, eight for children, eight concerned with education, six with health and hygiene, five with the cinema, two propagating the cause of Khadi 23 publishing stories, poems and literary matter, two meant exclusively for trade and commerce, five pertaining to the problems of the native states, eight pertaining to agriculture, one giving information about the library movement and one publishing random miscellaneous matter. Though addressed to the special interests, almost all these journals published matter pertaining to current political issues in varying amount. Especially their annual and special numbers were full of articles on these issues and pictures of the Congress leaders.

To sum up now the events succeeding the movement.. Gandhiji had undertaken a fast for 21 days during his detention to get some 'injustices' done to the Harijans (untouchables) redressed. Subsequently he was released. All other Congress leaders were also released and the British Parliament passed the Government of India Act of 1935 which came into operation in 1937 and under which a Congress ministry started functioning in the Bombay Province. The Congress Government restored the securities of the different papers and lifted various bans put on the press by its predecessor in office.

Popular Movement

To the different mass-movements launched by the Indian National Congress under the leadership of Gandhiji against the Government, one more was added with the passing of a resolution by that organization in August 1942, asking the British to withdraw from India. It is proposed now to examine the nature of the Gujarati press with reference to this mass movement known as the 'Quit India' movement and to give a picture of its further growth.

Hostilities were declared on 3rd September, 1939, between Britain and Germany, involving India once again. Those who were running the Gujarati press knew from the past experience the interest that the reading public showed in news about the war. They were aware of the fact that information about the war was in greater demand than before, because of the effect that the war had on Indian economic and more particularly political conditions. Now that war news was supplied by the news agency (the Associated Press of India in collaboration with the Reuter's news agency which was working on a global level) more rapidly than before, and also because the bigger printing machines (mostly cylinder and in some cases rotary machines) could print their copies more speedily, with the latest information and in bigger type, some of the Gujarati news papers brought out special supplements.

These supplements announced in big head-lines the outbreak of the war. The newspaper head-lines and comments pertaining to the war during September 1939 were, 'Poland has been a sufferer at the hands of the Nazis; German action is blind and brutal; Herr Hitalare chhadeehok kareli vachanbhangni parampara par prakash (A searchlight on the series of open breaches of promises by Herr Hitler); German jahajo par British vimani fojoe karelo hallo (The British Air Force attacks the German ships); Lokshahi Juthono Germanono Samno Karvano Nirdhar Determination of the democratic forces to meet the challenge of the (Germans). The Gujarati press thus evinced a support of Britain against the Nazis io the initial stages, as in the case of World War.

But the nationalist sections in the country viewed the situation in a rather different vein and wanted the people also to view it similarly. Hence the Working Committee of the Indian National Congress meeting at Wardha during September 1939 passed a resolution saying, among other things, that the British Government should declare its war aims in regard to Democracy and Imperialism in clearer terms. The resolution asked the British Government to indicate the place of India in any order envisaged. The resolution was commented upon by Gandhiji in the English weekly, the Harijan, dated 15th September, 1939, and its Gujarati version was published in the Harijanbandhu next week.

The Congress resolution was published by the Gujarati newspapers with big headings some of which read: Tamari neeti saaf saaf shabdoman janavo' (Declare your policy in categorical terms); 'Britainne Gandhijini chetavni' (Gandhiji's warning to Britain). 'Ahimsano antim vijay nishchit chhe' (the ultimate triumph of non-violence is certain); 'Congresse kareli spashta vaato' (The Congress talks plainly).

Thus the views of the Gujarati press on the Indian political situation tallied with those of the nationalist sections in the country. On 22nd October, 1939, the Congress called upon all ministries run by that party in the provinces to resign their offices by the 31st of that month. It also called upon the legislatures in such provinces to adopt a resolution asking Britain to declare her 'war-aims'. While all the Gujarati newspapers published this news with big headlines, some of the dailies and weeklies wrote editorials in which they expressed 'concern'.

Gandhiji commenting in the Harijanbandhu had said, 'The resignation of the Congress ministries was a necessity, but the next step is by no means clear. 'Congressmen seem to be expecting some big move'. Soon after this the Congress decided to launch Satyagraha by individuals who were to make propaganda against the war efforts of the Government and were to court arrest as a consequence. It started with the arrest of Vinoba Bhave on 31st October, 1939, following the arrest of almost all Congress leaders in the country. Vallabhbhai Patel was arrested in Ahmedabad on 17th November, 1940, followed by many congressmen in Gujarat who offered Satyagraha and courted arrest. The Gujarati newspapers had made arrangements to publish the names of the individual Satyagrahis, the details about their background, the notices that they had served on the Government and the manner in which they courted arrest. By December 1941 about 20,000 Congressmen throughout the country were held in detention but they were all released by the beginning of 1942.

By this time there were 22 Gujarati dailies, two bi-weeklies, 94 weeklies, 48 fortnightlies and 77 monthlies. The dailies included nine from Bombay, the Bombay Samachar, the Jame Jamshed the Sanj Vartman the Janmabhoomi the Vande, Matarama the Matrabhoomi, the Muslim Patrika, the Roznante and the Bharat Samachar; six from Surat, Gujarat Mitra one the Gujarat Darpan, the Deshi Mitra, the, Gujarat, the Pratap, the Jaybharat and the Vafaadar; two form Baroda, the Raj Huns and the Jay Gujarat; five from: Ahmedabad, the Gujarat Samachar, the Sandesh, the Prabhat the Sevak and the Rozgar.

The two bi-weeklies were the Kathiawad Times and the Sayaji Vijay from Rajkot and Baroda respectively. Among the 94 weeklies registered, 45 including the Gujarati, the Hindustan and Praja Mitra, the Kaisar-e-Hind and the Khilafat were published from Bombay; 11 including the Deshbandhu and the Dandiyo were from Surat; five including the Nav Gujarat, and the Praja Mandal Patrika from Baroda; the Arya Prakash from Anand; the Kheda Vartman from Kheda; the Gujarat Times and the Karmabhoomi from Nadiad; 16 including the Gujarati Punch, the prajabandhu and the Nav Saurashtra from Ahmedabad; the Jain from Bhavnagar; the Phoolchhab and the Bahurupi from Ranpur and one each from Wadhawan and Bhuj. Among these, 23 were found to be devoted exclusively to cinema matters while 24 were addressed to different castes, sects or religious minorities. These religious minorities included the Muslims who had by this time put up their claim for Pakistan a separate Muslim state. The Muslim Patrika, the Muslim Gujarat and later the Vatan were the exponents of this claim. As such they countered the demands of the Congress organization and emphasized the Muslim demands as an ethnic necessity The rest of the Gujarati journals decrying the Muslim claim supported the Congress. There was thus a marked polarization in the Gujarati press even as there was in the country at that time.

Three weeklies were devoted to crossword puzzles which were run by some Gujarati dailies; one was devoted exclusively to detective stories and one to market quotations. The 18 fortnightlies included the Bhageeni Samaj Patrika, the Sirohi Sandesh and six others from Bombay; the Jyotirdhar and one more from Ahmedabad, and, one each from Bulsar, Surat, Kheda, Bhavnagar. Jetpur, Songadh, Dhoraji and Anjar (Kuchh). Of these 18 fortnightlies, one, the Jyotirdhas, was the organ of some social reformists in Ahmedabad, two were trade-bulletins, one was a cinema magazine and the rest were meant for different castes or sects. The monthlies included the Navrachana and 13 others from Bombay; the Yuvak, the streejeevan, the Kumar, the Rekha and six others from Ahmedabad; two from Surat; the Patidar from Anand, the Sharda, the Gunsundari, the Pustakalaya, the Gramjeevan and 14 others from Baroda; the Samaj Sheekshak and two others from Navsari; the Jyoti, the Gharshala and 15 others from Bhavnagar; three from Rajkot and one each from Mehsana, Visnargar, Patan, Jamnagar, Wadhwan Jetpur, Gondal, Limbdi and Junagadh.

The dailies were of a uniform size-22 inches long and 17 inches broad with seven columns each, printed on bigger size cylinder or rotary machines. They contained mainly news procured through the news agencies and through accredited correspondents. In some cases the dailies -published weekly sections addressed to women or children, or devoted to health and hygiene and to religious matters. The weeklies and the bi-weeklies such as the Gujarati, the Prajabandhu, the Gujarati Punch and the Sayaji- Vijaya used to give weekly round-ups of the news, comments and literary articles. The monthlies like the Rekha were devoted to political and literary comment while others were full of diverse matter. Generally the weeklies were 17 inches in length and II inches in breadth while the monthlies were nine by six inches length and breadthwise. All these Gujarati journals-dailies, bi-weeklies, weeklies, fortnightlies and monthlies-contained advertisements which occupied considerable space. These advertisements, both display and classified, had increased on account of the war-time fillip that the economy received. It is to be noted here that the industrialists who spent profusely on advertisements were indirectly strengthening the press which was supporting the nationalist movement against the Government.

By the beginning of 1942 the war situation was becoming unfavourable to Britain. The British possessions in South East Asia were going over to the Axis. The war-news at that time was reported by the Gujarati press in a way which indicates a change after the nationalist sections in the country had become more active. The reporting provides, besides, a contrast to that of World War I when the nationalist sections had not grown so influential. The headings were: 'Britainne boom padavvani Gramin yojna' (German plans to gag Britain) "Japani sainyoni aage kuch' (Advances made by the Japanese troops); 'Sathi sainyoni lagaataar pichhe hath' (successive : retreats of the Allied forces).

Under these circumstances, the war-cabinet in Britain announced their decision on 11th March, 1942, to send Sir Stafford Cripps to India 'for consultations with the Indian leaders and for finding out some solution to meet the emergencies created by the war situation'. The announcement was made by the British Premier in the British Parliament and was reported in India by the Reuter's news agency. It was reported and commented upon by the Bombay Samachar by saying 'The arrival of Cripps is a Davpetch (a manoeuvre)': 'Cripps was coming to India to mislead the leaders (undha pata bhanavava)' and that 'the proposals must be devoid of any substance (Damvagarni)'. Similar comments were made by the Gujarat Samachar and the Vande Matram.

The negotiations lasted from 22nd March to 11th April, 1942, when Sir Stafford Cripps left India after an announcement of the failure of the negotiations was made. But some of the Gujarati newspapers which had made special arrangements to procure intelligence about the negotiations between Sir Stafford Cripps and the Congress leaders had started writing since March 30, in the following words: 'Crippsji bhens laya ke bada paap' (Cripps had defined expectations); Cripps yojana sicikarashe nahin (the Cripps proposals will not be acceptable).

Gandhiji had been writing on all these issues in his weeklies. On 11th May, 1942, he wrote an article captioned. 'To Every Briton'. Gandhiji had requested (as had the Congress organization in a resolution adopted earlier) Britons to support him in his demand for a withdrawal of British rule from India. That article appeared in the Gujarati Weekly Harijanbandhu dated 18th May under the heading, Angrejo Jav (Britishers Quit). The Gujarati press which had been quoting Gandhiji's articles took up this phrase in subsequent writings. It exhorted the people to 'respond to the call of the nation' and to 'be ready' for a fight till the finish.' Their reporting of the war-news was, as it were, providing a vicarious pleasure to the common man who liked to read about British reverses in the war. The war-news was captioned 'Dhari deshoni aage kuch' (forward march of the Axis); 'Britainni haroni parampara a series of defeats for Britain); 'Al Alamin sudhi pahonchela Germano' (the Germans have reached upto Al Alamin).

In view of the situation the Congress organization resolved, on 14th July, 1942, to request the withdrawal of the British rule from India and to launch a struggle under the leadership of Gandhiji, should negotiations between the Congress and the Government fail. This resolution was published by all the Gujarati dailies under big headlines and was commented upon from that day onwards. The Bombay Samachar said, 'Delhi had been shaken due to this resolution', and the 'Janmabhoomi and the Vande Mataram' said, 'still there is time for Britain to enter into a compromise with India'. Then these papers published the following words of Gandhiji, 'Bhale mari and bijaoni dharpakad they' (what of that if and others be arrested), and added that Gujarat would not 'lag behind in such an eventuality'. Then followed a series of addresses by Vallabhbhai Patel in Ahmedabad and Bombay from 25th July to 3rd August.

These addresses were given the front page treatment and were published under different heading' which read as: 'Koipan bhog apava taiyar raho; agnipareekshano samaya aavipabonchyochhe. (The moment for an ordeal by fire has come: be prepared to give any sacrifice).

Along with this the Janmahhoomi, the Vande Matram and the Bombay Samachar published the photographs of the different Congress leaders reaching Bombay during the first week of August and this practice of the press made the news more lively and the situation more tense.

The All India Congress Committee met as scheduled on 7th and 8th August. It adopted a resolution asking the British to quit and to declare India free. The meeting concluded late at night on the 8th and soon afterwards the Government declared the Congress organization as an unlawful association and arrested Gandhiji and Congressmen throughout the country in the early hours of the 9th. This led to a series of disturbances involving lathi-charges, tear-gas shelling and firing by the police throughout the country the Gujarati newspapers gave that news on the afternoon of the 9th in special supplements, and from the 10th onwards there were other reports of the disturbances from all parts of the country.

The Government's attitude towards the press in this respect took the form of a series of restrictive orders affecting the nature of comment and reports. Ever since hostilities were declared early in September 1939, the Government had passed the Defence of India Act and the rules inter alia which provided for 'a pre-censorship of material published in the press relating to certain matters'. When the Congress organization launched the 'Individual Satyagraha' movement in 1940, the Government had issued a notification according to which, 'the publication of any matter calculated directly or indirectly to foment opposition to the prosecution of the war and publish accounts of speeches, meetings, etc., calculated to that effect were prohibited. When the Indian National Congress adopted its August resolution asking the British to withdraw from India, the Government of India issued a fresh notification on 8th August, 1942. In that it was said, 'the printing or publishing of any factual news (which expression shall be deemed to include reports of speeches or statements made by the members of the public) relating to the mass-movement sanctioned by the All India Congress Committee or relating to the measures taken by the Government against that movement, except news derived from official sources or from the Associated Press of India or the United Press of India or the Orient Press of India or from a correspondent regularly employed by the newspaper concerned and whose name stands registered with the District Magistrate of the district in which he carries on his work, shall be prohibited. The Government issued a press note too, which said:

The declaration of various Congress committees to be unlawful associations renders liable to prosecution under the Criminal Law Amendment Act anyone who assists their operations. It follows therefore, that the editor of any newspaper who supports or encourages the mass movement sponsored by the bodies referred to above, or who opposes the measures taken by Government to avert or suppress that movement, will be guilty of an offence against the law. Moreover, the publication of factual news, both by the selection of events reported and by the manner in which they are displayed, can do even more to advertise and thus support the movement than editorial comment there on the responsibility of the press is, however, as great as its undoubted influence, and in order to ensure that, that responsibility may be exercised in a manner that will not bring the press into conflict with authority, Government consider it necessary:

(a) to exercise a measure of control over the origins of factual news relating to the movement so as to secure that what is published is derived only from recognized and responsible sources, and;

(b) while imposing no direct control over the expression of editorial views, to leave editors themselves in no doubt as to the limits beyond which it will not be in

> their own interests to go (But) Government wish it to be clearly understood that they do not propose to allow any newspaper to continue to publish matter, whether it takes the form of news or views, which in their opinion, will encourage the movement or incite people to take part in it or which will excite popular feelings in favour of the movement or against the measures that Government will be compelled to take to combat it.

The notification and the press-note have been quoted here at length to indicate the nature of the news and comments the press could publish about the mass-movement that had begun after the arrest of Gandhiji and other Congressmen in the country. Many a Gujarati journal had to close down and many more were called to book by the Government. Subsequent events were the cessation of war in Europe and the release of the Congress leaders followed by a series of negotiations, culminating in the transfer of power to India on 15th August, 1947. We have brought out that phase of the Gujarati press when it was associated with the mass-movements launched by the nationalist organization under Gandhiji's leadership.

It has been seen that the nature of content in the journals changed as a consequence and particularly because Gandhiji, during his stay in Gujarat, provided the Gujarati press with specific guidance and elaborate arguments-the latter through his weekly Navajivan. With increasing mass-awareness and popular participation in the movements, the nature of the news-coverage and press comment became such that the Government issued prohibitory orders restricting not only editorial comment but also the publication of factual news.

However, preoccupied with the news and views of the nationalists as the Gujarati press was, it secured a vaster readership throughout Gujarat. It kept up the popular interest in the mass-movements and received in turn a further fillip, functioning thus as an initiator and sustainer of the nationalist agitation till the British withdrew from India in 1947.

7

Freedom Struggle

Nature and Struggle for Indian Freedom : From Constitutionalism to Mass Satyagraha, Revolutionary Movements: Non-Cooperation, Civil Disobedience and Quit India, Indian Naval Uprising, Indian National Army, Role of Women in Freedom Struggle)

Indian National Congress

Although the idea of a common political organisation for the whole country was as old as the first stirrings of constitutional policies in India, it took decades to ferment and materialize. In the 1880's certain development gradually pushed the hesitant leaders of the various regional associations to common and concerted action.

In Calcutta Indian Association, the British Indian Association, the National Mohammedan Association and the Indian Union had worked together to call the National Conference. During November-December 1884 there were spontaneous demonstrations throughout India to mark Ripon's departure from India. These, demonstrations marked a spirit of organization which India had never known before.

Inspite of the universal desire among the Indian leaders to unite, unity seemed difficult. Interprovincial jealousies, clash of personalities and egoism of the Indian leaders stood in the way of their coming together in a common organization. They needed a neutral outsider to unite them. Such an outsider appeared on the Indian political scene in the person of Allan Octavian Hume. Hume addressed an open letter to the graduates of Calcutta University (and, through them, all educated India) encouraging them to form an association for national regeneration.

After publishing his open letter, he set up an Indian National Union, with branches in various cities. Hume met the Viceroy, Lord Dufferin, in 1885. Hume's idea was that a safety valve was needed for the escape of great and growing forces of discontent in the country. A Congress of educated Indians would provide the needed outlet. Dufferin was not opposed, and Hume got in contact with leading politicians in Calcutta, Bombay, Madras and other parts of the country. It was decided to convene a Conference of the Indian National Union in December.

On 28 December, 1885 the proposed conference met in the auditorium of the Gokuldas Tejpal Sanskrit College at Bombay, under the name of the Indian National Congress. The seventy-two invited delegates from different provinces were presided over by Woomesh Chandra Bannerjee, a Calcutta barrister.

As then defined, the party's principal objective were: (a) fusion into one national whole of all the different and discordant elements that constituted the population of India; (b) gradual regeneration along all lines, mental, moral, social and political, or the nation thus evolved; and (c) consolidation of union between England and India by securing the modification of such conditions as may be unjust or injurious to the later country.

The Congress then discussed and passed nine resolutions. The more important of these were in the form of demands to the Government of India for the:-

(i) Appointment of a Royal Commission to inquire into the working of Indian administration.

(ii) Abolition of the Indian Council (of the Secretary of State).

(iii) Creation of Legislative Councils for the North-West Provinces and Oudh and the Punjab.

(iv) Admission of a considerable proportion of elected members to the supreme and Local Legislative Councils with the right of interpellation and discussion of budgets, and the creation of a standing committee in the House of Commons to consider formal protests from majorities in the Councils.

(v) Reduction of military expenditure and its equitable apportionment between India and England.

(vi) Introduction of simultaneous Public Service Examinations in England and Indian and the raising of the age of candidates.

It is evident, however, that Hume simple gave form to what was by then an almost universally felt need. As an Indian historian has remarked, "the Congress was the natural and inevitable product of forces already at work in the country; it would have emerged soon enough, Hume or no Hume.' Furthermore, the 'safety valve' theory is only a small part of the truth.

More than anything else, the National Congress represented the urge of the politically conscious Indians to set up a national organisation to work for their political and economic advancement. Even Hume's motives were mixed ones. He possessed a sincere love for India and its poor cultivators.

In any case, the Indian leaders, who cooperated with Hume in starting this National Congress, were patriotic men of high character who willingly accepted Hume's help as they did not want to arouse official hostility towards their efforts at so early a stage of political activity. The Indians who actively worked for the creation of an all-India political organisation represented new social forces that were increasingly opposed to the exploitation of India for British interests. They needed an organization that would fight for India's political and economical advancement.

If Hume wanted to use the Congress as *'safety valve"*, the early Congress leaders hoped to use him as a lightning conductor. Gopal Krishna Gokhale was to point out later in 1913 that no Indian could have started the Indian National Congress. If an Indian had come forward to start such a movement, embracing all India, the officials would not have allowed it to come into existence.

In any case, there is no doubt that with the foundation of the Indian National Congress in 1885 the struggle for India's freedom was launched in a small, hesitant and mild, but organised manner. It was to grow in strength year by year and in the end involve the Indian people in powerful and militant campaigns against the foreign rulers.

Some of the great presidents of the National Congress during its early years were Dadabhai Naoroji, Badruddin Tyabji, Ferozeshah Mehta, P. Anandacharlu, Surendranath Banerjee, Ramesh Chandra Dutt, Ananda Mohan Bose, and Gopal Krishna Gokhale. Other prominent leaders of the Congress and the national movement during this period were Mahadev Govind Ranade, Bal Gangadhar Tilak, Sisir Kumar and Motilal Ghoshs Madan Mohan Malaviya, G. Subramaniya Iyer, C. Vijayaraghavachariar, and Dinshaw E. Wacha.

History in Brief : The founder of the Indian National Congress in 1885, was not sudden event, or historical accident. It was the culmination of a process of political awakening that had its beginnings in the 1860s and 1870 and took a major leap forward in the late 1870s and early 1880s. The year 1885 marked a turning point in this process, for that was the year the political Indians, the modern intellectuals interested in politics, who no longer saw themselves as spokesmen of narrow group interests but as representatives of national interest vis-a-vis foreign rule, as a 'national party' saw their efforts bear fruit. The All-India nationalist body that they brought into being was to be the platform, the organiser, the headquarter, the symbol of the new national spirit and politics.

Meanwhile, the Indians had gained experience, as well as confidence, from the large number of agitations they had organised in the preceding years.

The first major objective of the founders of the Indian national movement was to promote this process of becoming a nation, to weld Indians into nation. It was common for colonial administrators and ideologues to assert that Indians could not be united or freed because they were not a nation or a people but a geographical expression, a mere congress of hundreds of diverse races and creeds. The second major objective of the early Congress was to create a common political platform or programme around which political workers in different parts of the country could gather and conduct their political activities, educating and mobilising people on an all-India basis.

From the beginning the Congress was organised in the form of a Parliament. In fact the word 'Congress' was borrowed from North-American history to connote an assembly of the people. The proceedings of the Congress sessions were conducted democratically, issues being decide through debate and discussion and occasionally through voting it was in fact Congress, and not the bureaucratic and authoritarian colonial state, which indigenised, popularised and rooted parliamentary democracy in India.

If Hume and other English liberals hoped to use the Congress as a safety-valve, the Congress leaders-hoped to use Hume as lightning conductor.

The First Phase: Era of Moderates (1885-1905)

Objective and Method of Congress: The Indian National Congress, originally in the early years or phase, was under the influence of Moderates who were loyal to the British throne and did not talk of independence. The Congress at the time honestly believed that the English Parliament was the mother of democracy all over the world and that the British Constitution was the best of all constitutions.

The aim of the Congress was two-fold. First, is sought to educate public opinion. Secondly, the Congress was to persuade the rulers to effect various measures of political reform. The method adopted was constitutional agitation within the law, and slow, orderly political progress. They believed that if public opinion was created, organised and popular demands presented to the authorities through petitions, meetings, resolutions and speeches, the authorities would gradually concede these demands. Delegation of leading Indians were sent to Britain to propagate the Indian view. The three P's-Prayer, Petition and Protest-constituted their methods.

Congress Action Programme : The early nationalists wanted a larger share in the government of their own country and made an appeal to the principle of democracy. Their immediate demands were extremely moderate. They hoped to win freedom through gradual steps. From 1885 to 1892 they demanded the expansion and reform of the Legislative Councils. They demanded membership of the councils for elected representatives of the people and also an increase in the powers of the council. The British Government was forced by their agitation to pass the Indian Councils Act of 1892. By this Act the number of members of the Imperial Legislative Council as well of the Provincial Councils was increased. Some of these members could be elected indirectly by Indians, but the officials' majority remained. The Councils were also given the right to discuss the annual budgets though they could not vote on them.

The nationalists were totally dissatisfied. They demanded a larger share for Indians in the Council and also wider powers for them. They demanded Indian control over the public purse and raised the slogan that had earlier become the national cry of the American people during their war of Independence: 'No taxation without representation.' By the beginning of the 20th century, the nationalist leaders put forward the claim for Swarajya or self-government within the British Empire on the model of self-governing colonies like Australia and Canada. This demand was made from the Congress platform by Gokhale in 1905 and by Dadabhai Naoroji in 1906.

Demand for Economic Reforms : In the economic field the early nationalists complained of India's growing poverty and economic backwardness and the failure of modern industry and agriculture to grow. They put the blame on the policies of the British rulers.

The chief remedy they suggested for the removal of India's poverty was the rapid development of modern industries. They wanted the government to promote modern industries through tariff protection and direct government aid. They popularised the idea of Swadeshi or the use of Indian goods and the boycott of British goods as a means of promoting Indian industries. The nationalists complained that India's wealth was being drained to England, and demanded that this drain be stopped. They carried on persistent agitation for the reduction of land revenue in order to lighten the burden of taxation of the peasant. They also agitated for improvement in the conditions of work of the plantation labourers. They demanded abolition of the salt tax and reduction of land revenue.

Demand for Administrative and other Reforms : The most important administrative reform the Indians desired at this time was Indianisation of higher grades of administrative services. They put forward this demand on economic, political and moral grounds. Economically, Europeans were paid at very high rates and they sent out of Indian, large part of their salarie, this added to the drain of wealth from India.

Critical Evaluation : Later critics were to point out that the early nationalists did not achieve much practical success.

Very few of the reforms for which they agitated were introduced. The alien rulers treated them with contempt and sneered at their politics. Moreover, the early national movement had failed to acquire any roots among the common people and even those who had joined it with high hopes were feeling more and more disillusioned. Its critics ridiculed its methods as mendicancy or beggary through prayers and petitions. Their programmes confined with the narrow limits of capitalism. They could not visualise India's development except along capitalist lines. This inevitably limited the extent of their appeal among the common people and their capacity to move them to political action.

Achievements of Congress : The critics were, however, not quite correct in declaring the early national movement a failure. It was their very achievements in the wider sense that later led to more advanced stages of the national movement and made their own approach historically obsolete. Thus the early nationalists represented the most progressive force of the times.

They made possible a decisive shift in Indian politics. They succeeded in creating a wide political awakening and in arousing among the middle and lower-middle class Indians and the intelligentsia the feeling that they belonged to one common nation the Indian nation.

They made the people of India conscious of the bonds of common political, economic and cultural interest and of the existence of a common enemy in imperialism and thus helped to weld them in a common nationality. They popularised among the people the ideas of democracy and civil liberty. Moreover, a large number of nationalist political workers were trained in the art of modern politics, and the people familiarised with the concept and ideas of modern politics. Most of all they did pioneering work in mercilessly exposing the true character of British imperialism in India. They linked nearly every important economic question with the politically dependent status of the country. And, therefore, even though they were moderate in politics and political methods, they successfully brought to light the most important political and economic aspect of the Indian reality that India was being ruled by a foreign power of the purpose of economic exploitation.

Men like Dadabhai Naoroji, Ferozeshah Mehta, Dinshah Wacha, Gopal Krishna Gokhale, Surendranath Banerjee and others desired all-round progress and modernization of India-social reform, modern education, industrial and economic development. Their main achievements were the appointment of a Public Service Commission in 1886 which however caused disappointment, and the enactment of the Indian Councils Act of 1892 which did not modify the basic Constitution. Further, their efforts resulted in a resolution of the House of Commons (1892) for simultaneous examination for the I.C.S. in London and India and the appointment of the Welby Commission on Indian Expenditure (1895).

Bipan Chandra Says : "The period from 1858 to 1905 was the seed-time of Indian nationalism; and the early nationalists sowed the seeds well and deep. They evolved a common political and economic programme which united rather than divided the different sections of the people... In spite of their many failures the early nationalists laid strong foundations for the national movement to grow upon and they deserve a high place among the makers of modern India."

From the beginning, the Congress was conceived not as a party but as a movement. Except for agreement on the very broad objectives discussed earlier, it did not require any particular political or ideological commitment from its activitists. As a movement, it in corporated different political trends, ideologies and social classes and groups so long as the commitment to democratic and secular nationalism was there. From the outset the Congress included in the ranks of its leadership persons with diverse political thinking, widely disparate levels of political militancy and varying economic approaches. The basic objective of the early nationalist leaders were to lay the foundations of a secular and democratic national movement, to politicise and politically educate the people, to form the headquarters of the movement, that is,-to form an all-India leadership group, and to develop and propagate an anti-colonial nationalist ideology.

As for the question of the role of A.O. Hume, if the founders of the Congress were such capable and patriotic men of high character, why did they need Hume to act as the chief organiser of the Congress. The real answer lies in the conditions of the time considering the size of the Indian subcontinent, there were very few political persons in the early 1880s and the tradition of open opposition to the rulers were not yet firmly entrenched.

Growth of Extremism : Responsible Factors : Till 1905, Indian National Movement was led by the moderates. They followed constitutional methods to have their demand conceded. But when some national leaders found that no attention is being paid to their demands they changed their ideas. They realised that moderate policies, prayers and petitions before the English are not going to,bring about the desired results. Thus there came a new turn in Indian politics and there was rise of Extremism or militant nationalism in India. Bal Gangadhar Tilak of Maharashtra, Bipin Chandra Pal of Bengal and Lala Lajpat Rai of Punjab, the famous Bal, Pal and Lal were the chief leaders of the extremist group.

During the latter half of the 19th century political consciousness of the people and been growing steadily. But the leaders failed to obtain and concessions from the British rulers. At the same time, the colonial exploitation of the country continued. By the turn of the century, the general mood of discontent had spread to the rural gentry, the peasantry and the workers. It is not surprising, therefore, that the moderate leaders who went on pleading with the Government for reform were beginning to be less and less popular. The inevitable happened. The situation threw up a large number of new leaders who were more radical in their demands and who believed in a more militant form of nationalism. They came to be called Extremists. While the main support for the moderate leaders had come from the intelligentsia and the urban middle class, the new leaders who emerged appealed to a wider circle of the lower middle classes, the students, and even a section of the workers and peasants. It resulted in the rise of Extremism within the congress and that of Terrorism outside it.

(i) *True Nature of British Rule Earn of Knowledge:* The politics of the moderate nationalist were founded on the belief that British rule could be reformed from within. Politically conscious Indians were convinced that the purpose of British rule was to enrich England at the cost of India. The evil economic consequences of foreign rule were symbolised in the eyes of the people by the disastrous famines occuring between 1896 to 1900. The political events also disappointed the nationalists. In 1898 a law was passed making it an offence to excite feelings of disaffection towards the foreign government. In 1899, the number of Indian members in the Calcutta Corporation was reduced. In 1904, the Indian Official Secrets Act was passed restricting the freedom of the press.

The Natu brothers were deported in 1897 without being tried; even the charges against them were not made public. The anti-Congress attitude of Lord Curzon convinced people that it was useless to expect any political and economic advance under British rule. Even socially and culturally, British rule was no longer progressive. The Indian Universities Act of 1904 was seen by the nationalists as an attempt to bring Indian universities under tighter officials control and to check the growth of higher education.

(ii) *Contribution of Leaders :* Leaders like Tilak and Bipan Chandra Pal preached the message of self-respect and asked the nationalists to rely on the character and capacities of the Indian people. There was the realisation that only the masses could make the immense sacrifices needed to win freedom. Moreover, the nationalist leaders felt that political activity should be carried on continuously and not merely on the few days on which the National Congress or the provincial conferences met.

(iii) *Increasing Unemployment* : By the close of the 19th century, the number of educated Indians had increased perceptibly. Large number of them worked in the administration on extremely low salaries while many others increasingly faced unemployment. Many of them were attracted by radical nationalist politics. The educated Indians became the best propagators and followers of militant nationalism both because they were low paid or unemployed and because they were educated in modern thought and politics and European and World history.

(iv) *External Influence* : The rise of modern Japan after 1868 showed that a backward Asian country could develop itself without Western control. The defeat of the Italian army by the Ethiopians in 1896 and of Russia by Japan in 1905 exploded the myth of European superiority. Revolutionary movements in Ireland and Russia, Egypt. Turkey and China and the Boer War in South Africa convinced the Indians that a united people willing to make sacrifices could challenge even the most powerful of despotic governments.

(v) *Existence of a Militant Nationalist School of Thought* : From almost the beginning of the national movement a school of militant nationalism had existed, represented by leaders like Rajnarain Bose and Ashwini Kumar Dutta in Bengal and Vishnu Shastri Chiplunkar in Maharashtra.

In 1893, Tilak started using the traditional religious Ganapati festival to propagate nationalist ideas through songs and speeches, and in 1895 he started the Shivaji festival to stimulate nationalism among the youth. During 1896-97 he initiated a no-tax campaign in Maharashtra. He asked the famine-stricken peasants of Maharashtra to withhold payment of land revenue if their crops had failed. He set a real example of boldness and sacrifice when authorities arrested him in 1897 by refusing to apologise to the government. He was sentenced to 18 months' rigorous imprisonment.

(vi) *Portion of Bengal in 1905* : The worst and most hated aspect of Curzon's administration was the partition of Bengal into two provinces East Bengal and Assam in 1905. Supposedly this was done to stimulate the growth of the underdeveloped eastern region of Bengal. But documents not made public at the time show that one thereby weaken a solid body of opponents to our rule. These opponents were the Hindus of Bengal, politically the most advanced section of the country. The new provinces of Eastern Bengal and Assam was specially constituted so that Muslims would outnumber Hindus. This deliberate setting of one community against the other had as its inevitable result-an increase in communal tension. Hundreds of protest meetings were held, where Muslims as well as Hindus crowded to hear speeches by Surendranath Banerjee, Liaqat Hussain, and other leaders. Scores of petitions were sent to the government.

But this time the people realised that constitutional agitation would not be enough. Slogans of Swaraj, Swadeshi, Boycott and National Education emerged during the anti-partition campaign.

Action Programme Different from Moderates : The difference between the Moderates and the Extremists is apparent both in the means used and in the ends proposed. The Moderates were content to agitate through the spoken and written word along strictly constitutional lines. The Extremists condemned such methods as 'Mendicant Politics.' The time for prayer and petition was over, they said. The time had come for the Indian people to demand what was rightfully theirs.

Talented writers voiced the Extremists' position in the columns of fiery journals such as *Kesari* of Poona, *India of Madras* and *Bande Mataram* of Calcutta. The message was preached in giant open-air meetings; it was echoed from town to town, from village to village. Tilak gave utterance to the demand of the Extremists: "Swaraj is my birthright and I will have it." Bipin Chandra Pal wrote that India must attain absolute autonomy free from foreign control. Aurobindo Ghose gave bold expression of this demand for complete independence the necessary condition for national unity-in *Bande Mataram:* 'Liberty is the first requisite for the sound health and vigorous life of a nation.'

The sense of nationality, all but absent in 1856, was a vibrant reality fifty years later. The Moderates stuck in their old groove were unable to see this. Their failure to read the writing on the wall led to their eventual replacement by the extremists, and the acceptance of Swaraj, in the sense of complete independence, as the goal of the Indian National Congress. The methods and aims of the Extremists were naturally different from those of the Moderates.

Extremists differed from the Moderates in the following ways: (i) the Moderates wanted to work with the existing bureaucracy, but Extremists wanted to fight against it. (ii) The Moderates believed in improvement while the Extremists in reconstruction. (iii) The Moderates believed in cooperation but the Extremists in obstruction. (iv) The Moderates tried to win over the British but the Extremists wanted to turn them out. (v) The Moderates aimed at self-government but the Extremists at complete independence.

The distinctive political aspects of the programme of the militant nationalists were as follows: they believed that Indians themselves must work out their own salvation and make the effort to rise from their degraded position. They declared that great sacrifices and suffering were needed for this task. They deeply hated foreign rule and they declared in a clear cut manner that complete independence was the goal of the national movement. They advocated boycott of foreign goods, use of swadeshi goods, national education and passive resistance.

Partition of Bengal

The Partition of Bengal marks the turning point in the history of the Indian National Movement, which added impetus to the growth of nationalism in India.

Causes of Partition : Bengal was a vast province. It was not being administrated efficiently. Hence on July 20, 1905 Lord Curzon announced the partition of Bengal for administrative convenience. Actually, what the Government aimed with the partition was to end the increasing national unity in Bengal which was posing a threat to English empire. Lord Curzon partitioned Bengal into two parts. A new province was formed by amalgamating Eastern Bengal and Assam which were Muslim majority areas. Dacca was the capital of this new state. Administrative convenience was only an excuse on the part of the British government so that people may not oppose it.

Reaction of People : The people readily understood the trick of the government and a nation-wide opposition was registered at the partition of Bengal. The whole of Bengal echoed with the slogan of *'Vande Matram.'* There was political stir throughout the country. There were revolts at various places. Petitions and prayers to annul the partition were given a deaf ear by Lord Curzon. Surendra Nath Banerjee called the partition of Bengal as a national calamity and organised a forceful movement against it. The movement became a mass movement backed by the whole country.

People started boycotting foreign goods and adopting indigenous goods. The government suppressed the movement ruthlessly. But at last due to the vigorous resistance of the people, the partition of Bengal had to be annulled in 1911.

Effects of Partition

(i) This event led to a new awakening among the people due to anti-partition revolt. Swadeshi movement and slogans of *Vande Matram* added vigour to patriotism and the feeling of nationalism.

(ii) The emergence of a new sentiment for indigenous goods among Indians encouraged cottage industry in the country.

(iii) There remained no more faith in the justifiability of British in the minds of Indians. A few revolutionary organizations sprung up. The government tactics of ending the national unity resulted in Hindu-Muslim riots in the country.

Swadeshi and Boycott : The Anti-partition Struggle. The movement against the partition of Bengal took a concrete form in the Swadeshi Movement. The militant nationalists ardently believed in swadeshi and zealously propagated it among the people. Swadeshi was, according to the new nationalists, a weapon forged by the people to achieve industrial and general economic regeneration and advancement of India. Its implementation demanded great sacrifices especially, as Tilak remarked, from the middle classes who were the greatest consumers of foreign goods.

Boycott, conceived and organised by the militant nationalist was, on the other hand, openly and aggressively anti-British. It had a comprehensive programme and included not only the exclusion of British goods but also such items as the renunciation of titles and government posts and the boycott of councils and schools. The protagonists of the boycott used it as a weapon to compel the government to rescind the Partition of Bengal and stop repression. The 1906 session of the Congress at Calcutta adopted the swadeshi and boycott programme. All nationalist leaders, Tilak, Pal, Aurobindo, Barindra, Lajpat Rai and others organized a countrywide campaign through the press and the platform to popularize boycott. The campaign was successful and seriously affected the demand of British goods and gave a fillip to the Indian industries.

The Movement Spread Rapidly : British trade was appreciably curtailed. Mass meetings, demonstration, and hartals took place. *Kesari* and *Maratha* of Tilak in Bombay and *Sandhya, Bande Mataram* and *Yugantar* in Bengal educated the people in the new outlook and programme.

The government launched repression and increasingly intensified it. The Bengal Provincial Conference was dispersed by an executive order. Arrests and imprisonments of leaders, editors, propagandists and organizers of the movements took place. But the Swadeshi Movement spread to other provinces besides Bengal. It promoted the development of industries. In this respect, Bombay and Ahmadabad made considerable progress. The Swadeshi Movement had several consequences in the realm of culture.

Partition of Bengal and its Consequences

(i) There was a flowering of nationalist poetry, prose and journalism. The patriotic songs written at the time by poets like Rabindranath Tagore, Rajanikant Sen and Mukunda Das are sung in Bengal to this day.

(ii) Another constructive activity undertaken at the time was that of National Education. A National Council of Education was established to organize a national system of education. An engineering college founded by this council developed into the Jadavpur University after Independence.

(iii) A prominent part in the Swadeshi Movement was played by the students of Bengal. They practised and propagated Swadeshi and took the lead in organising picketing of shops selling foreign cloth.

(iv) There was active participation of women in the movement. From then on women took an active part in the nationalist movement. Many prominent Muslims joined the Swadeshi Movement including Abdul Rasul, Liazat Hussain and Guzavi. Many other middle and upper class Muslims, however remained neutral or, led by the Nawab of Dacca, even supported partition on the plea that East Bengal would have a Muslim majority.

(v) In spite of the popular character of the anti-partition movement and of the desire of the militant nationalists to take the national movement to the masses, the movement did not really affect and involve the peasantry of Bengal. It was confined on the whole to the towns and to the upper and lower middle classes of the province.

(vi) Though some of the Extremists unwisely alienated Muslims through over-enthusiasm and over-emphasis on Hindu religious symbols, leaders such as Surendranath Banerjee, Ashwini Kumar Dutta and Rabindranath Tagore repeatedly stressed Hindu Muslim unity.

(vii) The repressive methods of the Government, especially the brutal assault on the delegates to the Barisal Conference strengthened the resolve of the Extremists to carry on the struggle.

(viii) While Tilak was still for responsive cooperation, Aurobindo resolved upon aggressive resistance of the Russian terrorist type. What he meant became clear with the bomb attacks in Muzaffarpur and the discovery of the hideout of the terrorists at Maniktala. Tilak lent it moral support in the *Kesari*. He was sentenced to six years' transportation to Mandalay. Paranjpye, editor of The *Kal*, was jailed for nineteen months. Nine Bengali leaders were deported. Chidambaram Pillai of Madras and Harisarvottama Rao of Andhra were imprisoned.

The Government censored all newspapers, prohibited mass meetings and started prosecutions against the revolutionary associations.

With Aurobindo's escape to Pondicherry and his decision to give up politics and the national movement for religion, the open movement came to an end.

Split of Congress

On the issue of the partition of Bengal, extremists opposed the government and wanted to spread the Swadeshi and boycott movement throughout the country. But the moderates wanted to confine it only to Bengal and didn't want to come into direct clash with the government as they believed that it would obstruct constitutional growth of the country. The growing differences between the two came into limelight at Benaras Session where the extremists challenged the moderates for the first time. The fast growing popularity of the Extremists alarmed the Moderates. The rise of the revolutionary movement and the outbreak of Hindu-Muslim riots cooled their enthusiasm for the Swadeshi Movement.

Gokhale's negotiations with Morley raised their expectations or reform. The realized that their future and the country's future depended upon their maintaining hold over the Congress. In that crisis they did what all weak persons do in a similar situation. They took resort to secret manoeuvres for preventing the election of Tilak as President. A cable was sent to Dadabhai Naoroji who was on his way to England to return and preside over the Calcutta Congress (1906). He agreed and out of deference for the grand old man, Tilak withdrew from the contest. But even Dadabhai Naoroji could not stand the extremist tide.

As an astute politician, Naoroji in his Presidential address, announced the goal of Swarajya but to reassure the Moderates defined it as self-government of the colonial type. Dadabhai Naoroji maintained unity in both the groups through his ability and influence. But the extremists were successful in getting passed the resolution of swaraj, swadeshi and boycott and the resolutions pertaining to national education. After committing the Congress to their programme, the jubilant Extremists intensified their propaganda to rouse the people against the British.

The next session of the Congress was held at Nagpur. The Extremists proposed the name of Tilak for the Presidency once again. The reception committee got deadlocked over the issue, so the venue was shifted to Surat. On Mehta's advice, Rashbehari Ghosh was nominated as President. Tilak offered Rashbehari Ghosh to support him on the condition that the Calcutta resolutions should not be changed. The Moderates avoided giving him that assurance. Therefore, as soon as the session began and Ghosh took the chair, Tilak came to the rostrum to say that he had not been duly elected. There was and open rupture between the Moderates and the Extremists. The Congress was split. Its basic cause was the determination of the Moderate caucus to preserve their stranglehold over the organisation by. undemocratic means. Next day, i.e. on 28th December, the Moderates met under police protection. Only those who accepted the goal of colonial type of self-government and its realisation through gradual reforms and agreed to use strict constitutional methods to achieve it, were admitted to the meeting.

Lajpat Rai accepted these conditions and remained in the Congress. Tilak and Aurobindo refused to accept them and decided to stick to the Calcutta programme.

For the next nine years, the extremists were excluded from the national body. Deprived of the vitality of the younger men, Congress grew lifeless and inert. Attendance at the annual sessions dropped. Throughout the country, interest in political activity declined.

Conclusive Study

(i) The militant nationalists added a glorious chapter to the history of the national movement. They had clarified its objectives, taught people self-confidence and self-reliance and prepared the social base of the movement to include the lower middle classes, students, youth and women.

(ii) New methods of political organization and new modes of waging political struggles had been introduced. At the same time, certain old weaknesses persisted. The mass of the common people, the workers and the peasants, were still outside the mainstream of national politics. In spite of heroic talk of efforts at organizing mass struggles, such struggles were, on the whole, absent.

(iii) Passive resistance and non-cooperation remained mere ideas. The task of finding effective forms of political struggle was still unfulfilled and the country was still without an effective nationalist organization. Nor was the boundary of capitalism transcended. Tilak and others still saw social and economic development as bounded by capitalist enterprise.

(iv) Lastly, unlike the early Moderate nationalists, the militant nationalist did not realize the full significance of India being a country with many religions, castes and regions. While their militant anti-imperialism meant a great leap in national consolidation, the upper caste and Hindu tinge they imparted to it weakened the process of national unification and was to contribute to the bitter harvest of communalism in later years.

(v) The policy of the Extremists yielded good dividends. The partition of Bengal and annulment of it in 1911 gave a new self-confidence and self-assurance to Indian nationalists.

(vi) The aim of Swaraj, though denied by Lord Morley, was no longer looked upon as revolutionary demand and the shock of the First World War was required to compel the British Government to proclaim self-governing institutions as the goal of constitutional development in India.

(vii) However, the militant nationalists also failed in giving a positive lead to the people. They aroused the people but did not know how to harness or utilise the newly released energies of the people. Moreover, though they were radical in their nationalist beliefs, they remained constitutionalists in practice. But the people had learnt to take a bold stand in politics.

Revolutionary Activities—Rise and Growth : The enthusiasm that was denied an outlet in Congress politics found a more vehement one in revolutionary activities. This section, which the British called 'terrorists', advocated armed struggle. In this period, for the first time, militant resistance to British rule was organized effectively, though there had been incidents of armed rebellion from the moment the Company established itself in India.

Indian Revolutionaries

(i) In the nineteenth century, the Wahabi Movement—a Muslim religious crusade-developed into a major attempt to drive the foreigners from India. The Great Revolt of 1875 posed an even greater challenge to British supremacy. Not long after the Revolt was suppressed, Bengal and Bihar were rocked by the Indigo Rebellion. Indian cultivators of indigo were compelled to live on European-owned plantations in conditions that approached slavery. Between 1858 and 1860 the peasants refused to submit any more to forced cultivation. There were random attacks on the property of planters, and a violent uprising was feared. The cultivators' plight was publicised in Calcutta journals, and dramatized in the famous play, *Neel Darpan*. Ultimately, the government was obliged to set up on Indigo Commission, which gave some relief to the peasants After 1870, when the last Wahabis were suppressed, there was a period of relative quiet in the country. But the traditions of violent resistance did not die out entirely.

(ii) During the late 1870's the Calcutta student community was 'honeycombed' with secret societies. These amateur groups were not active, but in Maharashtra a serious effort was made at revolutionary organisation in 1879. Almost single-handedly, Wasudeo Balwant Phadke put together an armed band to rid the country of the British. His premature effort was crushed; but the spirit of rebellion lived on among the Marathas.

(iii) Tilak, the leader of the extremist group, had inflamed the tempers of some of his younger followers sufficiently to lead them to individual acts of terrorism. As early as 1897, two brothers Damodar and Balkrishna Chapekar of Poona, had assassinated two unpopular British officers. Later, Aurobindo Ghosh had actually planned some revolutionary activities.

(iv) The events following the partition of Bengal accentuated the revolutionary impulses of many Indians. They took to the bomb and the pistol and individual acts of terrorism.

(v) The *Jugantar* expressed their credo in an editorial in April 1906, after the Barisal Conference was broken up by the police, "The remedy lies with the people themselves. Force must be stopped by force." But these young terrorists, however, did not try to plan or organize a revolution based on violence and involving the whole country with the masses participation. They preferred to follow in the footsteps of the Irish terrorists and the Russian Nihilists and assassinated individual officials, who either because of their anti-Indian attitude or because of their repressive actions, had become unpopular. The idea was to strike terror in the hearts of the rulers and thus to arouse the people politically and ultimately to drive the British out of India.

(vi) By its very nature the planning and organization, the recruitment and training had to be secret underground activities. Many secret societies were set up, especially in Bengal and Maharashtra. Some of them functioned under the guise of physical culture clubs or associations. Of these the *Anusilan Samitis* of Calcutta and Dacca, the *Jugantar* of Calcutta and *Mitramela* started by the Savarkar brothers in Maharashtra became quite well known.

When V.D. Savarkar went abroad, his elder brother Ganesh started the Abhinava Bharat Society, which soon had many branches all over western India.

(vii) Public attention was seriously drawn to revolutionary terrorism by an attempt on the life of Kingsford, the District Judge of Muzaffarpur, by two young men, Khudiram Bose and Prafulla Chaki. The bomb, however, killed two innocent ladies. Khudiram was caught and Prafulla committed suicide rather than surrender.

(viii) A conspiracy case was started at Alipur against Aurobindo, his brother Barin and others, which was interrupted by the killing of the approver by the revolutionary terrorists within the jail compound. The officers in charge of the investigation and the prosecution were also assassinated one by one. While Aurobindo was acquitted, four others, including his brother Barin were deported to the Andamans and several others sentenced to long terms of imprisonment. Khudiram was hanged and Satyen Basu and Kanai Dutta who had killed the approved met with a similar fate.

(ix) Maharashtra, Nasik, Bombay and Poona became centres of bomb-manufacture. An attempt was made on the Viceroy's life. Jackson, District Magistrate of Nasik, was shot at a farewell party. Even before this, M.L. Dhingra killed Curzon-Wyllie, an official of the India

Office in London as a protest against the inhuman transportations and hangings of young Indians. He was executed.

(x) In Madras Province the people were excited by the eloquent speeches of Bipin Chandra Pal and Chidambaram Pillai who openly spoke of absolute independence. His arrest led to a serious riot in Tuticorin and Tirunelveil in which the police opened fire on a defiant crowd. Ashe, who had ordered the firing at Tirunelveli, was assassinated by Vanchi Aiyar of the Bharatha Matha Association. Unable to escape, Vanchi Aiyar shot himself.

(xi) The secret organizations of Punjab thrived on repeated famines and increase of land revenue and irrigation taxes. The *'beggar system'* caused irritation. Incidents in Bengal further inflamed the Punjabis. Assaults on Europeans took place at Lahore and riots broke out in Rawalpindi following the prosecution of Lajpat Rai's *Punjabi.* Ajit Singh was the heart and soul of this movement and he was helped by Aga Haider and Syed Hyder Riza. Deportation of Lajpat Rai and Ajit Singh quietened things for a while.

(xii) Rashbehari Bose, then a clerk at Dehradun, became the link between Bengal and Punjab. One of the bombs prepared in Bengal was thrown at the Viceroy, Lord Hardinge, as he was entering Delhi on 23rd December 1912, to prove that the repression-and-reforms policy would not pay. Some of the terrorist revolutionaries went abroad and established centres in Europe. Shyamji Krishna Verma, V.D. Savarkar and Lala Hardayal went to London. In Europe, Madame Cama and Ajit Singh were prominent.

(xiii) While the stimulus of the First World War was revitalizing the Congress, the revolutionaries decided to exploit the situation with the help of Germany.

Repressive measures of the Government had brought disarray in their ranks, but from 1912 they were re-grouping for a second trial of strength.

Revolutionaries Outside the Country : The Indian revolutionaries abroad added a new dimension to our struggle for freedom. They were not just individuals who had fled abroad to escape prison or death. Most of them were sent with a plan to organize centres in Europe, U.S.A., the Middle East and South-East Asia, where the cause of India might be propagated and arms and money collected to further revolution at home. They recruited fresh cadres from Indian students, businessmen and emigrant labour. They gathered the support of progressive or socialist movements wherever they went. With the outbreak of war they tried to establish contact with the Indian army units stationed abroad, prisoners of war and others hostile to British rule.

In collaboration with Germany, they planned to supply the Indian revolutionary organizations with recruits, funds and arms. They did not mean to be tools in German hands.

After Savarkar's arrest and abortive attempt to escape, the London revolutionaries dispersed. Virendranath Chattopadhyaya went to Paris and then to Germany. A committee of the resident Indians was formed in Berlin with German Foreign Office subsidy, which later came to be known as the Indian Independence Committee. Virenderanath became its secretary. It sent missions to Baghdad, Istanbul, Persia and Kabul to work among Indian army units and Indian prisoners of war. Raja Mahendra Pratap was sent to Kabul with Maulana Barkataullah and Maulana Obeidullah Sindhi, where they formed a Provisional Government of India.

Meanwhile Hardayal arrived in the United States where Taraknath Das and Sohan Singh Bhakna had already been spreading a revolutionary message among the Indian emigrants settled on the west coast and feeling rather embittered about the strict American immigration laws. They organized a party called *'Ghadar'*, taking the name of a weekly paper published from 1913, in commemoration of the uprising of 1857. Its programme included work among troops, assassination of officials, publication of revolutionary, anti-imperialist literature and procurement of arms. San Francisco became its headquarters and branches were set up all along the U.S. coast and the Far East. The idea was to bring about a simultaneous revolt in all the British colonies.

The *Komagatamaru* incident helped the activities of the *'Ghadar'* Party. This was a ship chartered to carry emigrants to Canada. When it arrived, the passengers were forced to return after two months of privation and uncertainty. When the *Komagatamaru* at last dropped anchor at Calcutta harbour, the passengers refused to board the train reserved for them by the Government. A riot ensued in which 20 to 40 were killed and many injured.

The *Toshamaru* met with a similar fate. The Punjabis abroad, inflamed by this news, hastened back to India and joined the victims to launch a vigorous armed campaign against British rule. Unable to secure German arms, they contacted the Bengal revolutionaries, among whom new leaders had emerged such as Jatindra Nath Mukherjee, Rashbehari Bose and Narendra Nath Bhattacharya. Seduction of Indian troops, simultaneous attacks on police lines and treasuries from Peshawar to Chittagong and an ultimate declaration of war with German arms were the major features of the plan. Unfortunately, however, treachery foiled the rising fixed for 21st February 1915. V.G. Pingle, an important member of the conspiracy, was arrested in the Cavalry Lines at Meerut in possession of bombs. Rebellious regiments were disbanded. Many of the conspirators were executed or transported to the Andamans. Rashbehari Bose escaped to Japan.

Jatin Mukherjee avoided isolated acts of assassination for a more ambitious scheme. A big haul of Mauser pistols, consigned for Rodda and Company, came in handy. The most memorable battle took place on the banks of the Buribalam river at Balasore between five Bengali terrorists waiting to unload German arms and a battalion of armed police, in which Jatin died of wounds he received while fighting heroically from a trench.

The revolutionary movements during the war failed because of a lack of coordination among the Indian leaders and a lack of communication between the Indian revolutionaries, the Berlin Committee and the *'Ghadar'* Party. The Government, suspicious from the beginning, persuaded the United States authorities to take steps to foil shipment of arms. Any activity in America was made impossible after she joined the Allies in the war against Germany. There was a trial of the *'Ghadar'* leaders in San Franscisco, which wiped out all chances of any further revolutionary activities based in the United States. The Government was quick to take steps against the revolutionaries. Local prisons and the penal colony in the Andaman Island were soon crowded with political prisoners. A series to conspiracy cases, stern penalties and harsh laws broke up the revolutionaries. The Newspaper (Incitement to Offences) Act, the Criminal Law Amendment Act, the Explosive Substances Act and the Indian Press Act were added to the armoury of the bureaucracy.

The terrorists added a colorful and inspiring chapter to the history of our freedom movement. Their desperate deeds and daring plans, cool action and indifference to death won them a lasting place in the memory of the nation. But with all their idealism and suffering, they were bound to fail. Acts of individual violence, however heroic, cannot mobilize the masses, and could be easily dealt with by an imperialism at its zenith. Secondly, most of the time the terrorists were working at cross-purposes without a common plan and central leadership. Thirdly, they had no base among the people. For one thing, being secret organizations they could not take the people into their confidence. But no sacrifice, so total, can entirely go waste. Few denied that the young activists who suffered imprisonment, deportation, or death, were deserving of the sacred name of martyr. Through their sacrifice, the urge for freedom grew stronger in the hearts of the people.

Famous Indian Revolutionaries

Ashfaquallah Khan (1900-1927) : Involved in nationalist activities from his school days, joined the Non-Cooperation Movement, became Bismil's trusted comrade, an important member of the Hindustan Republican Association, a leading figure in the Kakori hold-up of August 1925, caught by the Police in December 1925 through the betrayal of friend, tried in the supplementary Kakori case and sentenced to death.

Alluri Sitaramaraju (1897-1914) : In 1921 began to live among the tribals; the Girijans; in response to Gandhiji's call of Non-Cooperation, led the people to political agitation; arrested by the British authorities; atrocities committed on the tribals of Vishakhapatnam by the police and the officials for their participation in the anti-Government activities on which Sitaramaraju secretly organised them into an armed rebellion against the British authorities; surrendered to police hoping for fair trial and the settlement of his people's grievances; on 7th May 1924 treacherously shot dead by the police on the alleged ground of his attempted escape.

Bhagat Singh (1907-1931) : Born in a Sikh Jat Family of Lyallpur district, joined the Hindustan Socialist Republican Army in 1925; he initiated the militant youth organisation the *Naujawan Bharat Sabha* of the Punjab; in 1928 shot and killed Saunders to avenge the death of Lala Lajpat Rai who received injuries during the anti-Simon Commission agitation at Lahore; with Bathkeshwar Dutta exploded bombs in the Central Legislative Assembly on 8th April 1929; in the Lahore conspiracy case he was the main accused and received the death sentence; executed on 23rd March, 1931.

Chandra Shekhar Azad (1906-1931) : Arrested during Non-Cooperation Movement an flogged for ridiculing the court by giving his name as 'Azad', father's name as 'Swatantrata', and his address as 'the prison'; the name Azad stuck thereafter; joined the Hindustan Republican Association, involved in the Kakori conspiracy (1925), evaded the police, recordations the revolutionary movement and established links with the compatriots in Bengal; in September, 1928 when the party turned into the Hindustan Social Republican Army, he became its top leader and the "Commander of the Military Division"; reorganised with the attempt to blow up the Viceroy's train, the Assembly Bomb incident, the Delhi conspiracy, the shooting of Saunders at Lahore and the second Lahore conspiracy; surprised by an armed police party in Allahabad, died fighting a long battle.

Jatindra Nath Das (1904-1929) : Joined the Non-Cooperation Movement and was sentenced for six months imprisonment for pocketing; started manufacturing high explosive bombs for the revolutionaries; in June 1929 arrested in supplementary Lahore conspiracy case; in protest against the brutal treatment of political under-trials and prisoners and to enforce a distinct class for them, went on hunger strike in Lahore Borstal Jail in 13th July 1929; removed to the hospital and died there after 63 days of heroic struggle.

Khudiram Bose (1889-1908) : Gave up studies to join the Swadeshi Movement, associated with the Chhatra Bhandar an emporium for country-made articles in Midnapore. In 1908 the Jugantar group of revolutionaries decided to kill Kingsford, the notorious and oppressive Chief Presidency Magistrate of Calcutta; joined Prafulla Chaki. originally commissioned for the outrage; they hurled a bomb at Kingsford's carriage killing its occupants. Eventually arrested, bravely stood the trial and was executed on 11th August 1908.

Madam Bhikaji Cama (1861-1936) : Married into a loyalist family, had sharp differences with her husband and left for London in 1902; inspired by Dadabhai Naoroji and Shyamji Krishna Verma: in 1907 attended the Socialist Congress at Struttegart unfurling the flag of Indian freedom; in 1908 joined

Savarkar, Sardar Singh Rana etc. in patriotic extremism, organised the Indian youth in U.K and established the Free India Society, started Bande Mataram to propagate her revolutionary ideas; allowed to return to India in 1935, to take her last breathe.

Lala Hardayal (1884-1939) : Forced to give up his job for his political activities; elected general secretary of the Hindustan Association, later, the *'Ghadar'* Party; organised the Indian Independence Committee, and successfully enlisted the support of Germany in its favour; plans disrupted by Germany's defeat in the War; spent later years in U.S.A. advocating India's cause.

Rashbehari Bose : He launched an outrage on the Viceregal procession on 23rd December 1912 for which his associates were caught and received capital punishment, began operating from his Banaras hideout when a rising was planned in India during the First World War with German help, put plans discovered; organised a conference in Tokyo in March 1942 of Indians living in South East Asia, Which led to Indian Independence League at Bangkok, which under Rashbehari's leadership, formed the Indian National Army by recruiting Indian prisoners of war; later invited and passed over the leadership of the organisation to Netaji; died when Japan was collapsing in the war.

Ramprasad Bismil (1897-1927) : Involved in political activities from his early days; in 1923 became the acknowledged leader of the military wing of Hindustan Republican Association, led to Kakori train hold-up, sentenced to death and executed in Gorakhpur on 19th December 1927.

Sukhdev: Born at Lyallpur in the Punjab, drawn towards the secret revolutionary movement in North India, a close associate of Chandra Shekhar Azad and Bhagat Singh, took a leading part in the reorganization of the Revolutionary Parts into Hindustan Socialist Republican Army in September 1928 and looked after its activities in the Punjab and in the U.P.; tried as a principal accused in the Lahore conspiracy case;

received death punishment along with Bhagat Singh and Rajguru, executed on 23rd March. 1931.

Revolutionary Terrorism : Due to failure of the Non-cooperation Movement launched by Gandhiji, Revolutionaries became active again.

In 1924, Hindustan Republican Association was founded. Ram Prasad Bismil and Ashfaqulla, and few members of the organisation decided to loot the state treasury. At Kakori, near Lucknow, train was halted and state treasury was looted. But two traitors leaked the secrets-Bismil, Ashfaqulla, Roshan Singh and Rajendra Lahiri were arrested in the Kakori Conspiracy Case, 1925 and were hanged. Nearly all the major young revolutionaries of Northern India met at Delhi on 9th and 10th September, 1928, created a new collective leadership, adopted socialism as their official goal and changed the name of the party to the Hindustan Socialist Republican Association (Army). They were rapidly moving away from individual heroic action and assassination to mass politics. Lala Lajpat Rai's death, as the result of a brutal lathi-charge when he was leading an anti-Simon Commission demonstration at Lahore on 30th October, 1928, led them once again to take to individual assassination. So, on 17th December, 1928, Bhagat Singh, Azad and Rajguru assassinated, at Lahore, Saunders, a police official involved in the lathi-charge on Lala Lajpat Rai.

On 8th April 1929, Bhagat Singh and Batukeshwar Dutt threw a bomb in the building of Central Legislative Assembly in Delhi. Bhagat Singh, Sukhdev and Rajguru were sentenced to be hanged. That was carried out on 23rd March, 1931. In Bengal, too, the revolutionary terrorists started reorganizing and developing their underground activities. Among the several actions, was the attempt to assassinate Charles Tegart, the hated Police Commissioner of Calcutta, by Gopinath Saha in January, 1924. By an error, another Englishman named Day was killed. The Government arrested many under a newly promulgated ordinance. These include Subhash Chandra Bose and many other Congressmen. Gopinath Saha was hanged despite massive popular protest.

Among the new 'Revolt Groups' the most active and famous was the Chittagong group led by Surya Sen. Surya Sen's action plan was to include occupation of the two main armouries in Chittagong and the seizing of their arms with which a large band of revolutionaries could be formed into an armed detachment, the destruction of the telephone and telegraph systems of the city; and the dislocation of the railway communication system between Chittagong and the rest of Bengal. It became famous as 'Chittagong Armoury Raid'. On 18th April, 1930, a raid was organised. Surya Sen was arrested on 16th February, 1933, tried and hanged on 12th January, 1934.

Third Stage

The Gandhian Era : Struggle for Independence. The year 1919, constitutes an important landmark in the history of British India.

(i) The Rowlatt Bills and the reign of terror in the Punjab, culminating in Jallianwala Bagh massacre and barbarous enforcement of martial law in the Punjab.

(ii) The emergence of M.K.Gandhi of Satyagraha fame in South Africa the political leader in India.

(iii) Development of Pan-Islamism as a force in Indian politics.

(iv) The passing of the Government of India Act, 1919 on the basis of the Montagu-Chelmsford Report.

During the War years, Indian nationalism had matured. The movement has collected momentum and had become more forceful. The mood of the nationalist was one of expectancy, but if their hopes were belied, they were prepared to fight back.

During the First World War, Indians cooperated with heart, mind and money. British had assured the Indians to fulfil their legitimate demands after the war was over. But after the war, Indians were betrayed, which led to popular discontent. Contemporary national and international events encouraged revival of nationalism.

Non-cooperation Movement

Economic Exploitation : During the War, foreign imports had almost ceased, but Britain's wartime needs had increased. Some of these needs had to be met by India through increased production. Consequently, Indian trade and industry had developed to a certain extent. It had given the Indian industrialists a taste of high profits and property.

The Indian capitalists, however, could not take full advantage of the situation as India had few machine-making industries. Exports suffered by wartime controls and lack of shipping. Production trailed off towards the end of the war. Closures and unemployment followed. Prices of daily necessities had risen very high in the meantime. All these factors caused acute distress to the common people. The peasantry groaned under heavy rents and taxes. There was general anxiety about the future.

Immediately after the War, the economic situation took a turn for the worse. First, prices shot up. Foreign goods once again began to be imported. Indian industries faced heavy losses and even closure. To win popular support Britain, the United States, France, Italy and Japan had all spoken about the war to defend democracy and pledged themselves to stand by the right of self-determination of all countries and peoples.

World War Effect : After the War, however, they did not appear willing to put an end to colonialism. The peace treaties of 1919 belied the war aims of the allies and the 'fourteen points' of President Wilson. The Treaty of Versailles appeared to proclaim a rule of revenge. The distribution of the colonies of the defeated powers among the victors, the denial of self-determination to Central European peoples, the heavy burden of repartition imposed on Germany and, finally, the treatment of the Turkish empire, shocked Indians. After the end of war, Indians were not granted 'Swaraj' but in order to suppress the nationalists the Rowlatt Act was passed.

The Act of 1919 not Satisfactory : Of all the defects of the Act, from the nationalist point of view, particular attention may be directed to three points: 'Dyarchy', absence of even partialy responsible government at the Centre, and consolidation of Separate Electorates. 'Dyarchy' was too complicated to be smoothly worked. The perpetuation of Separate Electorates made it difficult for Hindu and Muslim to work together in the political field.

Revolution in Russia : Revolution broke out in Tsarist Russia in November 1917, and the Bolsheviks established the first socialist state in the world. While the Allies did the opposite of what they had preached, Soviet Russia created a great impression by unilaterally renouncing its imperialist rights in Asia. The Tsarist colonies were granted self-determination. The Asian nationalities in the U.S.S.R. were given equal status. The Revolution underlined the immense strength and vitality of the common people, who successfully withstood the intervention of the imperialist states and the strains of civil war. Lenin's decrees distributing land among the landless excited the intelligentsia. The Delhi Congress asked not only for India's right to self-determination but also for the declaration of the rights of the people of India.

External Effect : The proclamation of the Irish Republic by the Sinn Fein gave a further stimulus. In Egypt the Nationalist Party of Zaghlul Pasha had grown tremendously during the War. (Independence of Egypt was declared in March 1920). Almost at the same time Mustafa Kemal Pasha of Turkey was declaring war against the Allied occupation and setting up a provisional government. When the Allies allowed Japan to keep Shantung, which had been till then a German concession, there was violent resentment in China. The May Fourth Movement, in which intellectuals and students played an important part, organized a boycott of Japanese goods. The Chinese refused to sign the Treaty of Versailles. These new forces underlined the emergence of new challenges and the inauguration of new mass based national struggle.

Indian soldiers displayed exemplary heroism in the battles fought in Europe, Asia and Africa during the first World War and made conquests. The first World War also accounted for lowering the prestige of the Whites.

Passing of Rowlatt Act

The Government following the policy of concessions and repression made the fatal mistake presenting the nationalists with a strong dose of repressive legislation at about the same time. In December 1917 a committee was formed under the direction of Mr. Justice Rowlatt, the purpose of which was to investigate the revolutionary movement in India. The findings and recommendations of this committee were issued in April 1918 in the so-called Rowlatt Report. This document traced the growth of the revolutionary 'crimes' before and during the War. After painting an alarming picture, the committee recommended that many of the provisions of the Defence of India Act, which was due to lapse at the end of the War, should be made permanent. This would have meant the suspension of two of the most cherished principles of British justice—trial by jury, and *habeas corpus,* the rights safeguarding against illegal imprisonment.

Two bins embodying the committee's recommendations were speedily drafted and introduced before the Imperial Legislative Council in February 1919. One bill was enacted the very next month, despite the opposition of every Indian member of the Council.

Even before the Act was passed, popular agitation against the Rowlatt Bills had begun. This developed into nationwide campaign that soon outgrew its original concern with 'lawless laws' that were never actually enforced, and lifted Indian nationalism to a higher level. The leader of this movement that changed Indian and World history was Mohandas Karmachand Gandhi.

Emergence of Gandhi as Nationalist Movement Leader. Gandhi returned to his homeland in 1915. He established an ashram in Ahmadabad, and spent some time studying the conditions in the country. In 1917 Gandhi began his career of political agitation in India. He avoided the national political arena (which was then dominated by Tilak and Mrs. Besant) and concentrated on specific grievances. He campaigned against the 'indenture' system, under which Indian labourers were taken abroad to work under appalling conditions. Gandhi succeeded in getting the government to abolish the system. After this he fought for the rights of indigo cultivators in Champaran, Bihar, led a successful satyagraha campaign in the Kheda district of Gujarat, and brought about a settlement between mill-owners and workers in his own homebase of Ahmadabad. By the beginning of 1919, Gandhi had become one of the most prominent leaders in the country. His firmness and uncompromising idealism had won his many devoted followers and helped to focus nationwide attention on him and on his methods.

It was at this moment that the Rowlatt Bills were introduced. Gandhi immediately launched a *satyagraha* campaign against them. A general *hartal* all over the country was called from 6th April 1919, and this was to be followed by civil disobedience. The *hartal* was a unique success.

Massacre of Jallianwala Bagh

The Punjabi people had given a spirited response to Gandhi's call for non-violent protest. Successful hartals were held in Lahore, Amritsar, and other places. There were also occasional incidents of violence, to which the Punjabi authorities responded with severe repression. Two local leaders, Dr. Satpal and Dr. Kitchlew, were deported without trial. More disturbances followed, and the military was called in. On 12th April, 1919 Brigadier-General Dyer, an army commander, issued a declaration prohibiting public meetings in the town of Amritsar. Many people did not hear of the declaration, and a meeting was arranged for the next day, 13th April, 1919 in an enclosed plot of ground called Jallianwala Bagh. Dyer proceeded there at the appointed time. He found the Bagh filled with thousands of men, women and children. Dyer stationed his troops at the single entrance and. without warning the unarmed crowd, ordered his troops to open fire. The firing went on till the ammunition was exhausted. After the massacre, the wounded were left to die without medical help. It is difficult to estimate the casualties. They ran into hundreds.

After the Jallianwala Bagh massacre, martial law was proclaimed in the districts of Lahore and Amritsar. During its operation, all norms of a civilized government were suspended and efforts were made to intimidate and strike terror in the heart of the people. Students found shouting slogans were arrested. They were made to stand in the sun and then carried miles outside the towns before they were released. The more defiant ones were Hogged. All those who passed through the lane, where a missionary lady named Miss Sherwood had been assaulted, were made to crawl like vermin. Even the provincial government felt outraged by the order and it was withdrawn. Censorship was clamped in order to prevent the news of these excesses from leaking out. But notwithstanding the precautions taken by the authorities, some information came out. A wave of resentment swept over the country. Protests were made by the national leaders.

Rabindranath Tagore renounced his knighthood as a mark of protest and Sir Shankaran Nair resigned from the Executive Council of Viceroy. The A.I.C.C. demanded an enquiry into the 'atrocities' committed by the authorities. To pacify the Indians Lord Chelmsford appointed the Hunter Committee, to hold an enquiry into the Punjab 'disorders'. Simultaneously a bill was passed to indemnify the officers who were likely to be found guilty. The Congress decided to boycott the Hunter Committee and appointed its own committee to find out the truth. It was composed of Gandhi, Motilal Nehru, M.R. Jayakar and Abbas Tyabji.

These events which exposed British imperialism in its nakedness failed to shake Gandhi's faith in British justice. He continued to entertain the illusion that the guilty officers would be punished and the Government would make amendments. Therefore, when George V gave his assent to the reform bill on December 24th, 1919, proclaimed an amnesty and called upon the officials and the people to cooperative with each other. Gandhi, in the annual session of the Congress which was held at Amritsar in December 1919, shortly after the King's proclamation, strongly pleaded for cooperation with the government.

The Khilafat Movement. Soon after the Amritsar Congress, certain events took place which induced Gandhi to revise his decision to cooperate with the British. In the first place the British showed no sign of repentance for the excesses done in the Punjab. At this moment a third great wrong was added to the Rowlatt Acts and Punjab atrocities. This was the harsh treatment meted out to Turkey after its defeat in the First World War. The Sultan of Turkey, ruler of the Ottoman empire, was considered by many to be the Caliph or successor of the Prophet Muhammad. As such he was looked on as the head of the world-wide Muslim community. His dominion, the caliphate (Khilafat), was greatly reduced by the terms of the treaty ending the War. Many Turkish territories, including certain sacred placed of Islam, were taken away from the Caliph.

India's Muslims were outraged over this attack on the integrity of their religion. A Khilafat movement was started and soon gathered momentum. Ali Brothers, Maulana Azad, Hakim Ajmal Khan, and Hasrat Mohani formed a Khilafat Committee. Mahatma Gandhi embraced the cause of his Muslim fellow-countrymen, and in November 1919 he was elected president of the All-India Khilafat Conference. He also clubbed with it the demand for Swaraj, to annul Rowlatt Act and to make amends for the atrocities of Jallianwala Bagh. As the year 1920 opened, it was evident that India was gearing itself up for an unprecedented effort.

First Gandhian Movement

On 1st July 1920 Gandhi duly notified the Viceroy about his decision to launch Satyagraha on the twin issues of Khilafat and the Punjab wrongs. The Non-Cooperation Movement was launched on 1st August 1920 after the expiry of the term of the ultimatum. Fortuitously, Tilak's death during the preceding night removed the only leader who was capable of organizing an opposition to the Gandhian programme. In the special session of the Congress at Calcutta in September 1920 all the old leaders were opposed to the Gandhian programme of non-cooperation. Mrs. Annie Besant, C.R. Das, Motilal Nehru and M.A. Jinnah were all opposed to Council boycott. The idea of boycotting the schools and colleges also did not appeal to them. But Gandhi managed to get his policy of 'progressive non-violence, non-cooperation' adopted.

Non Co-opeative Movements Objectives and Progress : Gandhi described his Movement as 'a stage of peaceful rebellion' and called for defiance of 'ever single state-made law'. The objective was two-fold: first, to raise a fund of Rs. 1 crore in the name of Tilak to finance the country's non-cooperation activities; secondly to enroll a volunteer corps of one crore members to help promote various boycotts—social, educational legal and economic. There was to be a boycott of law courts by lawyers; of schools and colleges owned, aided or recognized by the government; of elections to the Central Legislative Assembly and the Provincial Councils; of honours, titles and official functions; of British goods. Swadeshi was to be encouraged as also the use of Khaddar; there was to be prohibition on drinking all liquor.

Before starting the movement, Gandhiji toured the whole of the country and acquainted the people with the movement.

The Tilak fund was soon over-subscribed. This apart, the Movement evoked an enthusiastic public response. Lawyers of the eminence of C.R. Das, Motilal Nehru, Rajendra Prasad, C. Rajagopalachari gave up their lucrative legal careers; thousands of students came out of college while many new national institutions were founded (e.g. the Kashi Vidyapeeth, the Jamia Millia Islamia). Subhash Chandra Bose quit his career in the I.C.S. and Jawaharlal Nehru his practice at the bar in Allahabad.

The number of students in colleges and secondary schools fell, as did excise revenues. As for the boycott of elections, Moderate politicians and sundry others did contest, but Congressmen and their sympathizers abstained from voting, thereby exposing the unrepresentative character of those elected. The boycott of foreign cloth adversely affected the import of British piece-goods.

By July 1921, the Non-Cooperation Movement had thoroughly roused the country, although it appears to have made little immediate impression on British policy. Thus, when the Prince of Wales (future King Edward VIII) visited India in November 1921, there were large-scale popular demonstrations against him. Prince of Wales was boycotted through out the country.

Movement Called Off : Meanwhile, the Moplah Rebellion in Kerala had raised the ugly spectre of Hindu-Muslim antagonisms while the Chauri Chaura holocaust demonstrated how the seeds of violence were imbedded deep in the national psyche. On 6th February 1922, the day following Chauri Chaura, Gandhi decided to suspend the Movement and at the same time abandon the proposed civil disobedience campaign at Bardoli in Gujarat. In Chauri Chaura, a village in Gorakhpur district, UP, twenty-two policemen were brutally killed after they had fired on a political procession. For Gandhi this was the last straw. There had already been disturbances in Madras, Calcutta and elsewhere, not to mention the Bombay riots. The Chauri Chaura incident convinced him that the country was not yet ready for mass civil disobedience. He prevailed upon the Congress Working Committee, which met at Bardoli on 12th February 1922, to call off the movement.

The sudden and abrupt countermanding of the Movement, which had raised popular enthusiasm to a high pitch, created strong resentment and even political confusion. The Congress was sharply split, as were the Khilafatist. Seizing the opportunity, the Government, which had hesitated hitherto, arrested Gandhi on 10th March and sentenced him to six years in jail.

Non Co-operation Movement and its Impact : The Non-Cooperation Movement brought Gandhi into the limelight of all-India politics. He now emerged as the logical heir of Tilak. Another significant impact was that the imprisonment of thousands of people from all walks of life removed from the popular mind the sense of terror and ignominy associated hitherto with jail entry; it became respectable and presently a badge of honour. Again, the fear complex inspired by alien authority, thus far a dominant feature of public life, dissolved. People were no longer afraid.

With the boycott of foreign goods, Indian Cottage Industries developed. Instead of English, Hindi got encouragement because the Congress had accepted it as a national language. National educational institutions which were founded gave impetus to nationalism, because they furnished information about Indian culture.

Indian Muslims had been attracted to the Non-Cooperation Movement because of the Khilafat issue. The fate of Turkey, however, was not really a question that concerned India in its struggle for freedom. The Khilafatists were inspired mainly by feelings of pan-Islamic internationalism. Such sentiments, however laudable, helped little in the building up of the Indian nation. In 1922 the Turkish people deprived the sultan of political power. Two years later Kemal Ataturk abolished the office of caliph and established a secular state.

The demise of the Khilafat hastened the breakdown of the precariously balanced harmony between the Indian Muslims and Hindus.

Civil Disobedience Movement : Gandhi was placed in charge of the Civil Disobedience Movement by the Congress Working Committee. On March 12th, 1930 he left Sabarmati Ashram as the head of its 78 male and female inmates and set out on foot for Dandi on the West Coast. He walked nearly 375 kms. On 5th April, they reached Dandi. Next-day he violated the salt laws by picking up a lump of salt form the shore. It was a signal for the beginning of Civil Disobedience Movement. C. Rajagopalachari led the salt satyagraha in the South. The programme of non-cooperation, whose whole emphasis was on boycott, non-payment of unjust taxes and civil disobedience of unjust laws were added for this movement. All congressmen were called upon 'to abstain from participating directly or indirectly in future elections (to the Legislatures). The sitting Congress members in the Legislatures were called upon to resign their seats.

In the large towns all over India, a fever of enthusiasm grew among the lower-middle classes. One expression of this was the entry of women into the civil disobedience movement. The police made countless arrests, but there were always more Satyagrahis ready to offer themselves for imprisonment. In May there were spectacular non violent 'raids' on salt factories in Dharsana and Wadala in Gujarat. The government replied, as usual, with repression. In June, Congress and its affiliates were declared illegal, and Gandhi and other leaders were arrested. Soon almost a lakh of men, women and children had been put in jail. The press was gagged, and newspapers could not report on the dozens of police firings that took place. Scores of people died in these incidents.

Most Muslims, taking their cue from Jinnah, stood aloof from the passive resistance movement. But in the North-West Frontier Province, the warlike Pathans rallied around Khan

Abdul Ghaffar Khan, 'Frontier Gandhi'. His followers known as Khudai Khidmatgar (Servants of God), or Red Shirts, became the most powerful political force on the Frontier.

Civil disobedience spread to every part of the country and took many forms. No-tax campaigns were started in Gujarat, Bihar, Bengal and UP. In Maharashtra, the Central provinces and Karnataka, Satyagrahis organized peaceful violations of the forest laws. In Eastern India, the villagers refused to pay Chaukidari (Watchman) tax. The peasants refused to pay land revenue. The women also actively participated in picketing shops, selling foreign cloth or liquor. Foreign goods were boycotted. It was not always possible to maintain strict non-violence. In Peshwar, Khudai Khidmatgar volunteers rioted after the arrest of their leader, 'Badshah Khan.' But Hindu soldiers of the Garhwal Rifles, called in to put down the riots, refused to fire on their Muslim compatriots. In Sholapur the arrest of Gandhi sparked off strikes and rioting. The people took control of the town for a week and set up a sort of parallel government. In the North-East, the Manipuris joined in, and the young Rani Gaidinliu led her Naga people against the British.

The Government resorted to repressive policy against the Civil Disobedience Movement. Unarmed crowd was lathicharged and fired at. Over 90,000 Satyagrahis including Gandhiji and the other Congress Leaders were imprisoned. The Congress was declared illegal. People were also beaten up for wearing Khadi or Gandhi cap. Newspapers were censored. According to official figures, more than 110 persons were killed and more than 300 were wounded as a result of police firing.

Second Stage : The Government reacted to the second phase of the Civil Disobedience Movement with the most severe measures of repression that it yet had resorted to. Congress was again outlawed, and more than a lakh of persons were arrested. Inhuman treatment was meted out to men, women and children. British Prime Minister McDonald made a declaration on 16th August, 1932 which is known as McDonald Decision. Gandhiji began fast unto death even in jail (20th September, 1932). The Indian people refused to be cowed into submission. There was picketing of cloth and liquor shops, salt satyagrah, forest-law violations, and non-payment of rent and to revenue. The national flag was hoisted in many places. The banned Congress held an illegal session in Delhi, and Congress activities went on despite police arrests. But it was difficult to keep up a high pitch of enthusiasm over a long period of time. Yet the people persisted, until finally the Movement was suspended by Gandhi in May 1933.

Comments : A healthy aspect was that the Movement helped to inculcate among the people qualities of fearlessness, self-reliance, sacrifice. The agelong dependence on the British and their promises was shattered. Another revealing facet was the coming into its own of Indian womanhood.

The Civil Disobedience Movement, the second nationalist mass struggle in the history of Indian nationalism, had a greater mass basis than the movement of 1920-21. It proved increased political awakening among the Indian people. Even the peasants were drawn into the nationalist struggle to a great extent. They had also evolved their own independent political and economic organizations which was not the case in the first movement.

Quit India Movement

The Quit India Movement followed in the wake of the failure of the Cripps Mission. Cripps' failure to resolve the political impasse created what appeared to Gandhi a moral crisis; Gandhi was determined, as he put it, to free Britain from the taint of hypocrisy and, at the same time, restore the dignity, self-reliance and integrity of the Indian people and convert their ill-will into goodwill. It has been suggested that the term 'Quit India' was coined by an American journalist during an interview with Gandhi. Writing in *The Harijan* on 26th April the Mahatma had instead used the expression 'orderly and timely British withdrawal from India.'

On 14th July the Congress Working Committee appealed to Britain to withdraw from India with goodwill so that a provisional government might be established which would cooperate with the United Nations in resisting aggression. The committee, however, affirmed that "should this appeal fail the Congress will then be reluctantly compelled to utilize all the non-violent strength it might have gathered since 1920". As scheduled, the AICC convened in Bombay on 7th August 1942 and adopted a resolution which justified the demand for the British to 'quit India' and explained its implications. *Inter alia,* it formulated the broad outlines of the constitution of a provisional government including its composition and aims, outlined a solution to the communal problem and declared India's aspirations for world peace and amity.

The All-India Congress Committee endorsed this, 'Quit India Resolution' on 8th August 1942. It authorized 'the starting of mass struggle on non-violent lines on the widest possible scale'. The evening after the Quit India resolution was passed, Gandhi addressed these memorable words to the Indian people: "Every one of you should from this moment onwards consider yourself a free man or woman and act as if you are free....I am not going to be satisfied with anything short of complete freedom. We shall do or die. We shall either free India or die in the attempt."

The next morning Gandhi and all other important Congress leaders were arrested. The Government hoped this would stifle the movement. But the rulers had not correctly guaged the changed mood of the people. Spontaneous acts of protest—*hartals,* strikes, processions—followed the arrests. Students played a major role in organizing these demonstrations, which at first were mostly non-violent. Very soon the situation went completely out of control. The people had no guidance, most of the leaders were in prison, some had gone underground and passion's were raging high. Individuals and groups interpreted the situation to the best of their understanding and acted as they thought best. The continuing police repression and 'Ordinance Raj' further inflamed the feelings of the people.

There were strikes in factories, colleges and schools. Police stations, post offices and railway stations which were considered the symbols of British authority in the country were attacked, set on fire or wrecked. Later some acts of sabotage were also indulged in. Telephone wires were cut and attempts made to derail trains. There was continuous exhortation to peasants to withhold tax payments. In many areas, the peasants set up alternative regimes, where the writ of the Government did not run for days and weeks.

The Government reacted sharply and let loose a reign of terror. Every canon of morality and human decency was violated in the name of preserving law and order. Authority made frequent use of bullets in quelling disturbances. The disturbances lacked both coherence as well as sound planning. The result was that in a few weeks the peak of their fury had been reached, to be followed by a rapid decline in overt action while the movement was driven underground. The Government did not relax its whip hand until satisfied that there was little chance of the movement reviving. Thereupon, it ordered the release of Gandhi on 4th May 1944, 21 months after his arrest.

Comment : The Revolt of 1942 achieved two things. It had given utterance to India's anger against imperialism and her determination to be free, in a striking and unmistakable manner; it was a living testament to the white hot intensity nationalist feelings had reached and the limits to which the people were prepared to suffer and sacrifice in exercise of their right to be free. Secondly, after the Revolt of 1942 there could have been no doubt left in the minds of the British rulers that the days of imperialist domination of India were strictly numbered. In one sense the revolt of 1942 marked the culmination of the Indian freedom movement. After the August 1942 uprising it was only a question of time and determining the actual mechanics of the transfer of power and the pattern of

Government the country was to have after independence. There were no doubt many political developments and much parleying and bargaining between the 1942 Revolt and the actual coming of independence in 1947. But that the freedom struggle was bound to win was no longer in doubt.

Royal Naval Mutiny

The ratings (non-commissioned sailors) of the Royal Indian Navy at Bombay harbour resented the racial discrimination in food and pay and the derogatory remarks made by British Officers in day-by-day life in the ships against Indian national character. Their sense of loyalty eroded as the Congress and communists launched anti-British propaganda.

The intermingling of Indian sailors with troops of Allied power during the war transformed the thinking of Indian. The discontentment erupted when the British Indian Government awarded seven years' rigorous imprisonment to Indian National Army official Abdul Rashid. On 18th February 1946 the ratings numbering 11000 mutinied, responding to the call given by Bombay students for a *hartal.* They took control of some ships, mounted the guns and were all set to open fire.

The protest received mass support and it spread to Calcutta and Bombay, where general public burnt government property. The agitation received much support from the left parties. The Mutiny of the naval ratings demonstrated to the British rulers that they could no longer depend on the loyalty of the armed forces.

Subhash Chandra Bose and the Indian National Army : Originally attached to the aims and policies of the Congress, Bose frequently disagreed with the official policy of the Congress High Command. Bose found the outbreak of the Second World War to be a convenient opportunity to strike a blow at the English for the freedom of India. But he found it hard to convert Gandhi to his views. In July 1940 he was arrested under the Defence of India rules. After a few months he was released on the ground of ill-health but was interned in his house under strict police surveillance. But on 26th January 1941, eluding police vigilance, he disappeared from his residence in Calcutta and, travelling secretly through Peshawar and Russia, reached Berlin on 28th March. There he tried to raise an Indian legion. The Indian community in Germany acclaimed him as their leader—Netaji—and greeted him with *Jai Hind*. He made frequent use to Berlin radio for broadcasting to India, urging countrymen to rise in arms against the British. The outbreak of war in the east created a new dimension in Bose's efforts to free India. Rashbehari Bose, who had settled in Japan, organised a conference in Tokyo in March 1942. Another conference was held, in Bangkok in June 1942. Out of these conferences was born the Indian Independence League and a decision to form an Indian National Army (Azad Hind Fauj) for the liberation of India from British subjection. A Council of Action was formed with Rashbehari Bose as its President and Mohan Singh as Commander-in-Chief of the Army. Shortly afterwards the high-handed attitude of Mohan Singh led to his arrest and Rashbehari Bose assumed control of the whole movement.

The Bankok Conference had sent an invitation to Subhash Chandra Bose to come to East Asia. He arrived at Tokyo on 13th June 1943. The Japanese authorities promised to extend all help to Bose to expel the British from India and to enable India to achieve full independence. In the beginning of July, Subhash Chandra Bose went to Singapore where he was handed over the Presidentship of the Indian Independence League by Rashbehari Bose.

Subhash Chandra Bose immediately formed the Provisional Government of Free India whose object was to bring about the expulsion of the British and their allies from the soil of India. He called upon the Indian people to 'rally round our banner and to strike for India's freedom'. He assumed command of the Indian National Army and gave it the famous battle cry:

'Chalo Delhi' (onwards to Delhi). Within a few days nine world powers including Japan, Germany, Italy, Burma, Thailand and Nationalist China accorded their recognition to the Provisional Government of Free India.

In 1944 the Indian National Army commenced its military career. In May battalion No. 1 of the 'Subhash Brigade', of the INA entered Indian territory. The Brigade captured Mowdok, an outpost situated south-east of Chittagong, and held it for several months. Meanwhile, the main body of the Subhash Brigade had proceeded to Kohima in Nagaland. Unfortunately, by this time the fortunes of war had turned against the Japanese. They were obliged to send all their available aircraft to the Pacific Front. Without air support, it became impossible to capture Imphal before the start of the monsoon. In June 1944 Japanese and INA troops withdrew into Burma. During the offensive, Indian soldiers had advanced 150 miles inside their country. Four thousand Indian lives were lost in this courageous attempt to liberate the country.

In the winter of 1944-45 the British counter-attacked. The Japanese retreated leaving Rangoon in Indian hands. The city was occupied by the British in May 1945, and 20,000 INA troops were obliged to surrender. Netaji had meanwhile escaped to Singapore and thence to Bangkok. In one of the disastrous days of August 1945, Subhash Chandra Bose is reported to have lost his life in an air crash.

It is true that many leaders did not like the idea of India winning freedom with the assistance of a country like Japan and her Fascist allies. But, during the closing years of the war, Subhash Chandra Bose and the INA served to hold up the drooping spirits of the nationalist Indians at home who were feeling helpless and frustrated; they set before all sections of the Indian people, including those serving in the army, an example of courage and patriotism which was both inspiring and ennobling. Therefore, when the Government announced their decision to prosecute three of the INA officers for treason because they had broken their oath of loyalty to the British Crown, there was a wave of nationalist protest. There were persistent demands that the officers should be released. Not only the Congress, but almost the entire political leadership of the country, was opposed to the trials and expressed themselves emphatically in favour of releasing the INA officers. The Congress set up an INA Defence Committee which consisted of such eminent lawyers as Bhulabhai Desai, Tej Bahadur Sapru, Kailashnath Katuju and Asaf Ali. Nehru also was a member of the committee. A great sense of drama gripped the nation as these national leaders stood up to defend the INA officers in the historic Red Fort at Delhi. The INA officers were found guilty by the Court Martial, but their sentences were remitted.

Before the three accused were given full liberty, there were gigantic demonstrations in Calcutta demanding their immediate release. This showed the British the depth of the popular feelings against the government. Public opinion was so emotionally charged that the Government had to yield. The sentences were suspended and the INA officers set free.

Role of Women

Women's participation in the Freedom Struggle added to the legitimacy of Indian nationalist movement participation in active politics not only changed their goals but also organised their activities. This was made possible by the deliberate attempt of progressive nationalist leaders to involve women in their struggle. Women themselves were amazed to find their political participation being approved and encouraged by men who otherwise wanted then to behave like perfect wives as in the religious texts.

Though the number of women was quiet small yet far exceeded their expectations. The nature of their work demonstrated how women saw themselves and how others saw their contribution.

In 1905 the British portioned the province of Bengal. Along

with men, women also participated in large numbers in boycotting foreign goods in favour of swadeshi. Many women burnt and destroyed their own foreign goods and clothes. On numerous occasions women silently made significant contribution to national movement by sheltering the fugitives, hidding weapons and in covering the revolutionary activities of men. Similarly in active politics women regenerated Indian womanhood by participating as women delegates in Indian National Congress. Their came up two distinct categories of behaviour of women, public and private, whereby the general role, duties of women were redefined. A women no longer remained a wife or mother but also developed as an individual who could play a significant part in politics.

With the coming of Mahatma Gandhi a new phase began in the history of women's role in the freedom struggle. On April 6, Gandhi addressed a meeting of women of all classes and asked them to join satyagraha. In the meeting of Jallianwala Bagh, along with men women were also massacred.

To induce women to join freedom struggle Gandhiji worked India's sacred legends like Ramayana. He said that restoration of the rule of Ram was possible only if women emulating the brave Sita united with men to overthrow Ravana i.e. British and establish Ram Rajya. Sucheta Kriplani once said that Gandhi's personality was such that it inspired confidence not only in women but also in guardians of women.

With the launching of the Non-Cooperation Movement, Sarojini Naidu decided to form a women political organisation. This was the *'Rashtriya Stree Sangha'*. C.R. Das urged women to participate actively by coming out of their houses. In Bombay in November 1000 women demonstrated against the visit of Prince of Wales to India.

In 'Young India 'Gandhi' urged women to come out openly against the British appeal was not restricted to so called 'respectable' women but extended it to those who stood on the margins of middle class society. Women followed Gandhi not only because their men accepted his leadership but also due to their personal admiration for him.

In the Civil Disobedience movement due to the cosmopolitian nature of the city, the women of Bombay took the lead in picketing and demonstrations. This was possible because Gandhi was able to construct a new image for the Indian women where their passivity and self suffering became a strength.

Women of Bengal also came forward but their demonstration were smaller but more radical. Here also women made and sold salt, picketed shops of cloth and labour, preached the value of Khaddar. Earlier women were merely supporting the revolution by hiding them, collecting funds or spreading their propaganda. But now were making and transporting explosives and were directly involved in revolutionary acts.

Rani Lakshmi Bai : Rani Lakshmi Bai, the second wife of the ruler of Jhansi, Gangadhar Rao, was born probably at Banaras. When her husband died without a issue in 1853 she was not permitted by the British authorities to adopt a successor. Her territory was later annexed under the "right of lapse" and a mere pension was offered to her.

She was reported to have declared them: *"Main Jhansi nahin dungi"* (I shall not surrender my Jhansi).

When the revolt started, the spirited Rani was drawn into the thick of the struggle and she became the authority of her region. She heroically defended Jhansi against Sir Hugh Rose's protracted siege, although ultimately she bad to escape. Later Rani Lakshmibai joined Tatya Tope and surprised the British by their capture of Gwalior. When Sir Huge Rose renewed the British attack on Gwalior Fort, the Rani—fighting valiantly was killed in action. An estimate of the Rani's heroic personality has thus been made by Sir Hugh Rose himself: "...the high descent of the Rani, her unbound liberality to her troops and retainers and her fortitude which no reverses could shake, rendered her an influential and dangerous adversary."

Annie Besant : Mrs. Besant, a British Socialist turned Theosophist, came to India in 1893. At first she confined her activities to religious social and educational fields. She pleaded for the equal rights of women, the organisation for workmen and the reform of land laws. She ' also campaigned for better housing, school, meals for the poor chilren and for the Scouts Movement. A critic of child marriage, Mrs. Besant opposed the rigidity of caste system and championed the cause of depressed classes.

Mrs. Besant emerged as a political leader in 1915, when she was successful in bringing a compromise between the Moderates and the Extremists of the Congress. She founded the Home Rule League in 1916 and started two journals, the *New India* and the *Commonwealth.* Mrs. Besant was imprisoned for her political activities and on her release in 1917 she presided over the Calcutta session of the Congress. Later, in consultation with Indian leaders, she drafted the well-known commonwealth of India Bill.

Mrs. Besant was responsible for starting several institutions including the Central Hindu College at Banaras in 1890, which was the nucleus of the Banaras Hindu University.

Rani Gaidinliu : Nagaland produced a brave women in Rani Gaidinliu who at the age of 13 responded to the calls of Gandhi and the Congress and rebelled against foreign rule. The young Rani was captured in 1932 and sentenced to life imprisonment. She wasted her youthful years in the cells of various Assam Jails, to be released only in 1947 by the Government of free India.

Rajkumari Amrit Kaur : Belonging to the ruling family of Kapurthala in the Punjab, Raj Kumari was born at Lucknow and educated in England. She came in contact with Gandhiji in 1919 and soon became his close follower and a life-long associate. She also served him as a Secretary for sixteen years.

Amrit Kaur was prominent among those women who gave up their riches and a life of luxury for the cause of India's freedom. Joining the Congress, she took an active part in the Salt *Satyagraha* of 1930 and the Quit India Movement of 1942 and suffered imprisonment. She served the independent India as its first Health Minister.

Amrit Kaur gave most of her time, money and energy to the many-sided reconstruction programme of Gandhiji and she was more involved in social service than in politics. She concerned herself with the progress of women and the Harijan upliftment and endeavoured to eradicate the early marriage, purdah and illiteracy. She was the founder-member of All India Women's Conference and the founder-President of Indian Council for Child Welfare. She also guided the Indian Red Cross movement during crucial years.

Kamla Nehru : Born in a Kashmiri family settled in Delhi, Kamala received her education at home and was married to Jawaharlal Nehru in 1916. When her husband joined the Non-Cooperation movement she gladly followed him. Kamla took prominent part in political processions, organised various activities of the Congress and thus endeared herself as the *Pride of Allahabad.* In 1930 she joined the Congress Volunteers' Organisation and led the Civil Disobedience movement. She was arrested for this on the New Year's Day in 1931. On the eve of her arrest and imprisonment Kamla left a brief message: "...I am confident that the people will leave no stone unturned to uphold the dignity of the national flag."

An ardent patriot and a devoted wife, Kamala fought against her illness with the same vigour and steadfastness with which she upheld the cause of her country. Bravely bearing the unhappy separation from her husband, who was often in jail, she dismissed every suggestion of the Government for a conditional release of Jawaharlal, even when she needed his presence most.

Sarojini Naidu : Born in a family reputed for its scholarly background, Sarojini was educated in England. She showed a marked flair for literature at an early age which later found expression in beautiful English verses and earned her the title "Nightingale of India".

Sarojini poems were typically Indian finding expression through a Western language and partly, western influence.

Turning a Home Rule League in 1916 at the call of Mrs. Besant, Sarojini relegated her literary and domestic activities to the background. She then placed herself in the forefront of the national struggle and distinguished herself as one of the chief lieutenants and confidants of Gandhiji. She was the first Indian lady to preside over the Congress (Kanpur, 1925). During the Salt *Satyagraha* she took over the supreme charge of the Civil Disobedience movement and led the salt raids at Dharsana in 1930. She also played an important role in all the subsequent political movement. At the beginning of the Quit India movement in 1942, she was arrested and detained with Gandhiji at the Aga Khan Palace, Poona. She toured the foreign countries several times to put forward the Indian point of view. Chairman of the Asian Relations Conference in 1947, she was the first Indian lady to become the Governor of Uttar Pradesh in free India.

8

Towards Freedom

The British-owned *Pioneer* of Allahabad was an early instance of Indianization of newspaper ownership. Under the editorship of F.W Wilson, an able and vivacious journalist the *Pioneer* made good progress in circulation. But he was a thorn in the side of the bureaucracy and the management terminated his services. After this the newspaper's fortunes declined and in the early 1930's the proprietors sold the paper to some Indian landlords and businessmen of the United Provinces.

The process of Indianization was stimulated by the negotiations for the transfer of power that began as the war drew to a close. Like the owners of many plantations and industrial units, the British proprietors of newspapers decided to sell their interests and repatriate the proceeds; they feared that restrictions might be imposed by the government of a free India on the remittance of foreign exchange. Bennett Coleman sold the *Times of India* to Seth Ramakrishna Dalmia, a leading industrialist who had interests in banking and airlines. The Madras *Mail* also changed hands. The *Statesman* too eventually came under Indian management after independence.

The Partition

Partition was the other, and gruesome, side of the medal of independence. The Hindu-Muslim riots set off by the Muslim League's 'direct action' on 16th August 1946 made it impossible for many Hindu-owned newspapers to function in Pakistan; and for *Dawn to* continue publication in Delhi. Prominent among newspaper counterparts of the refugees who fled to India from West Pakistan were the, *Tribune* of Lahore which shifted first to Ambala and subsequently, to Chandigarh; and the Urdu *Pratap* and *Milap* which moved from Lahore to Delhi.

More far-reaching than these physical displacements were the psychic effects of partition. The scenario in post-partition India was that though the eligible voters among Muslims had voted almost to a man for the Muslim League and its two nation theory in the 194546 elections, most of them stayed back in every Indian province except Punjab. Gandhiji and Nehru wanted that the millions of Muslims who chose to remain in India after the creation of Pakistan should be able to live in safety and dignity, irrespective of how Hindus were treated in Pakistan. This was a high morality of unilateral right doing, far above the ordinary human morality of reciprocal obligation. Not many could rise to that height.

A curious feature of the newspaper scene in the post partition years was that several Hindu-owned Urdu newspapers campaigned against, Urdu, and for Hindi. Urdu was perceived as a symbol of the Muslim domination of India prior to British rule, and of the re-establishment of Muslim rule in the western and eastern wings of the sub-continent in 1947 as the result of partition. Many Muslims for their part, and for long, had looked upon Urdu in the same way as a symbol of Muslim supremacy. When the government of the United Provinces passed an order on 8th April 1900 to the effect, that law courts and government offices should entertain petitions written not only in Urdu but in Hindi in Devanagari script, many Muslim politicians objected and held protest meetings. They said it would lower the status and prestige of Urdu.

If the post-partition campaign against Urdu in a section of the Indian Press betrayed pique, Urdu was soon to attract much solicitude from politicians, both Muslim and non-Muslim, many of whom are moved not by genuine concern for Muslims and for the language which they regard as theirs, but by calculations of the number of Muslim votes they could gain by espousing Urdu as 'the language of the minority'.

Another psychological effect of the vivisection of India in order to create an Islamic State was the feeling generated among some Hindus that what remained of India should, logically, be a Hindu State. A prominent exponent of this view was Seth Ramakrishna Dalmia, who urged that India should be proclaimed a liberal religious State. He said in the course of a statement in July 1950, published prominently by the Times of *India:* "The only right course for saving the country from economic collapse, ending refuge distress, establishing cordial relations with Pakistan and assuring complete protection to the Muslims in India is to declare India a liberal religious State, which is beyond doubt the wish of an overwhelming majority of India's citizens." He expressed regret that "though the country had not recovered from the shock of the tremendous human tragedy created by the influx of East Bengal refugees, the outbreak of the Korean war has diverted the attention of Government to international politics. Neglecting the country's most urgent domestic problems, all are busy speculating about the possibilities of a third world war."

The suggestion that India should be a religious State, even if a liberal one, was directly opposed to the thinking of Jawaharlal Nehru, educated in England and nurtured in rationalism and Marxism. He had been unhappy with Gandhiji's description of the ideal State as Ram Rajya because of its evocation of India's Hindu heritage. Nehru must have been irked also by the dig at his propensity to interest himself at least as much in the problems of the world as of India. The Prime Minister's aversion to Seth Dalmia was to be a factor in the formation of India's first Press Commission and in the framing of its terms of reference.

News Flow Emancipated : There were two aspects of the operations of Reuters in India as a limb of the British empire. One was its total control of the flow of news from and to India, and the other was its dominant role in news gathering and distribution within India.

An early instance of bias in reports of world events supplied by Reuters to Indian newspapers related to the Russian revolution of 1917 and subsequent events in the Soviet Union. In an article that Jawaharlal Nehru wrote for the *Hindu* (3rd April 1928) on his return from a visit to Russia the previous year, he said: "It is right that India should be eager to learn more about Russia. So, further information has been largely derived from subsidised news agencies inimical to Russia, and the most fantastic stories about her have been circulated. The question most frequently asked me has been about the alleged nationalisation of.women!" Nehru went on to pour ridicule on the fictitious 'Riga correspondents' who sat in London or Paris and concocted stories denigrating the infant Soviet State.

News sent out from India by Reuters to the rest of the world tended to be governed by Britain's imperial interests. The viewpoint of the Muslim League, after it became separatist and implacably hostile to the Indian National Congress, was enthusiastically projected abroad, as will be seen from the following instance.

When the Congress Working Committee met at Bardoli during December 1941, C. Rajagopalachari persuaded the Committee to revive the offer made by it earlier, in July 1940, to support the war effort if the British government agreed to recognise India's independence at the end of the war and to form immediately a provisional national government. At this point the British Viceroy, Lord Linlithgow, decided to use reuters to publicise abroad the Muslim League's objections to the Congress proposal. The historian S. Gopal writes: "The Viceroy, having no wish to cooperate with the Congress, disliked the Bardoli resolution. He therefore saw to it that Reuters cabled the full text of Jinnah's statement criticising the resolution, and urged Amery to give the statement the fullest weight in Britain and use it in the United States. 'If, under pressure from liberal quarters in the U.K., Rajaji and his friends were able to stifle me in their close embrace, I feel quite sure that the Mahatma would emerge once again upon the stage to give the *coup de grace* to British influence in India'.

Then, in the spring of 1942, there was, a, gaffe about the supposed death of Subhas Chandra Bose in an aeroplane accident. Bose had effected a dramatic escape from house detention in January 1941, and made his Way to Germany to canvass aid for India's freedom struggle in the belief not shared by Mahatma Gandhi, Jawaharlal Nehru and the great majority of the nationalist leadership that imperialist Britain's enemies should be regarded as India's friends. The whole country was shaken with grief. The Congress president and Gandhiji sent telegrams of condolence to the aged mother of Bose. When the allegedly dead Indian leader broadcast a talk from Radio Berlin, Reuters tried to disclaim responsibility for the report.

More grave was the failure of Reuters to make known abroad the firm opposition of the Congress leadership to the plans of Subhas Bose to liberate India with German and Japanese assistance. Mahatma Gandhi wrote in *Harijan* of 26th April 1942: "It is folly to suppose that aggressors can ever be benefactors. The Japanese may free India from the British yoke, but only to put in their own instead. I have always maintained that we should not seek any other power's help to free India from the British." Again, Viceroy Linlithgow cabled to Secretary of State Amery a summary of a report, intercepted by Intelligence, of an interview with Gandhiji on 15th May 1942 of a group of Bombay Congressman led by the former Chief Minister, B.G. Kher. The report, sent by Sharaf Athar Ali, a Communist, to P.C. Joshi, then secretary of the Communist Party of India, quoted Gandhiji as telling Kher (who had asked whether civil disobedience at that point would not mean help to the Japanese): "Oh, no. We are driving the British (out). We do not invite the Japanese. I disagree with those who think them liberators. Chinese history points that out. In fact I believe that Subhas Bose will have to be resisted by us. Subhas has risked much for us; but if he means to set up a government in India under the Japanese, he will be resisted by US."

The Viceroy, who had got Reuters to cable Jinnah's anti Congress statement, did not organise similar publicity for these anti-Axis views of Mahatma, Gandhi. The Viceroy apart, if Reuters had performed properly its duty as a world news agency, the British Press and public opinion would not have been as grossly misinformed as they were: "In the London Press, libellous propaganda was made by publishing on the front page of certain newspapers a huge headline, 'GANDHI'S INDIA-JAP PEACE PLAN EXPOSED!' The 5th August 1942 issue of the London *Daily Sketch carried* a photograph of Miss Slade (Mira Behn) with the caption, 'ENGLISH WOMAN GANDHI'S JAP PEACE ENVOY!' Punch cartoons were unspeakable. The London *Daily Herald, too was* clotted by the contagion."

Reuters' monopoly of news flow from and to India was a matter of concern to many members of the Indian and Eastern Newspaper Society. Reuters responded to this in its own fashion. At a meeting of the Society in New Delhi on 15th February 1943, F.R. Jones of the Reuters' office in Bombay suggested that "if members desired an additional service they might as well get it from the Associated Press of America through Messrs Reuters Ltd. for an additional fee." Objection was raised on the ground that it would merely be a new Reuters service specially charged. Amritlal Seth *of Janmabhoomi* urged that a competitive service to Reuters was necessary in the interest of newspapers.

The end of Reuters' dominant role in the gathering and distribution of news within the country became inevitable with the British decision, after World War II, to withdraw from India.

Transfer of proprietorship of the Associated Press of India to Indian newspapers had been urged by Arthur Moore of the *Statesman* during the four years of his presidentship of the Indian & Eastern Newspaper Society from its inception in 1939. A liberal who believed in unimpeded flow of information, he also pressed for the abolition of the monopoly clause in Reuters' contract with Indian newspapers which bound them not to utilise any competing world news agency, and for a reduction in the Reuters subscription rate in consonance with the lowered Press cable rate.

Arthur Moore questioned the stand taken by Reuters that the issue of the transfer of API's ownership to Indian newspapers should await the end of the hostilities. Referring to the change in ownership of Reuters in October 1941 when publishers of the London newspapers, organised in the Newspaper Proprietors Association, came in and held an equal number of shares with the Press Association comprising publishers of the provincial newspapers of Britain, Moore said: "If it could be possible for the main body of Reuters to change hands in wartime, it should not be impracticable to effect a change of ownership of the Associated Press under the same conditions."

With the pressure mounting, over the years, for transfer of control of domestic news to Indian newspapers, Reuters thought of a way to ensure at least the continuance of its exclusive distribution of foreign news in India. The expedient thought of was to make the Indian successor to API a partner in Reuters. The new approach was embodied in a draft resolution that was presented at the 21st general meeting of IENS held in Bombay in mid-December 1943: "The Society is of the opinion that the time has arrived for a further and direct discussion of the question of Indian newspapers securing representation in Reuters' central organisation and assuming the management of their Indian concern (Eastern News Agency, which distributed foreign news) and of the API. With a view to the formulation of definite proposals thereon, the Society suggests:

(a) the deputation of two representatives of the Society to visit London, if necessary, for such discussion; and

(b) pending the final fulfilment of these objectives, the establishment of closer association between Reuters and API."

The terms that Reuters initially offered to Indian newspapers would have retained the cream of the profits, as well as control, for Reuters. These terms were acceptable to the British-owned newspapers represented in IENS. Unlike the All India Newspaper Editors' Conference in which the editors of both Indian and British owned newspapers took a common stand as professional journalists against restrictions on publication of news ever since they first met in November 1940, IENS was an association of newspaper publishers and a divergence in approach was not surprising. The story of Reuters' one-sided formula has been told by A.S. Bharatan, who became the first general manager of Press Trust of India which eventually took over API:

> "Reuters' attitude in the early stages was based on the belief that they could part with the minimum and hold on to the maximum. After prolonged discussions a scheme emerged under which Reuters were to retain full control of the foreign news service and transfer the internal news agency, API, to the new Indian company. The annual income of these two agencies was in the proportion of two-to-one... This amounted to transferring a deficit-making agency to the Indian company and keeping the profit-making part in Reuters' own hands."

Even the Indian newspaper publishers among the members of IENS were divided in their approach to the question. Eventually the following resolution was adopted: "The IENS is indebted to Mr. Sadanand and Mr. Goenka for the proposals put forward by them for organising a news service owned by newspapers in the country. The Society has in the past strongly expressed the view that steps should be taken by the newspapers in India to acquire complete control of the API and an interest in the Reuters services in the country, with a view to reorganising them on cooperative lines. To put forward concrete proposals to this end, the Society hereby appoints the following subcommittee: the president (H.W. Smith of the Times of *India), K.* Srinivasan, S. Sadanand, and Ramnath Goenka."

The name Press Trust of India for the new agency emerged during discussion at a meeting of this Press Agency Sub Committee held at Madras in February 1946. The company was incorporated at Madras on 27th August 1947, within two weeks of Independence Day. The salient features of PTI's constitution as amended from time to time are:

(i) No distribution of profits to shareholders. Any profits are to be applied entirely to expanding the range and improving the quality of PTI's services to its media and non-media subscribers.

(ii) Membership is restricted to owners of newspapers published in India and subscribing to one or more of the agency's services.

(iii) To ensure the integrity, independence and freedom from bias of PTI's news service, no person can hold more than 1,000 shares of the company, and no member is entitled to more than five votes in all.

(iv) In order to guard and promote the wider public interest, there is provision for the appointment of up to, four Directors unconnected with the newspaper business.

Meanwhile, rapid political developments in the subcontinent made Reuters give up its old approach of dictating terms to IENS. It agreed to a total transfer of its operations in India, and invited an Indian newspaper delegation to visit England and negotiate an agreement under which PTI would become a shareholder in the main Reuters organisation. The members of the IENS delegation-K. Srinivasan, Devadas Gandhi, Sadanand, Goenka and C.R. Srinivasan-assembled on 20th May 1948 in London for the negotiations, which dragged on for thirty days.

In the meanwhile, Prime Minister Nehru made a critical reference to Reuters in the Indian parliament on 12th March, 1948. He said in reply to a question that the news agency had not fully and correctly covered the speeches of Indian representatives in the United Nations Organisation. He also said that the Government were aware that Reuters gave different versions of the news relating to Kashmir, in India and Pakistan. The Prime Minister finally announced that the Government had decided to discontinue, after due notice, the arrangement for the supply of Reuters news, on payment, to government offices in India and for use in the broadcasts of All India Radio. Yet it was a favourable nod from the Indian Government in mid-1948 that eventually resulted in the acceptance by IENS of the draft agreement with Reuters that the delegation led by K. Srinivasan brought from London. Did the Nehru government hope that PTI, by entering into partnership, could reform Reuters from within?

Failure Experiment : Kasturi Srinivasan's biographer writes. "The delegation was a divided house right from the beginning. Sadanand and Goenka were both strongly antagonistic to Reuters and preferred an arrangement with an American news agency instead. Devadas Gandhi, who was not particularly opposed to Reuters, was still of the view that prior commitments had been made with the Associated Press of America and it would have been much better if an agreement had been arrived at with that agency. C.R. Srinivasan was the only member of the delegation who stood by Kasturi Srinivasan all the time.

"The main points for negotiation were the terms for the transfer of API to Indian ownership, and the basis on which Reuters should supply world news to PTI. In regard' to the latter, two alternatives had been suggested: one, bulk purchase of news from Reuters on a seller-buyer basis without PTI becoming a partner of Reuters; and the other, a partnership in Reuters on terms similar to those that had been obtained by the Australian and New Zealand Associated Presses. But the Reuters sub-committee throughout pressed only for the conclusion of a partnership arrangement and consequently no other proposition was canvassed during the negotiations." Sadanand and Goenka, however, preferred bulk purchase of news by PTI from Reuters, without entering into partnership. The Indian delegation's mandate was that four signatures were necessary for it to conclude any agreement. Since this majority was not forthcoming, the delegation returned with a draft agreement. Its main features were as follows:

On taking up 12,500 shares, PTI would nominate one Director and one Trustee of Reuters.. Apart from the share capital, PTI would bear its portion of the running costs of the organisation. The day PTI took its shares, API would be transferred to PTI for a value to be agreed to by the auditors of both parties.

PTI would operate as a national news agency in India and would be responsible for providing Indian news to Reuters, transmitting news outside India at Reuters' cost. Reuters might, send correspondents to India on special occasions in consultation with PTI, and while in India these would be under the discipline of PTI.PTI would set up an Indian Desk in London and its Chief Representative there would be responsible for the contents of the world news service sent to India by Reuters. He would advise Reuters' Managing Editor on this, as well as on the use of incoming Indian news, and be under the discipline of Reuters. The Indian Desk would take over from Reuters the despatch of news services to Ceylon, Burma, Pakistan, Malaya and also certain Far Easter countries. The PTI Director on Reuters would have special responsibility for the contents of the service to these countries.

The area from Cairo in the west to a point eastwards to be fixed in consultation with the Australian Associated Press would be called the Indian Zone. Subject to the general responsibility of Reuters' Board, the primary responsibility of collecting news and supervising the work of correspondents in the zone would vest in PTI. A number of correspondents nominated by PTI would be added to the Reuter set-up in the zone. Reuters would introduce Indian journalists at the executive level into their world news organisation. A PTI man would be appointed in New York to cover the United Nations, and another would be appointed in Washington.

PTI would have exclusive use of Reuters news in India for the Press as well as the radio. PTI could sell its own news anywhere outside and should consult Reuters if it intended to sell the service to a competing world agency.

The scene shifted to India. At a four-day general body meeting of IENS in Bombay which began on 21st July 1948, the president of the Society, Tushar Kanti Ghosh, read out a letter received by him from Sardar Patel. In the course of this letter the Home Minister, who also held charge of. Information & Broadcasting, said that "having regard to the totality of the circumstances and taking a broad view of the agreement, I feel it is demonstrably in the interests of India and should be accepted." The agreement was endorsed by the Society and formally announced on 21st September 1948.

PTI had to raise funds quickly for buying the shares of Reuters. It issued 10,000 debentures of Rs. 100 each, carrying interest at 4 1/2 per cent. Sardar Patel, with whom Bharatan had good rapport, helped by persuading the ruler of Baroda to buy a large portion of the debentures. PTI remitted the money, and became a partner of Reuters with effect from 1st February 1949. Reuters' Agreement of Trust was suitably amended. The PTI Board appointed C.R. Srinivasan as its Trustee and Devadas Gandhi as Director of Reuters. Ramnath Goenka was appointed as alternate Director. PTI took over the operations of API on lst February 1949.

What nullified the potential of the partnership agreement for PTI emerging as a major player on the world news scene was PTI's lack of resources to deploy correspondents to cover adequately the zone of operations allotted to it. The newspaper publishers who owned PTI were interested in securing the staple of news at the cheapest possible rate, supplementing it with their own correspondents in some of the world capitals. Even these few correspondents posted abroad sent home as many of them continue to do news letters rather than spot news. The publishers did not share the vision that had impelled Jawaharlal Nehru to say at the Allahabad session of the All India Newspaper Editors' Conference on 16th February 1946: "I should like the owners of all newspapers present here to think of starting your own foreign news service. A number of newspapers could combine for the purpose and appoint their agents. I would particularly like them to go to places which are not sufficiently covered by other agencies-in South East Asia, the Middle East and the rest of the world."

PTI was without a correspondent in Moscow till 1963, and except for a two-month visit in 1949 by M. Sivaram, there was none in Peking till November 1980. It had, a maximum of only five correspondents at any time in the whole Indian zone, making do with, stringers at other places. The tenuous presence of PTI men was compounded by PTI's misjudgement in making Bombay-which did not have direct communication links with the capitals in the Indian zone-the controlling centre. It would have been more appropriate to give operational control of the Indian zone to the Chief Representative in London.

To direct the Indian Desk at the headquarters of Reuters in London, the PTI Board chose as its Chief Representative G Parthasarathi, who had been assistant editor of the *Hindu* since 1936. K. Gopalan, a senior member of the staff from the API days, was assigned to assist him. They found on arrival, in April 1949, that the 'Eastern desk' which was supposed to select and edit the news file of the world service that would go out to India and to a large number of other Asian countries consisted of six men who, except for one person, were professionally mediocre: "Five had no knowledge of Indian conditions and even Indian geography. The sixth had a distant acquaintance with India by virtue of his having been a sub editor on the Statesman of Calcutta about twenty years ago. But he was long past the age of retirement." It was only after a personal discussion in Bombay, during a visit to India by Parthasarathi that PTI's management was persuaded to strengthen the Indian desk by replacing three of the Englishmen by Indians.

Meanwhile the Englishmen on the Indian desk presented problems not only of ignorance of the region they were expected to serve but of political prejudice imbibed over years of work in Reuters. When dealing with despatches from the United Nations the English sub-editor, Gopalan says, tended to apply as before "the British news agency treatment of five hundred words to the British delegate, hundred to the American and twenty words to say that 'the Iraqi, Pakistani, Egyptian and Indian delegates also supported the motion' or some such thing."

In, addition to its work of processing for the Indian zone the Reuters world service which was "eighty per cent British in concept and content " the Indian desk contributed to coverage from the Indian and Asian viewpoint of international events in London like the conferences of Commonwealth Prime Ministers. The posting of D.P. Wagle at New York led to better coverage of United Nations proceedings. From Indonesia, N. Rajamani who had close links with Dr. Soekamo and other nationalist leaders did some fine reportage. When talks opened at the Hague on the political future of Indonesia, Reuters initially relied entirely on the ANP news agency of Holland. The Indian desk sent a special correspondent, on PTI account, to the Hague to ensure that justice was done also to the Indonesian nationalist viewpoint in Reuters despatches.

These limited gains were more than offset by another factor which militated against the partnership arrangement from the start, namely the conflict between India and Pakistan which were the two most important countries-at any rate at that time-of the zone allotted to PTI. Indo-Pakistan hostilities were in full swing when the PTI-Reuters agreement was being negotiated, a ceasefire coming into effect only, at the end of December 1948.

Altaf Hussain, president of the Pakistan Newspaper Editors' Conference, stated in Karachi on 8th March 1950 that Pakistan "has never accepted and will never accept" the position of being treated as a part of the Indian zone mentioned in Reuters' agreement with PTI. When there was a massive exodus that year of members of the minority Hindu community from the eastern wing of Pakistan (now Bangladesh) to India, PTI sent two correspondents to Dacca. Both were arrested by Pakistan authorities. Reuters, instead of helping to find a practical solution to the problem of news blackout in a situation of widespread human distress, sent its general manager to conduct negotiations with the Eastern News Trust of Pakistan for the operation of a separate Pakistani beam by Reuters. This new beam would additionally cover several countries which were already included in the Indian zone under the agreement with PTI which had come into force only the previous year.

Another irritant for the Indian partners of Reuters was the posting of a British correspondent in New Delhi on a regular basis, whereas the partnership agreement had visualised that "Reuters may send correspondents from headquarters to India on special occasions in consultation and in cooperation with the PTI." When the four-year partnership agreement expired at the end of 1952, it was not renewed. Instead, PTI entered into a contractual relationship with Reuters as between buyer and seller for the supply of the Reuters news and commercial service to PTI and for the supply of the PTI service to Reuters. This was what Sadanand and Goenka had urged from the beginning.

With the ending of the unequal partnership in Reuters, PTI became free to augment its sources of foreign news, including pictorial coverage, through arrangements with other international news agencies besides Reuters.

Freedom Fighters

Kasturi Srinivasan had told his colleagues of the All India Newspaper Editors' Conference in October 1942 that the Indian Press could not be fully free till the country became free. But it soon turned out that, in certain respects, each State is like every other, whether it be alien and autocratic or native and democratic, capitalist or socialist. None of them will tolerate attempts at subversion through sedition and violence, or the disclosure of State secrets.

Sadanand's *Free Press journal* learnt this to its cost. When Indian ratings of the Royal Indian Navy mutinied in Bombay in February 1946 against racial discrimination, "*FPJ* stood foursquare behind the R.I.N. boys of 'Talwar' and other ships and establishments and allowed them the full use of *FPJ* columns to air their grievances, even though the R.I.N. mutiny came at a time when the Congress had started negotiations with the British Cabinet Mission and frowned on the mutiny. *FPJ* went a step further. It employed two of the R.I.N. boys sacked by the Navy and pilloried the authorities editorially. This was something Sardar Patel could never forgive."

As the war ended and it become clear that India's independence could not be long delayed, Sadanand made plans for starting an Indian international news agency with the same during-do that he had shown in organising the Free. Press of India news agency in the late 1920's. He visited Cairo, London and New York during 1945-46 and entered into agreements with American and other news agencies and individual journalists to launch the Free Press of India World Service. The project ended in smoke when the *Free Press Journal* disclosed in September 1947 that Indian naval and land forces were being moved towards Junagadh. The Muslim ruler of that overwhelmingly Hindu majority State on the Gujarat coast had acceded to Pakistan; and while the people demonstrated in protest, the Nawab was preparing to bring in outside armed support.

The story of the movement of Indian forces was broken by B.C. Dutt, who was working on the FPJ and the afternoon *Free Press Bulletin.* He recalls: "Through the grapevine I still maintained with the navy, I heard a startling piece of news. Ships and some army units were heading for Junagadh by sea and land. Natarajan (the editor) could not doubt the authenticity of the news, as I had managed to smuggle out a carbon copy of the movement order." The story was banner-headlined in the *Free Press Bulletin* on a Saturday and the news agencies sent it on teleprinter for the Sunday papers which carried it on the front page. On Monday morning the editor, S. Natarajan, called B.C. Dutt and told him how angry Sardar Patel, Home Minister, who was also in charge of Information & Broadcasting, was: "He is furious that we published news about the armed forces without official clearance. The phone almost burnt up by the time he hung up on Sadanand last night."

The Indian government denied to Sadanand the lease of teleprinter lines and other facilities he needed, though he had placed a large order for teleprinters. This was the beginning of his financial decline and serious ill-health. He died in 1953, a heroic and tragic figure in the history of Indian journalism.

9

Other Side of Polity

(Politics of Regionalism, Communalism, Backward Class and Dalit Movements, Tribal People Movement, Struggle for Gender Justice)

Caste and Class

Political institutions cannot remain oblivious of the social atmosphere in any democratic set up. They are either based on the existing organisational structures in the society or they create new structures for themselves. Very often it so happens that a democratic society combines both the old and the new institutions. At times, the national progress lags behind because of these old institutions, but as long as the new institutions do not become an integral part of the new society, condemning the old institutions serves no purpose. A discussion on the role of caste in Indian politics is, therefore, futile unless one realises that a developing society is neither modern nor conservative but it is in a constant flux transforming both the institutions and the thinking process in a state.

An analysis of the Indian political system would reveal that it is functioning in a society which is considerably flexible and fairly accommodative. It is a society which provides for an open expression of the interests and their competitiveness and on change can occur unless it goes through the medium of such a competition and the clash of interests.

Caste and religion are dominant factors in Indian public life. The general elections held in the country have been indicative of their influence. Their influence is not confined to the regions of South India which are considered to be the strongholds of caste but are equally obvious in the North. It is therefore said that while the candidates may belong to different political parties, they, in fact, represent their respective castes. The elections for Panchayats, municipalities and the assembly and even the Parliament prove that the caste influence is fairly strong. In fact, the Panchayati Raj system has strengthened the caste system.

Caste in Indian society refers to a social group where membership is largely decided on the basis of birth. This section comprises a local group whose members do not enter into martial relationship with outsiders. Originally this group was associated with a specific profession. The mutual relationship of one caste with the other is established on the principle of lineage and the resultant purity of blood, making the relationship between one and other caste distant.

The definition of caste is, however, incomplete, Usually a caste is fragmented into several sub-castes whose members are more unified. Each group maintains its identity and establishes relationships with similar groups spread over a large geographical area.

This definition leads us to castes like the Reddys, Kammas, Okkaligas Kurmis, Bhuriars, Rajputs and others who despite being residents of different geographical divisions develop an affinity based on caste.

Caste in Indian Politics

The importance of caste should be realised in order to understand its impact on the political arena. Caste through a united effort of its members to assert themselves, has today intruded in both politics and administration mainly through franchise and institutions like the Panchayati Raj. Politics is, of course, accommodative and flexible enabling caste to step in. Yet while caste influences politics, politics also influences caste and shatters its solidarity. Caste solidarity is conductive to political power and strength but political power in turn tends to weaken Caste consolidation by creating internal competitions leading to new alignments at times cutting across the caste barriers. For instance, the dominant Reddy group in Andhra politics has often relied upon and mobilised the non-Reddy support outside its own caste structure whenever a competitive situation arose within the Reddy group.

Despite the two seemingly contradictory features of casteism—politics and the secularisation of caste—there is no doubt, that in every part of the country castes are trying to emerge in a big way by assuming political forms on a competitive basis. One should also admit that these castes also violate some of their own traditions for gaining certain common economic and political benefits.

However, if we do not recognise that, in India all politics is caste politics both at the central and state level and our work would be incomplete without a study of the clash among caste groups, Whether it is the factionalism of Indian political parties or the nomination of candidates and the mode of election campaign—most things can be explained through caste interests and caste balance. Politics in Andhra for instance, cannot be understood without an intensive study of the triangular fight among the Reddy, Kammas and Velama communities.

Similarly, the Okkaligas and Lingayats in Karnataka, Nayars and Ezhavas in Kerala, Maratha Brahmins and Mahars in Maharashtra, Banias and Patiders in Gujarat, Bhumihars, Kayasthas and Rajputs in Bihar and Jats, Brahmins and other weaker sections in Uttar Pradesh offer explanations to the most active forces in the State policies at the regional level. In all these States historically speaking, the political positions were, to start with, monopolised by certain high castes like the Brahmins due to their initial advantages. These castes were referred to as entrenched castes. At a later stage, however, the competitive situation within the entrenched castes was so tierce that its members had to look beyond their own group and mobilise those placed lower in the caste hierarchy who in turn were challenging to get into the ruling section.

At a still later stage when the expansion of political support became inevitable due to inter-caste competitions, the remaining or lower castes were not included in the power structure.

It may be borne in mind that a caste does not lose its identity after its transformation into a political group. It is likely that its influence at the social level is a bit reduced but to imagine that the influence of caste has swaped and would continue doing so in the framework of a modern democratic and industrial society would be to believe the experience of the last thirty years. Those who believe that the competitive situation among different caste groupings is a violation of caste principles which provide for mutual dependence, forget that the competition continues despite dependence.

As a separatist notion, however, caste is a challenge to secularism but if caste creates separation it also brings the people together as a group. The social universe of the rural poor is limited to a period of 15 to 20 miles and one does not expect them to identify themselves with bigger groups other than caste. The only social group they understand is caste. Caste is thus a centre for loyalty and those who speak of only bigger loyalties not only give a sense of security but also promote a healthy desire for progress. The caste operations are thus the first step in a democratic process of involvement and change which in the long run are likely to first step in a democratic process of involvement and change which in the long run are likely to lead to it dissolution.

Democracy, undoubtedly, increases the activities of the

caste groups. As the political power of the ruling elite gradually passes on the people in a mass society the impact of castes is felt much more. Sometimes one caste dominates over the other, due to social conditions. In Maharashtra, for instance, when the Brahmins took to English education they dominated others in matters of public employment.

The caste became important in politics because politics is highly competitive. Its purpose is to gain power for certain ends. It, therefore, exploits all kinds of loyalties in the society to gain and consolidate certain political positions; organisation and articulation of support are important in the above process of politics in our country. Caste is one such organisation with which the people are associated. The linkage between politics and caste is thus important and in the process both interact so closely that they are transformed. While politics exploits the caste organisations, caste also gets an opportunity to assert its identity and its position. Politicians utilise both the structures to consolidate power but in the process they change the form and expression of caste.

Thus the influence of caste varies with situation. While in certain electoral constituencies caste may be the sole deciding factor, in others its influence may be minimal. Party programmes also cut across caste loyalties and members of one caste may be divided on the basis of ideological affiliations.

The analysis reveals that the political connection is a reflection of the social reality and politics is one instrument which a particular class or group exploits to strengthen itself. It is, however, certain that the caste institutions are influenced in a dynamic and developing society, by urbanisation, industrialisation and modernisation. No political party can function with a style of caste group and thus it has to look beyond the caste structure and appeal to all castes through its programme. This is bound to weaken the caste structure. It is none the less difficult to say whether caste has used politics more than politics has utilised caste.

Politics on Class Basis

In the modern society the Political System is an important determinant of social system. A democratic political system aims to abolish the social distinctions and establish social equality which means that no person will be treated high or low on the basis of one's income, occupation or birth.

An aristocratic political system, on the other hand, starts with the belief that some are born to rule and other to be ruled. Such a system stratifies the society into distinct classes of rulers and ruled. In every society rulers have enjoyed a higher status. In democracy also, the legislatures and ministers enjoy a higher prestige though some of them may even be illiterate.

A class is one of two or more broad groups of individuals who are ranked by the members of the community in socially superior and inferior positions.

Karl Marx gave an economic interpretation to the meaning of the class. Thus, he differentiated between the bourgeoisie who own the means of production and the proletariat who do not. The bourgeoisie enjoy his status in society because they own property while the proletariat's status is inferior because instead of owning the means of production they rather work upon them. According to Marx, therefore, ownership of the means of production determines status of individuals. Max Weber also conceived of class as the product of economic factors. It may, however, be seen that according to Weber class is the result of economic distribution rather than of economic production. According to Marx, though the worker forms an essential part of productive system, yet he has no voice in the management of the factory or the mine where he works.

In order to augment the capital, the capitalists degrade the workers to the level of an appendage of machine. Marx contended that with the accumulation of capital the lot of the worker grows miserable. This gives rise to class consciousness among workers, who find their interest antagonistic to the interest of the capitalists. Thus Marx views the class in purely antagonistic terms, possessing irreconcilable class interests.

Generally there is a close co-relationship between the three hierarchies of caste, class and power. The Brahmans have the highest position in the caste hierarchy, while the untouchables have the lowest position and in between the two there are large collection of castes which have no fixed position. Similarly, there is close relationship between the status of a caste and its economic position. The higher castes tend to be land owners, while the tenants are mostly from the middle castes and agricultural labourers come mostly from the untouchable castes. Similarly all position of power and influence are in the hands of higher castes. Thus we find an intimate co-relationship between caste, class and power.

Some scholars have tended to argue that in the urban areas class is slowly replacing caste and that caste values are being discarded by those urban classes which now look to the west for new ideas and values. However, Prof. Srinivas does not agree with this view. He says. "There is a wide spread impression among educated Indians that caste is on its legs and that the educated, urbanized and westernized members of the upper classes have already escaped its bonds. But these impressions are wrong. These people may observe very few restrictions, marry outside the caste and even religion, but this does not mean that they have escaped entirely the bonds of caste. They show caste attitude in a surprising contexts. And they interact closely with the relatives who are steeped in attitudes. On occasions they are not averse to make use of caste times.

While we can not deny the hold of the caste on politics it is also true that the socio-economic status has a close relationship with political activity. This means that if the low status castes can raise their socio-economic status they can also raise their levels of political involvement and activity.

Politics on the Basis of Regionalism

India is a vast country inhabited by people of different races, speaking different languages, having many religious who are further divided into various castes, sub-castes and sects and subsects. Geographically also it is of a continental size. Some of the ethnic, religious and linguistic groups have a concentration of populations in certain areas which they regard as their own. They are primarily interested in the economic development of these and at the same time want to preserve their cultural identity. To protect their economic interest they do not want outsiders to settle there. All these economic political and cultural factors have combined together giving birth to regionalism which appears in various forms.

Regionalism Based on Language : One of the most important forms of regionalism is linguism. Regionalism in its linguistic form has asserted itself in three forms in,

(i) forcing the Centre to reorganise the States on linguistic basis;

(ii) preventing the Centre to make Hindi, the sole official language within a period of 15 years as originally provided in the Constitution; and

(iii) committing violence against linguistic minorities within States.

(i) *Reorganisation of States on Langauge Basis :* Though linguistic reorganisation of States was done in 1956 on the basis of the report of the States Reorganisation Commission headed by Justice Fazal Ali, it did not satisfy many social segments. It rejected in principle the monistic approach of linguism for the creation of States, yet in practice it followed except in case of Punjab and Bombay which were kept bilingual. The Commission rejected the claim of certain social segments for separate statehood because of their small size on the one hand and on the other, many unwidely States such as U.P. and Bihar remained as before and some more unwidely States were created in the process such as Madhya Pradesh and Andhra This left some social segments dissatisfied. Hence, they had to agitate again and because of these agitations both violent and non-violent, Bombay was bifurcated into Maharashtra and Gujarat in 1960; Nagaland was created in 1962 by bifurcating Assam. Punjab was bifurcated into Punjab and Haryana in 1966 and out of Assam, Meghalaya was created as a separate State in 1971; Mizoram and Arunachal were created in 1971 as Union Territories.

(ii) *Official Language Problem at the Centre :* The linguistic regionalism has also created the problem of official language both at the Centre and in the States. The Constitution provided that Hindi in Devanagari script would be the official language of the Union, but for a period of 15 years English would be continued to be used for the purposes of the Union for which it was being used immediately before the commencement of this Constitution. As a matter of abundant precaution the framers, however, provided that even after the expiry of 15 years Parliament may be law provide for the use of English for such purposes as specified in law (Art. 343)

Though the decision mentioned above on Official language was taken by the Constituent assembly unanimously, the Southern States in general and Tamil Nadu in particular refused to accept it. When Hindi became the Official language in 1965, there were widespread linguistic riots in Tamil Nadu and to ensure non-Hindi speaking people that Hindi would not be forced on them. Parliament passed the Official Languages Act in 1967 which provided that English shall continue to be used as an associate Official language unless resolutions of its discontinuance have been passed by the Legislatures of all States which have not adopted Hindi as their Official language.

Though this act is a sufficient guarantee that Hindi would not be imposed on non-Hindi speaking people, the Tamil Nadu government (both DMK and AIADMK) has refused even to accept the three language formula as an education policy for schools which provides for the use of regional languages, English and Hindi. It is following only a two-language formula, in schools of Tamil Nadu where only Tamil and English are taught. In fact, in 1968 the Tamil Nadu Assembly decided to scrap Hindi from the schools altogether. Their slogan is 'English ever and Hindi never'. It even opposes the use of Hindi commands in the army and it has done away with NCC training in colleges because of commands in Hindi. It is also against voluntary spread of Hindi. Even the use of Hindi in the U.N.O. by an Indian representative was criticised. This has created a difficult situation from the point of view of national unity and integrity because Hindi, a language spoken by the largest number of people in the country, should not be hated at least.

(iii) *Violence against linguistic Minorities in the States :* Moreover, inspite of the linguistic reorganisation of the States, there is a linguistic problem at the State level. For example, there is rivalry among Kannada, Tamil and Urdu in Karnataka, between Hindi and Urdu in Bihar and U.P., between Konkani and Marathi in Goa, between Assamese and Bengali in Assam and between Hindi and Punjabi in Punjab.

This shows that the linguistic regionalism is also asserting itself very powerfully. Since in every State there are linguistic minorities and the linguistic majority is discriminating against them either by denying them the facilities to educate their children through their mother-tongue or by forcing them to learn the language of the linguistic majority, in some States there are linguistic clashes between them. For example, there was a violence against Tamilians in Karnataka in 1984.

Demand for New States

Though the process of linguistic reorganisation continued till 1971, even thereafter there are demands for further reorganisation of States both on linguistic and non-linguistic basis. For example, there are demands for the creation of Mahakoshal and Madhya Bharat in Madhya Pradesh, of Jharkhand (by Tribals) in Bihar, Madhya Pradesh, West Bengal and Orissa; of Gorkhaland (consisting of Darjeeling, Siliguri, Dooars in Jalpaiguri) and Utarkhand in West Bengal; of Udayachal, and Purbachal and Karbi Anglong in Assam; of Vidarbha in Maharashtra; of Saurashtra and Kutch in Gujarat; or Bhojpur (in East) and Bundelkhand (in South) in U.P. and of Telengana in Andhra. Even in Manipur, the tribal students who are anti-Meiteis want a separate State.

Boundary Disputes among States : The existence of inter-State boundary and water disputes is also a manifestation of regionalism at present. This problem in the form of boundary disputes came into existence because of linguistic reorganisation of States in 1956 and thereafter. At present there are boundary disputes between Maharashtra and Karnataka on Belgaum, between Karnataka and Kerala on Kasargod, between Punjab and Haryana on Chandigarh and Fazilka, between Assam and Nagaland, on Rengma reserved forests in Rangapani area and on some villages in Desoi valley, between Assam and Meghalaya on Langpih, Hakumari and Jingiram river area of garo hills, between Assam and Arunachal on Pasighat subdivision.

Water Disputes among States : Inter-State water disputes like 'sons of soils theory' is a form of economic regionalism. There are such disputes between Haryana and Punjab on Ravi-Beas and Sutlej waters; among Gujarat, Madhya Pradesh, Maharashtra and Rajasthan on Narmada waters, among Tamil Nadu, Karnataka and Kerala on Cauvery waters, among Andhra, Madhya Pradesh, Maharashtra and Karnataka on Godavari waters.

These territorial and water disputes have defied their solution because of sensitive feelings of regionalism.

Full Statehood Demand

Demand for full Statehood is another form of regionalism. Since some of the Union Territories such as Himachal, Manipur and Tripura have been granted full Statehood, the Union Territories of Andaman, Laccadives, and Delhi have also demanded full Statehood. In fact, the Goa Assembly passed a resolution in 1976 asking for full Statehood.

Sate Autonomy Demand

The demand for State autonomy is also another form of regionalism and the regional parties such as DMK and AIADMK in the South, Akali Dal in the North are spearheading this demand. Telugu Desam, which has just emerged as a new regional party in the south.

Politics of Language

India is a federation of twenty five states and seven Union Territories, with a Central Government in New Delhi and a corresponding governmental machinery in each of the states, the powers and responsibilities of the Centre and the states being laid down by the Indian constitution. A decentralised system of government prevails, with policy making and implementing powers being distributed between the Union and the state governments. At the Union level the bicameral parliament is the supreme law making body, as are the various state legislatures in the respective states. In case of a clash between a Union and a state law, the Union law prevails, but this clash has often been avoided because of the dominant role played by a single party—the Congress—in the Union and state governments since independence.

In the case of language policy making, the official language of the Union has been laid down by the constitution of India (Article 343), which has also identified, in its Eighth Schedule, the various languages of the country to be used for purposes specified in Article 345 of the constitution. Further, the constitution has put all authority in the hands of the Central Government both for formulating and implementing the language policy. For example, it is the responsibility of the Centre to safeguard the cultural interests of the minorities and to see that they have adequate facilities for receiving at least primary education through their mother tongue (Article 350A). It is also the special responsibility of the Centre to develop and spread the official language (Hindi) of the Union (Article 351). The state governments, however, are left free to adopt either a regional language or the official language of the Union for the official purposes of the state (Article 345).

According to the Indian constitution, education for long has been (now it is a concurrent subject) a States subject (Article 246). From the strictly legal point of view the Government of India has had no authority to make any policy decisions in the field of primary and secondary education. Policy statements made by the Centre, therefore, like the National Policy on Education (1963) have served only as guidelines for the states. With regard to the tertiary level of education, however, the Centre is required to coordinate and maintain standards in higher education. With the adoption of the technique of Five Year Plans and the creation of the Planning Commission, there has been a trend towards centralisation in educational policy making. The Planning Commission lays down broad policies with the help of various Central and State authorities. Proposals regarding educational planning are submitted to it at the state level by the education departments and Universities at the national level by the Ministry of Education and the University Grants Commission. Responsibility for implementation lies in the case of the states with the education authorities of each state and in case of the Centre with the Ministry of Education.

The Chief Ministers of the various states are also important participants in national policy making through the Conference of all the Chief Ministers. In the particular field of policy making concerned with the official language, the role of the Chief Minister's Conference held in August 1961 accepted the Government's proposal for the continued use of English as the associated official language and endorsed the three language formula for adoption at the secondary stage of education for the teaching language subjects.

There is very little scope for policy formulation at the local level in India. In the sphere of education, there are some institutions, mostly primary and secondary schools which are managed by District or Municipal Boards of Education. However, since most of these receive grants from the state government, they have very little say in policy matters. Nevertheless, they take into account local conditions in deciding the languages to be taught and the medium of instruction. Regarding the official language in use at the local level, the Union Government memorandum of 1956 lays down that districts having 70 percent or more of its population speaking a language other than the official state language should have the status of unilingual areas with that language superseding the official state language.

Is Hindi an Official Language Really? : The unbroken history of a single language being used as the official language of the country is absent in India where the language of the rulers is known to determine the language of the government—Persian during Muslim dominance and English during British rule. Political independence in 1947 brought with it demands for cultural an emotional independence. The adoption of an Indian language for official purposes of the Union constituted a major demand in this direction.

The importance attached to the question of the official language of India is evidenced in the lengthy and detailed provisions made by the Indian constitution. The constitution distinguishes between the fifteen 'languages of India' and the 'official language' for all-India official purposes. Article 343 lays down Hindi, in the Devanagari script, as the official language of the Union. Clause 2 of the same Article stating that English "shall continue to be used" for such purposes as might be specified by law upto 1965. Article 346 provides for the use of the official language for official communication between a State and the Union or between one state and another. Article 345 leaves the choice of the state official language to the state governments. The language provisions of the constitution were the product of a heated debate and dissatisfaction and controversy over it still continues. The non-Hindi regions, in general regard Hindi only as the first among equals and resent its being chosen the official language of the Union.

The Multi-party System and the Hindi-English controversy: In the multi-party political system of India the various political parties have served largely as pressure groups influencing the post-independence modifications in the official language policy. For nearly three decades after independence the Congress remained dominant both at the Centre and in a majority of the states, without facing a single, strong opposition. Interestingly though, the party itself has been known for its eclectic tradition and has been composed of desperate political ideologies, groups and purposes. Consequently, the Congress Party as a whole did not have a language policy acceptable to all its members, and most of the solutions offered were in the nature of a compromise. Pressures for amending the official language policy, therefore, came as much from within the ruling party as from outside.

The two main issues now were the relative positions of Hindi and English in the official sphere, and the implementation of the 1965 deadline for replacing English by Hindi as the official language of India. As the fifteen year time limit for switching over to Hindi began to come to an end, it was feared, chiefly in the non-Hindi areas, that the removal of English as an associate official language would not only be difficult but disastrous. Apart from technical considerations, the main political objection to Hindi as the official language is that it places the non-Hindi areas (particularly South India, which belongs to a different language family) as a disadvantage in relation to the rest, English, on the other hand, being a foreign language is believed top lace an equal linguistic burden on both the Hindi and non-Hindi regions.

The Official Language Commission had, in 1956, endorsed the constitutional provisions thereby aggravating the non-Hindi opposition which perceived the implementation of the official language provisions as a threat to the political status of the non-Hindi regions, a restriction over their participation in national politics, and as disturbing the balance of power between regions.

As a result of the political significance attached to the official language question, a Special Committee of Parliament appointed to review the Commission's report, cautioned against a too hurried switch over to Hindi. Within the Congress Party, opinion was divided. Nehru, G.B. Pant and other leaders favoured a go-slow policy, and at the Pragiyotishpur session of the Congress in 1958, Nehru pleaded for a consensus of the opinion on the language question and criticized the imposition of majority decisions on a minority. He repeatedly assured the non-Hindi areas that English would remain an associate official language as long as the non-Hindi regions wanted it. At the same time, advocates of Hindi like Govind Das and P.D. Tandon insisted on a rigid implementation of the fifteen year deadline and showed their impatience at the delay in making Hindi the official language.

Their intolerance and failure to come to a compromise only served to unite the various groups from the non-Hindi areas. The latter, if previously demanding an equal role for their respective languages, now united in their support of English and opposition to the move to treat the 1965 deadline as a rigid one. The result of the agitation was the Presidential Order of April 1960 which indefinitely extended the time limit for a final switchover, followed by legislation in 1963 to establish the 'associate language' status for English.

The passing of the Official Language Act, 1963 should be examined against the background of the changed composition of the Congress Parliamentary Party following the 1962 general elections. India's third general elections weakened the Hindi group within the party. While representation from the non-Hindi states of Gujarat, Maharashtra, West Bengal, Orissa and Madras increased from 100 to 124, that from the Hindi states dropped from 186 to 150. Moreover, within the Hindi states the Congress suffered significant losses, so that as pointed out by Weiner, the Hindi region was "threatened with the possibility of five years of uncertain government." Significantly, opposition within the Hindi areas the comprised largely of Hindi communalist political parties like the Jana Sangh and the Samyukta Socialist Party, which identified Hindi with Hindi political interests.

This adversely affected Hindi's chances of being accepted as the official language of India. The changed political atmosphere, with a weakened Hindi group in the Lok Sabha, facilitated the introduction and passing of the Bill providing for the continued use of English for official purposes after 1965. Section 3 of the Official Languages Act, 1963 provides that English may be used for official purposes after 1965.

Though the 1963 Act legalized the go-slow policy of a section of the Congress, it appeased neither the pro nor the anti-Hindi groups. If champions of the non-Hindi cause such as Frank Anthony and S.K. Chatterjee objected to section 3 of the Act which provided that English 'may' be used, and not that English 'shall' be used; advocates of Hindi argued that the introduction of Hindi had been needlessly slowed down. The latter insisted that a time limit ought to have been laid down for a changeover to Hindi. Supporters of English felt that English should have been designated as associate official language for an indefinite period.

Communal Thinking

In religious matters, the people are very sensitive and throughout the world religion has played an important role both in integrating and disintegrating the societies. If on the one hand, "it had the effect of unifying large sections of people who would otherwise have remained fragmented on the other religion has also led to sharp ad severe divisions between man and man, group and group, nation and nation." Religions wars in middle ages in Europe and communal riots in India at the time of partition created havoc. Even now in India communalism continues to be a subject of continuing interest to the students of government and politics.

With the passage of time the members of the principal communities have increasingly organised themselves on communal lines and religious fundamentalists have again become very active. Because of their role, India, though a secular State is not a secular society because "India like some of the Asian countries is drifting into the morass of obscurantism religious fundamentalism and communal fanaticism." The communal fantacism has expressed itself in the following form :

(a) *Communal Violence* : India is a land of minorities where there is an acute problem of communalism which had led to more than nine thousand communal riots in the country since independence. In fact, between 1967-1978, every year there have been more than 170 incidents of communal riots. These communal riots have taken place in many States such as Andhra, Karnataka, Kerala and Tamil Nadu in the South in 1978. Again in 1982 there were communal riots in Kanyakumari district of Tamil Nadu (between Hindus and Christians) and also in Hyderabad and Travancore Cochin in December 1982, in Kashmir (at the temple town of Mattan), Bihar (at Jamshedpur in 1979 on the occasion of Ram Naumi procession), Delhi, U.P. in the North, in West Bengal (at Kaliachak in Malda district in 1978), Tripura and Assam in the East, in Gujarat (at Godhra and Baroda in 1978 and 1982 respectively) and Maharashtra in the West This shows that the communal riots have been breaking out in one part of the country or the other with distressing frequency and no part of the country from Kargil to Kanyakumari and from Guwahati to Chaupati has been free from communal riots which has made our democracy the greatest functional anarchy in the world in which the riots of communalism are deeper than democratic norms. Aligarh, Meerut, Moradabad, Baroda and Hyderabad are the most troubled cities in this respect.

(b) *Sectarian Riots :* In addition to the communal riots, there have been sectarian riots as well. For example, Lucknow has been the traditional centre of Shia-Sunni conflict and Kanpur and Amritsar that of Sikhs and Nirankaris. There is also tensionbetween the orthodox Sikhs and Sikhs following Radhaswami sect in Punjab. Though there have not been communal riots in Sikkim, the people have organised themselves into two hostile groups, namely, Lepchas and Bhutias. In Meghalaya, Manipur, Tripura and Mizoram also there is a conflict between tribals and non-tribals.

(c) *Destruction and Forcible Occupation of Religious Places :* Demolition, burning and forcible occupation of religious places is another form in which communalism has shown its ugly head. For example, in Arunachal Pradesh some of the churches were demolished and Christians were persecuted. Chruches were burnt in Srinagar during Pro-Bhutto demonstration in 1979 because Bhutto's hangman was a Christian. Even in Jalandhar, a part of Sodal temple premises has been forcibly occupied by Nihangs. In 1984 some temples in Punjab and some Gurudwaras in Haryana were also burnt.

(d) *Creation of Muslim Majority District :* In Kerala even the districts have been reorganised on communal considerations. For example, one Muslim majority district was created in the mid-sixties by the CPM government of Namboodaripad under the pressure of Kerala Muslim League which was a partner of the then coalition government. In 1982, the Congress government headed by Karunakaran agreed to create another Muslim majority district and as a reaction, thereof the Kerala Christians have also demanded the creation of Christian majority district. The reorganisation of districts on communal lines is most unfortunate and it should be avoided.

(e) *Misuse of Religious Places for Political Purposes :* Misuse of religious places such as temples, churches and Gurudwaras for political purposes is another form of communalism. For example, the Akali Dal has been organising its marches (campaign) from the Golden Temple for achieving its political demands. It is also a fact that many extremists and persons indulging in anti-national and secessionist activities were hiding in Guru Nanak Nivas which the SGPC considers a part of the temple complex where the army had to be used in June 1984 in 'Operation Bluestar' to flush out the extremists. This is unfortunate because religious places should not be used for political purposes.

Growth of Communalism

Though the problem of communalism is a colonial legacy, it will be a travesty of truth to deny the fact that a great extent we too are responsible for allowing it to take the present form. This is so because our faith in secularism is skin deep and therefore we have failed to rid the body politics of this deadly virus of communalism. The main causes of communalism in India are as follows :

(a) *Communal Legacy Past :* One of the main causes of communalism in the country today is the historical communal legacy. In order to curb the rising tide of nationalism in India the British government adopted the policy of divide and rule. For this purpose they encouraged the Muslim minority to establish their own educational institutions, publish their own literature to remove the stigma of disloyalty encouraged them to advocate the interests of Muslim minority on the basis of communal representation—an idea which was given to them by Mr. Archbold, the Principal of M.A.O. College, Aligarh, which was established in 1875.

Bengal was partitioned in 1905 by Lord Curzon in order to create a Muslim majority province. Though Bengal was reunited in 1911, the idea of partition on communal lines remained. In fact this was the beginning of communalism. Because of the encouragement of the British government, the loyal Muhammadans founded their own political party, namely the Muslim League, in 1907, at Karachi and on the demand of the Muslim League, Lord Minto, the Viceroy, recommended separate and weighted representation to the Muslim and the British government granted this under the Minto-Morley Reforms Act 1909. According to Ramsay, Macdonald, the British officialdom was responsible for the demand of separate and weighted representation because it accepted the character of demands presented by Sir Aga Khan, the leader of the Muslim delegation to the Viceroy. Lord Minto was briefed by Archbold himself who earlier also had arranged a meeting between the Viceroy (Lord Minto) and the Muslim delegation at Simla in 1906 through Col. Dunlop Smith, the Private Secretary to the Viceroy.

Thereafter, this principle of separate and weighted representation was extended to Sikhs, Europeans, Anglo-Indians and Christians by the Montagu-Chelmsford Reforms Act of 1919. The Macdonald award of 1932 further extended this principle to the depressed classes which was annulled only when Gandhiji went on a fast unto death in Poona jail. By the time the Government of India Act 1935 was passed, Muslim communalism was at its height which ultimately resulted in the partition of the country in 1947.

When the country was partitioned there were communal riots on an unprecedented scale and lakhs of Hindus and Muslims were killed. A very large number of Muslims decided to remain in India. Those who remained in India lost their privileged position in politics and services because the separate electorate with weighted representation and reservation in services for minorities were abolished by the new Constitution. This adversely affected their political and economic position.

(b) *Communal Sectarian Parties and their Politics* : The second cause of communalism in India is the existence of communal parties and organisations such as Muslim League, Jamait-e-Islami, Jamaite-Tulba (Kashmir), Itahadul Musalmeen, Hindu Maha Sabha and Akali Dal and organisations like the RSS, Patit Pawan Sangathan, Vishwa Hindu Parishad etc., even after independence. These political parties, through their communal propaganda have prevented the development of nationalist outlook and many a times encouraged communal violence. For example, in 1980, communal riots in Hyderabad started because of fatal stabbing of a Janta Party worker by a member of the Majlis-e-Musalmeen. In 1979, the RSS played a prominent part in Jamshedpur riots. In 1980 communal riots took place in Pune and Sholapur because of the role played by Vishwa Hindu Parishad which reacted sharply against the conversion of Harijans to Islam. So long as the communal parties are allowed to operate freely in the name of secular state, the situation is not likely to improve much in this respect.

(c) *Institutions with Communal Prefixes* : Existence of institutions with communal prefixes such as the B.H.U., Muslim University Aligarh, Khalsa College Amritsar and Christian Colleges encouraged the development of communal outlook. In fact the virus of communalism is spreading speedily though these institutions among the students, who instead of developing nationalist outlook develop communal tendencies. In spite of these drawbacks it is important to note that the Minority Commission recommended that the minority character of AMU should be restored by amending the Constitution to overrule the judgement of the Supreme Court in Azeej Pasha's case in 1967. The allegedly financed institute of Islamic studies has also come into existence in Baroda.

(d) *Religious Fanaticism* : In certain parts of the country the revivalist movements are very active which have resulted in frequent rioting. For example, in Baroda which witnessed 18 riots within 15 months (between September 1981-82) Ganpati, Navaratri and Tazia processions were taken out on an unprecedented scale. Shivaji Jayanti was never celebrated in Baroda even when Gaekwad rule it but it is done now. The use of loudspeakers in mosques, gurudwaras, temples and at other religious festivals has now become common and this not only disturbs the public but also results in social tensions. In Kerala an ancient stone cross was found at Nilakal and the Christians built a church overnight at the place with fabricated material which was taken as an affront to the Presiding deity at Sabarimala many miles away by the Hindus. Similarly, overnight Nishan Sahib was hoisted in Sodhal temple in Jalandhar which created a rift between the Hindus and Sikhs.

(e) *Social Factors* : Since the partition of the country, the Hindus and Muslims are suspicious of each other. The Muslims who want to preserve their separate identity, are afraid of being culturally assimilated by the Hindu majority and as a result thereof, there is a fundamentalist upsurge among them. Because of this upsurge, they have started the process of conversion of Harijans to

Islam. Though the process of conversion of Hindus to other religions such as Islam, Christianity, Buddhism, Jainism and Sikhism has been going on since long, the Hindus do not like conversion to Islam and Christianity in particular. Therefore O.P. Tyagi introduced "Freedom of Religion Bill" in the Lok Sabha in 1978. Justice Ansari, then Chairman of the Minority Commission, opposed it and said that the Bill is "a subtle move to prevent minorities from propagating their religion in the name of protection of freedom of religion. The Bill has not been passed so far and the conversions continue. Recently in 1979 in Tamil Nadu, (Meenakshipuram, Tiruneveli, and Ramanathapuram districts) Andhra and Karnataka many Scheduled Caste Hindus adopted Islam and this attracted the attention of some of the Hindu organisations like the Arya Samaj. Questions were asked in Parliament but the Government did not agree to ban conversions because in a secular state, this cannot be done. However, at any time these conversions may affect the Hindu-Muslims relations. The celebration of the first mass conversion of the Harijans to Islam in Tirunelveli district of Tamil Nadu in which the Union Muslim League leaders Sulaiman Sait, G.M.Banatwala (MPs) and others participated in 1982 is likely to worsen the situation sooner than expected.

It is important to note that in 1947 the Muslims constituted 5.1 per cent of the population but in 1979 the figure increased to 11.20 per cent. The Muslim population in India has increased because of illegal entry of Muslims into India particularly in West Bengal, Assam and other Eastern states, lack of interest in Family Planning among Muslims and lastly because of the conversions.

(f) *Economic Factors* : Economic rivalry between small sections of both the communities is another cause of communal flare ups. How the economic factor can trigger a communal carnage can be illustrated by the Moradabad riots. There is no denying that partly the rising prosperity of the minority community accounted for it. Traditionally, Muslim artisans have been producing the brass goods for which Moradabad is famous while their sale and export have been largely controlled by the Hindus. But during the last few years, some Muslims connected with the brass industry, who did well, have been able to muscle into the export trade as well, cutting into the profits of Hindu middlemen. Not surprisingly, the Hindus are unhappy. Similarly in Baroda, communal riots took place in 1981 because of rivalry between Bhois and the Muslims on illicit-liquor and gambling rackets. According to Ashgar Ali Engineer, a social scientist at Biharsharif and Godhara and acquisition of wealth by Muslims and resultant economic rivalry between them and Hindus were the causes of riots.

(g) *Political Factors :* Because of the improved economic conditions of Muslims now they have started asserting in local politics as well, which is not liked by some of the communal Hindu leaders. Hence, they skilfully, manipulate religious sentiments of the people by creating social tensions to achieve their political ends. It will not be out of place to mention here that in Kerala, a Muslim majority district was created on the basis of political consideration. The Muslims of Kishtwar and Tehsil in Ladakh have also been encouraged to ask for a Muslim majority district of Kishtwar.

(h) *Law Enforcement Agencies with Communal Outlook :* In communal riot sometimes, even the role of law enforcement agencies has not been impartial and in fact, in certain cases the police itself committed excesses on the minorities as it happened in Aligarh in 1978 and at Jamshedpur in 1979. It is important to note that

Morarji Desai, then Prime Minister accepted that in Aligarh, in U.P., the Provincial Armed Constabulary committed excesses. In Jamshedpur a three-member inquiry commission headed by Jitendra Narain, a Judge of the Patna High Court found that Bihar Military Police was partisan.

In the end, it can be said that while provocations of religious controversies relating to the observance of festivals and disputes over land and property continued to be the major factors responsible for communal trouble, a few incidents happened over trivial matters.

A quarrel among boys over kite-flying, eve-teasing or a drunken brawl had led to serious trouble in certain cases. Again playing of music loudly by one community in front of a place of worship of another community could cause it.

Summing up the root causes of communalism Satinder Singh has said :

"In sum, the main factors responsible for the current widespread riots are : far from happy historical memories; uneven economic development of the two major communities, virtual absence of a fairly strong Muslim middle class; largely selfish new Muslim leadership; total ignorance of the rulers of basic problems of the Muslim community; the stark poverty of an rampant illiteracy among the Muslim masses; and the growing aggressiveness in a sizable section of the Hindus."

If the communal riots are to be stopped then the fire fighting approach of the Government will have to be drastically changed and the causes of disturbances particularly on festivals anticipated preparations to tackle them should made in advance.

Secondly, the communal parties and organisations should be banned. It should be noted that on the basis of the Jitender Narain, Commission report, the Bihar government banned the holding of public meetings by the RSS and Jamati-e-Islami an educational institutions in 1981. The Minority Commission has also recommended the banning of the para-military training of communal organizations such as the RSS, The Hindu Maha Sabha, the Akali Dal, Jamat-e-Tulba, Kashmir Liberation Front and the Peoples League are communal parties/organisations.

Thirdly, an anti-riot force with substantial minority representation should be set up.

Fourthly, communally sensitive areas such as Aligarh, Moradabad, Hyderabad, Biharsharif, Jamshedpur, to name a few, should be kept under close surveillance and for that purpose more police stations should be created. In all there are sixteen such sensitive district in the country.

Fifthly, there should be special courts to try cases of communal violence so that those who now indulge in them may be punished immediately.

Sixthly, the Government should impose cumulative fines on the people living in sensitive areas, who frequently indulge in them.

Seventhly, mixed peacekeeping Mohalla Samities should be appointed.

Eighthly, strict watch must be kept on places of religious worship and they should not be allowed to be used by anti-social and communal elements. Some of these places are being used for these purposes. For instance, 15,000 country made bombs were recovered from an underground factory inside a mosque in old Lucknow. The Akali Dal has also used gurudwaras for giving shelter to extremists to achieve political ends. This should be checked.

Movements of Backward Classes

Backward class movement is one of the important arenas on social change. For decades these group of people were subject to inhuman conditions and often become victim in the hands of the high caste groups. When they became aware of their extreme exploitation it became intolerable for them to accept inhuman treatment from other high caste groups and started challenging the power of the high caste. Such movements definitely helped the lower caste to enhance their social position though not ritually and it enabled them to avail of facilities.

In Madras, non-Brahmin caste found themselves in a disadvantageous position because the Brahmin caste on account of their education, were holding higher posts. The non-Brahmin movement laid stress on two aspects: with respect to reservation in admission to college courses and with respect to the recruitment to government jobs. In both, they wanted that the reservation should be according to the population proportion. Both the demands created a good deal of resentment among the Brahmins who now found themselves being discriminated on the ground of their caste. The members of the aggressive groups of Dravida Kazhagam and Dravida Munnetra in Tamil Nadu carried on a virulent campaign against Brahmins.

But in North India when the lower castes claimed higher status, there were violent clashes. The Sudra castes sanskritized themselves and wanted to put on the sacred thread in order to register themselves in the census as members of the Vaisya or the Kshatriya caste. This led to violent clashes between the Brahmins and Kshatriyas on one hand and the Shudra castes on the other.

Many of their movements took a political turn. The non-Brahmin leaders of the old composite state of Madras formed the South India Liberation Federation in 1916 to advance and protect the interests of the non-Brahmins. The federation later on called itself the Justice Party. It started newspapers in English and other languages to educate and put forward the case of the non-Brahmins. In the same way many weeklies were started in various languages by caste organisations in different parts of India.

Thus the aim of backward classes movement was to limit the Brahmin monopoly in the two fields of education and appointment to government posts. But this was not a mass movement. The opposition of Brahmin dominance did not come from the low and the oppressed castes but from the leaders of the powerful rural dominant castes such as the Kammars and Reddis of Andhra Pradesh, Tamil Nadu and the Nayars of Kerala.

These backward classes include tribes, Hindus etc. Various steps have been taken up to improve upon the lot of the backwardness such as the positive discrimination, Mandal commission.

The backward class commission was appointed according to the Article 340 of the Constitution. The Commission was to determine the criteria to be adopted to provide concessions to 'Socially and Educationally Backward Classes' besides the scheduled castes and scheduled tribes. The Commission was also asked to prepare a list of such classes.

But the commission's report of backward classes on the basis of caste was not the criterion to be taken into consideration. The commission submitted its report in 1955 by listing 2399 castes as backward but it was rejected since caste was taken as the criterion of identifying the backwardness instead income was taken into consideration. The commission also recommended to include certain sections of Sikhs, Christians, Muslims to be included in the backward classes.

Economic backwardness is the result of many social evils. With respect to criteria of backwardness, the Commission recommended for general guidance (1) Low social position in the traditional caste hierarchy (2) Lack of education in the major section of the community (3) Inadequate or no representation in government service and (4) Inadequate representation in the field of trade, commerce and industry. The list of other Backward classes were published by the Education Ministry and by the State Governments. The commission also revised the list of SC and ST on the basis of such available information. The Commission noted that the great majority of the Backward Classes were ignorant, illiterates and poor. This was due to the traditional exploitation practised by the high social caste groups.

Resulting from the various benefits offered to these backward class groups, many of these groups have improved upon the socio-economic conditions that the economic status has been improved, they have their political representations. But at the same time, one should not ignore its negative implications. That it fails to create capable men of merit in the job market plus there has been conflict between those who avail of these facilities and those who are deprived of these facilities but belong to the same economic position. Further there has been clamour on the part of many who try to get a place in the backward class group so as to avail of these facilities through reservation.

Backward Classes who manage to get all the benefits are the most vocal in their professions for the welfare of the backward sections of their caste or group. It is also true that these sections of the caste make full use of the backwardness of their group to consolidate their own political power. Because of this, there is also a clamour for more and more to include in the list of backward class.

M. N. Srinivas explained that the rise of the backward class for education and economic opportunities was fundamentally a movement to achieve mobility on the part of the groups which had lagged behind the Brahmins in westernization. In the process of participating the modern political and other processes assumed significant changes.

(1) Freeing the caste from its traditional local and vertical matrix, within the local matrix the emphasis was on the independence of castes or local section of castes.

(2) The coming into existence of new opportunities educational, economic and political, brought about an increase in horizontal solidarity.

M.N. Srinivas maintains that reservation policy in an attempt to bring equality has improved the conditions of the backward class. Social movements have not been but without ideological backing for example S.N.D.P. movement in the south, the Mahar movement in Maharashtra, the Telengana Movement in Andhra Pradesh.

The SNDP movement exemplifies the principle of re-interpretation as those of the protest ideology. The Izhavas of Kerala suffered from conditions of acute relative deprivation within the framework of the caste system as characterized by the principle of purity and pollution. This principle was legitimised by the priests of orthodox Hinduism (Brahmins) and by the kings who wielded secular authority.

During British rule, these two sources of legitimacy were undermined to a great extent, and new sources of status were established, based on occupation, income, education and an egalitarian value system. Under such conditions, the leaders of the deprived sections were awakened to alternative sources of identity. Two ways of protest were open to them. One was to reinterpret Hinduism and claimed a new identity within its fold, and the other was to abandon Hinduism and embrace another religion and culture. The Izhavas choose the former, although they did make several attempts to choose the latter, because of the presence of a charismatic leader, Sri Narayana Guru Swamy.

Sri Narayana Guru Swamy established a new identity for the Izhavas of Kerala based on a re-interpretation of orthodox Hinduism. He denied the existence of a plurality of Gods, religions and castes. He argued against the criterion of birth as the basis of differential access to the highest forms of spiritual knowledge, and demonstrated the efficacy of training in gaining this knowledge. He established a set of beliefs, rituals, temples and priests which was parallel to those of the upper castes.

The world-view of his re-interpretation of Hinduism was both enlightening and simple, on the basis of which Izhavas were able to claim a new identity with honour, esteem and self-respect. This movement was basically known as Self-respect Movement.

Further Sri Narayana developed Dharma Paripalana movement among the Izhavas (toddy-tappers) of Kerala. Until 1935, the Izhavas belonged to the schedule castes. They were considered to be untouchables by the clean castes. The Izhavas. who formed about twenty-six per cent of Kerala's total population, suffered from many religious, educational and political disabilities. It was he who gave them a new lease of life. Temple entry movement was organised by him. The Mahar movement in Maharashtra completely rejected Hinduism and adopted its sect which stressed on egalitarianism such as Buddhism.

The Mahars were deemed as an important section of the scheduled castes of Maharashtra constituting about ten per cent of the state's population. They served as village watchmen, messengers, and removers of cattle carcasses. These services were hereditary and were paid for in kind. The Mahars were also weavers, petty traders, carpenters and cultivators. Thus, they occupied educational and political disabilities. In the third decade of the present century, the Mahars organised themselves under the leadership of Dr. Ambedkar. Dr Ambedkar vacillated between adopting one of two themes of identity to tight against the discriminations imposed by the upper castes—whether to stay within the Hindu fold or to abandon Hinduism altogether. He finally resolved the dilemma in 1956 by accepting Buddhism and abandoning Hinduism which also meant giving up caste. A large number of his followers embraced Buddhism which upheld egalitarian values.

Thus these Backward Class movement did not occur in vacuum. Exploitation, social injustice provided the fertile ground for such movement. These movements have been dominant in establishing new identities among the Backward Classes, characterized by conflict with the dominant groups.

Because of this new identity, it becomes a threat to the dominant groups since this dominant position socially and economically has been challenged by the new emerging class.

Mandal Commission Report

The Mandal Commission, its chairman as B.P. Mandal was constituted to look into two issues of other Backward class so as to implement various measures pertaining to reservation of education and jobs.

The main recommendations of Mandal Commission are :

* Socially and educationally backward classes should be accorded 27 per cent reservation of seats in educational institutions, in jobs under the control of Central Government, Public sector and Private sector, receiving financial assistance from the Government in one form or another.
* Candidates belonging to OBCs recruited on the basis of merit in an open competition should not be adjusted against their reservation quota of 27 per cent.
* The above reservations should also be made applicable to promotion quota of all levels.
* Reserved quota remaining unfilled should be carried forward for a period of three years and reserved thereafter.
* Relaxation in the upper age limit for direct recruitment should be extended to the candidates of OBCs in the same manner as done in the case of SCs and STs.
* A roster system for each category of posts should be adopted by the concerned authorities in the same manner as presently done in respect of SC and ST candidates.
* The above scheme of reservation should be made applicable to all recruitment to public sector undertakings both under the central and state government as also to nationalized banks.
* All private sector undertakings which have received financial assistance from the Government in one form or other should also be obliged to recruit personnel on the aforesaid basis.

* All universities and affiliated colleges should also be covered by the above scheme of reservation.

To give proper effect to these recommendations, it is imperative that adequate statutory provisions are made by the Government to amend the existing enactments rules, procedures, etc. to the extent they are not in consequence with the same.

An intensive and time bound programme of adult education should be launched in selected pockets with high concentration of OBC population. Residential school should be set in these areas for backward class students to provide a climate especially conducive to serious studies. All facilities in these schools including boarding and lodging will have to be provided free of cost to attract students from poor and backward homes. Scats should be reserved for OBC student in all scientific technical and professional institutions run by Central as well as State Government. Those stales which have already reserved more than 27 per cent seats for OBC students will remain unaffected by this recommendation.

Suitable institutional finance and technical assistance is made available to such members of village, vocational communities who want to set up sway scale industries of their own. Similar assistance should also be provided to those OBC candidates who have obtained special vocational training.

Some State Government like Karnataka and Andhra Pradesh have already set up separate financial corporations etc, for OBCs. Separate financial institutions for providing financial and technical assistance shall be established for the backward classes. All the state government should be directed to enact and implement progressive land legislation to effect structural changes. Certain sections of some occupational communities like Fishermen, Khatives, Banafares etc. suffer from the stigma of untouchability in some parts of the country. They have been listed as OBCs, by the commission, but their inclusions in the list of SC/ST may be considered by the

Governments. Backward class Development Corporation have been set up both at the Central and State levels to implement various socio-educational and economic measures for their advancement. A separate Ministry/ Department of OBCs at the centre and states should be created to safeguard their interests. With a view to giving better representation to certain backward sections it is recommended that areas of concentration may be carved out into separate constituencies at the time of delimitations.

At present no Central Assistance is available to the State Government for implementing any welfare measure for other Backward Classes. All development programmes especially designed for Other Backward Classes should be financed by Central Government in the same manner and as to the same extent in the case of the Scheduled Tribes and Scheduled Castes.

The entire scheme should be reviewed after twenty years. OBCs should be re-divided into two categories i.e. Intermediate Backward Class and Depressed Backward Class. The former is awarded 12 per cent and latter is awarded 15 per cent in the OBC reservation scheme. In Chairman, Mandal's opinion Article 15 (4) of the Indian Constitution will not permit such a provision.

The Mandal Commission reviewed; (a) Various court judgements with reference to reservation schemes, (b) The related debates in various state assemblies and parliament, (c) The reservation schemes now in force in various states, (d) Opinions of State Government and Central Government in the question answer format, (e) Ideas and suggestions from General Public and (f) Reports of the previous Backward Class Commissions set up by the Central government. It also gathered opinions from Central and State Government, VI and VII parliament members, voluntary organizations, social workers, intellectuals and the public.

Emergence of Dalit Consciousness : Dalits and the social groups occupy the lowest position in the local hierarchy of castes. They are the out caste made up of former 'outcaste' groups of 'exuntouchables' who form the inner core of poverty, adopted the nomenclature of 'Dalits' following the original usage of the term by Mahatma Jyotiba Phule (1827-1899) backward caste Maratha social reformer to describe the outcastes and untouchables as the oppressed group.

Dalits existed from the time of Rig Vedas. Purusa Hymn mentions the existence of four castes. The Brahmin was his mouth, of both his arms was the Rajanya (Kshatriya) made, his thighs become the Vaisya, from his feet the Sudra was produced." Thus the origin of the existence of Dalits is attributed to religion.

On the basis of the hymn we understand four-fold division of society existed. But many scholars believe that this hymn has been composed at a later time and therefore does not represent Rig Vedic period. But at the same time it is also true that Dalit problem took root at the time the hymn was written. In the Upanishad period, the problem seems to have been crystallized and is becoming deeper and clearer. The Chhandogya Upanishad not only refers to the first three upper castes but also compares Chandala (outcaste). They are born against the rule of endogamy. It refers to only three upper castes and fourth caste Sudra was not mentioned. Instead it refers to Chandala.

In Manu Smriti, references to mixed castes are made—the Chandalas and how and where they were supposed to live. During this time the negative development of the Dalit problem or state had reached its climax. In the recent years when British ruled India, their situation remained status quo and they followed the policy of non-interference, actively upholding the distinctions in Hindu society.

During British period a number of small movements came into existence, who showed concern for the Dalits for various reasons. Even before this, during Muslim period Bhakti movement helped the cause of the Dalits particularly in spiritual sphere. This happened through Bhakti Saivas who belong to backward class or they themselves were Dalits. These efforts had little impact on improving the condition of Dalits.

Mahatma Jyotiba Phule, Dr. Ambedkar, Mahatma Gandhi, E.V.R. of Chennai, Sri Narayana Dharma Paripalan of Kerala and reform movements of Karnataka, and Pant movement in Punjab were few leaders who fought for the Dalit Cause.

Among all the social reformers, Jyotiba Phule's contribution for the cause of Dalit is notable. It was in 1873 that he started Satyashodhak Samaj. He strongly condemned the tyranny of caste system. His revolt was against caste in so far as caste denied ordinary human rights at all. In 1851 he started a primary school for untouchables in Poona. He criticised Manusmriti because it was a stumbling block in the way of social change. Mahatma Phule made efforts to unite all the non-Brahmins and the Dalits and to remain united for their own cause.

The depressed classes were used in place of scheduled caste in British India, and also by the members of various reform movements. But till 1932 the latter expression was used more or less for all kinds of depressed people including the untouchables', until then no effort was made to differentiate it, to define on the basis of religion. In 1932 for the first time the term 'The Depressed Classes' was used for people with an untouchable background. At that time the British Government was also trying to help all the other communities such as Muslims, Christians, etc. which according to them, were not covered under Depressed Classes with special benefits, like separate electorates in the aftermath of independent India.

Religious and legal sanctions against discrimination made the scheduled tribe accessible for political and constitutional rights through positive discrimination.

With the numerical majority the political democratic structure created potential vote banks among the scheduled castes. The Reservation of electoral candidates for parliament and Assembly was the last straw with which all leading political parties dilly dalied for creating fusion and fission among the scheduled caste members. Parallel and vertical caste organizations marked cleavage of social and economic and political between them to usurp power.

The legal and democratic rights, with numerical strength made the homogeneous groups make use of the existing situations. The access to power through political emancipation was easy and principle of hierarchy has been rejected and egalitarian and competitive ideologies prevail and caste consciousness among the Harijans has been consolidated all the more.

But developmental awareness of the Dalits depends much on the personality of their leader.

Movements of Tribal People

Alienation from Land : The history of land alienation among the tribes began during British colonialism in India when the British interfered in the tribal region only for the purpose of exploiting the tribal natural resources. Coupled with this, in many places, tribal lands have been occupied by moneylenders, zamindars and traders by advancing them loans etc. Opening of mines in the heart of tribal habitat and even a few factories provided wage labour as well as opportunities for factory employment. But establishment of factories and mines did not always bring increased, more secure and paying employment; on the other hand, destitution and displacement. On the legal fiction that the land not settled belonged to the Government, and shifting cultivation land was traditionally occupied and owned by villagers or clans without specific recognition by the Government-mines could be opened on 'Government' land without compensation and rehabilitation, and even without warning.

The fate of those who lost settled lands to factories is not less worse but only differently affected. In Rourkela area, 1231 families were dispossessed of their house-site and agricultural land.

The tribes were promised employment in factories which never happened in reality and the tribes because of their acculturation were inclined to participate in various opportunities and avenues opened for them. But training was denied to them. Funds which was to be invested for tribal development were grabbed by authorities and it was never utilised for their welfare, the Madras Agency Tracts Interest and Land Transfer Act, 1919 was meant to protect the aboriginal's land from alienation to non-tribal. But despite these laws, the tribals were made deprived of their land. Thus the national policy was implemented in order to look into the problem of tribal land alienation.

In the beginning it was believed that the forests were under the administrative control of the "Rajas' or estates under whose jurisdiction the area came. For all practical purposes, the tribal population inhabiting the jungle area were free to make independent use of the forest resources. After the British came to power, the Forest Policy of the British Government was more inclined towards commercial considerations rather than human. Some forests were declared as reserved ones, where only authorised contractors were allowed to cut the timber, and the forest-dwellers were kept isolated deliberately within their habitat without any effort to ameliorate their economic and educational standards. The expansion of railway in India and in England heavily devastated the forest resources in India. The Government started reserving teak, sal and deodar forests for the manufacture of railway sleepers. The Indian Forest Act of 1855 was enacted, asserted state monopoly right over the forests. The forest dwellers were however free to use the forest produce, subject to an annual payment of fixed rent The post-independence forest policy in India essentially derives its root from the policies of 1865 and 1878. No doubt, it was amended several times till the National Forest Policy of 1952.

The Committee on Forests and Tribals in India, with Prof. B.K. Roy Burman as its chairman, observed that the individual tribal, the local tribal community and the national interest should be regarded as the three corners of a triangular forest policy" and hence, there should be ample provisions in the National Forest Policy to implement comprehensive plans for an integrated development of the tribals and the forest on equal footing, so that commercial and humanitarian aspects of the policy go side by side.

Forest land and its resources provide the best means of livelihood for the tribal people and many tribes including the women engage in agriculture, food gathering and hunting, they are heavily dependent on the products of the forest. Therefore when outsiders exploit the tribal's land and its resources, the natural life cycle of tribal ecology and the tribal life is greatly disturbed.

Poverty and Indebtedness

Majority tribes live under poverty line. The tribes follow many simple occupations based on simple technology. Most of their occupation falls into the primary occupations such as hunting, gathering, agriculture. The technology they use for these purposes belong to the most primitive kind. There is no profit and surplus making in such economy. Hence their per capita income is very meager, much lesser than the Indian average. Most of them live under abject poverty and are in debt in the hands of local money lenders and Zamindars. In order to repay the debt, they often mortgage or sell their land to the money lenders. Indebtedness is almost inevitable since heavy interest is to be paid to these money lenders.

The demands of the supernatural, sometimes too insistent to be neglected, especially in times of family crisis, and those of the creditors quite out of proportion to the principal advanced and the demands of the petty officials, not to speak of those of the close relatives, do not leave much for the household after what was saved from the wild animals, rats and weeds. Even then festivals and occasional celebrations in honour of guests eat heavily into their lean resources. The local creditors have no hesitation in advancing loans, for not only heavy compound interest, but also pre-emptive rights to purchase the standing crops at rock-bottom prices as their privilege. However pressing the claims of others may be, the creditor knows that the Adivasi will honour his word. And the Adivasi knowing no arithmetic always leaves a comfortable arrear in favour of the creditor. Thus the vicious circle becomes inescapable. One way to break this vicious circle was to go for alternate employment, another to sell land and repay the outstanding debt as the creditors demanded, and the third way led to virtual serfdom known as debt bondage or bonded labour. This is a system of labour whereby "a person on receiving some advance in money or kind engages himself to be a labourer of his creditor for agricultural and domestic purposes as long as the loan together with the interest remains unpaid". In 1962, a study by the Assistant Commissioner for Scheduled Tribes and Castes, showed that in Koraput district of Orissa, a few persons with, more than 15 acres of agricultural land had become bonded labourers with a maximum advance of Rs. 2000 taken. Bonded labour had become almost a way of life, so much that even tribal money lenders engaged bonded labourers from among their fellow-tribals. In a study it was found out that most frequent and important factor in becoming a bonded labourer was the repayment of parental debts. At the time of meeting demands of life crisis and of various life cycle related ceremonies such as death, birth, initiation ceremony, meeting food scarcity, crop failures, payment of loans from another creditor, purchasing land and catties etc, are accountable for the tribal people's indebtedness to local money lenders. When they fail to pay them back, their land is handed over to those money lenders and in turn they become the bonded labourers of these local exploiters. Thus a tribe is born indebted and dies indebted. It is the most unfortunate and sad scene.

The indebtedness of tribals multiplied at an exorbitant rate through the cunning ways of the Sahukars, often resulting in the transfer of tribal lands to the moneylenders. Indebtedness eroded the economic base of the tribal family, even as the very reason for indebtedness was the erosion of land settlement pattern. The shifting cultivation assured to the tribals was snatched away, and thus they were bound to lose their land and access to land. Consequent erosion of their earning power led them to seek loans from the money lending communities. Illiterate tribals were exploited. A study points out that 61 per cent of the households in tribal areas arc debtors and the incidence of debt is very high in the case of landless households. From the total loans only one-fourth of the amount is advanced by the officials and governmental agencies. The study also points out that 67 per cent of loans arc used for consumption purposes. The tribals find it difficult to get out of the debt traps. Their wages arc so low that they cannot clear off their debts. The studies on the Minimum Wage Policy also suggest that while laws exist in the statue books, they are not even enforced. The low wages account for their poor standards of living, they cannot afford even their minimum needs like food, health and education.

Health and Nutrition Problems

The normal health of the tribal people cannot be said to be very bad but they become chronic after repeated infections. They suffer from many diseases but water borne diseases happen to be the worst threatening one due to poor drinking water supply. Water is available for the tribes in plenty but is highly dirty and contaminated one. Consequent upon these, they get infection from various water borne diseases such as diarrhoea, dysentery, cholera, tapeworms etc.

Tribal people suffer from other diseases due to deficiency in minerals and other good nutrients. These problems differ from region to region, for example (he tribes in the Himalayan region, suffer from goitre due to lack of iodine. Some of the common diseases among the tribes are tuberculosis. Yaws is a common disease among the Andhra Pradesh tribes. Leprosy is also a common problem among the tribes in India.

Study, on fertility and mortality trends among the tribal

population of India have been found to be fragmentary and isolated. Limited studies are available on infant mortality and hardly any study is available on maternal mortality among the tribal population. Basu and Jindal (1990) studied in depth a primitive tribal group, that is, Kutiya Kondhs of Tumdibandha Block of Phulbani district, Orissa. The average age of menarche among Kutiya was found to be 14.5 years. It was observed that the average number of pregnancies per month was 5.09 and 3.89 respectively among completed and incomplete mothers of reproductive life cycles.

Infants mortality was found to be very high, that is, 179.75/1000. The fertility record of Kutiya Kondh mothers in various age groups indicate a total fertility of 5 estimated on an average in the age group of 45-49.

Basu and Kshatriya (1992) studied the fertility and mortality trend among the Dudh Kharia of Sundergarh district, Orissa. They reported that the estimated total fertility, crude birth rate, crude death rate and infant mortality rate are 5.39, 38.5, 11.80 and 102.4 respectively. All these demographic parameters show higher value than the Indian national population level according to 1981 census but these are similar with other Indian tribal populations.

The health and nutrition problems of the vast tribal population of India are as varied as the tribal groups themselves who present a bewildering diversity and variety in their socio-economic, socio-cultural and ecological settings. The nutritional problems of different tribal communities located at various stages of development are full of obscurities and very little scientific information on dietary habits and nutrition status are available due to lack of systematic and comprehensive research investigations. Malnutrition is common and has greatly affected the general physique of the tribals. Malnutrition lowers the ability to resist infection, leads to chronic illness and in the post-wearing period leads to permanent brain impairment. Maternal malnutrition which is quite common among the tribal women is also a serious health problem.

The nutritional status of pregnant women, directly influence their reproductive performance and the birth weight of their children, a factor that is crucial to an infant's chances of survival and to its subsequent growth and development. Nutrition also affects lactation and breast feeding which are key elements in the health of infants and young children and a contributory factor in birth spacing.

Tribal diet are generally grossly deficient in calcium, vitamin A, vitamin C riboflavin and animal protein. Diets of South Indian tribes, in general and of Kerala in particular are grossly deficient even in respect of calories and total protein. A high incidence of malnutrition was observed in some primitive tribal groups in Phulbani, Koraput and Sundergarh districts of Orissa and also among Bhil, Garasin of Rajasthan, Radar, Rabri and Charan of Gujarat and Benda of Orissa. Studies of tribal communities in Orissa conducted by Ali (1982) have found that an ecological imbalance caused by rapid deforestation has resulted not only in-depleting food resources, but in prolonged droughts, adding to hunger and starvation of the tribes.

Sexually transmitted diseases are also popular diseases in tribal areas. VDRL is a very sensitive test to diagnose if a person was suffering from syphilis or not. VDRL was found to be positive in 17.12 per cent cases (reactive in dilution of 1:8 or more) of polyandrous Jaunsaris of Chakrata, Dehradun. Out of 17 per cent, 9.92 per cent was found among males and 7.19 per cent among females. Among the Santhals of Mayurbhanj district, Orissa, 8.90 per cent cases (reactive in dilution of 1:8 or more) of VDRL were observed, of which 4.99 per cent were females and 3.91 per cent were males (Basu et al, 1993). The prevalence of STD was also reported to be high in the polyandrous Toda tribal group of Nilgiri hills. While conducting morbidity studies among the Kondha tribe of Phultani district, Orissa, Swain et al,(1990) found syphilis (10 per cent) in Desia Kondhs (reactive in dilution 1:8 or more) whereas it was not diagnosed among primitive Kutia Kondh tribal groups. The presence of STD is also reported among Andamanese, tribal groups of Madhya Pradesh, Rajasthan, Mysore, Lacadive and Minicoy islands.

Because of the extensive felling of trees by vested interest, the distances between the villages and the forest areas have increased, forcing the tribal women to walk longer distances in search of minor forest produce and firewood. In this rapidly changing milieu, tribal are confronted with an extraordinary workload. Given this additional workload, even women in advanced stages of pregnancy are required to work in the agricultural field or walk long distances to collect fuel and minor forest provides. The overstrain on tribal women however is not adequately compensated due to the non-availability of minor forest produce and decrease in foodgrain production.

To malnutrition and additional workload, one has to add the destruction of traditional herbs through deforestation and the lack of access of the tribals to modern medicine with the increasing ecological imbalance, results in diseases such as TB, stomach disorders and often malaria.

Child-bearing and Maternal Mortality : Child bearing imposes additional health problems on women-physically, psychologically and socially. The complication of health and of childbirth and of illegally induced abortions in areas where environmental and health conditions are adverse, result in large numbers of female deaths. Poor nutritional status and its concomitant problems of poor body weight, and height, poor weight pregnancy, low hemoglobin levels, is one of the primary underlying causes of maternal poverty in India.

Maternal and child health care practices have been found to be largely neglected in various tribal areas. From the inception of pregnancy to its termination, no specific nutritional diet is consumed by women. On the other hand, some pregnant tribal women reduced their food intake because of simple fear of recurrent vomiting and with the belief that the baby may remain small and the delivery may be easier. The consumption of calcium and vitamins during pregnancy is poor. "The habit of taking alcohol during pregnancy has been found to be usual in tribal women and almost all of them continue regular activities including hard labour during advanced pregnancy. More than 90 per cent of deliveries are conducted at home attended by elderly ladies of the household. No precautions are observed at the time of conducting deliveries which resulted in an increased susceptibility to various infections. Further they are alien to outside nurses and doctors and they have their own way of diagnosis and cure.

From all the aforementioned discussion on health and nutrition and often such related issues the speedy spread of health education among the tribals is very crucial.

Most tribes are illiterate. Therefore, audio-visual methods may be adopted to put across to them the basic principles of health and sanitation. For raising the standard of health and nutritional facilities of the tribals, cooperative endeavour is necessary among the states, the centre, the medical personnels and non-governmental organisations with community participation.

Education in Tribes

Educationally the tribal people are at different levels of development but, overall, the formal education has made very little impact on tribal groups.

Before the year 1950, the Indian government had no direct programme for direct tribal education. With the adoption of the constitution and through the provision of reservation policy the government has become responsible for tribal education. The census figures of 1931 disclosed that only 0.7 per cent of the tribal population were literate, it rose to 32.60 per cent in 1991 against 52.5 per cent for the entire country so the total picture of tribal education is not very encouraging. Since education is probably the most effective instrument for ensuring equality of opportunity the tribes lag far behind others due to lack of education.

The reasons for this state of affairs are :

Social Cause : Formal education has not been necessary for the members of tribal society to discharge their social obligations. Hence they should be prepared to accept education. Superstitions and myths play an important role in rejecting education among the tribes for example some tribal groups believe that their gods shall be angry if they send their children to schools run by outsiders.

Economic Cause : Most tribes live in abject poverty, it also accounts for their lack of interest in education that it is not easy for them to send their children to schools. According to the present education system any economic benefit a tribal child can bring to his family is after 10 years of schooling, the parents have neither the patience nor the foresight to wait for such a long period.

Low Education : The tribal children cannot follow the same syllabus and curriculum taught at other institutions. They have no taste for this kind of education since their socialisation and exposure has been done in different environment. Instead of teaching them about formal syllabus they should be taught about their local cultures, folklore, music, art and the environment they are dwelling in.

Lack of suitable teacher is one reason why many tribal children fail to go to schools. Most teachers approach tribal people with a sense of superiority and treat them as sevage and uncivilized and hence fail to establish proper rapport with the tribal students, so there is a gulf between tribal students and teachers.

Lack of facilities, infrastructure, lack of staff, ecological condition, technical facilities could be other factors accountable for low rate of tribal education.

Tribal Identity Issue

A tribe is an endogamous group having a common territory, possessing a common dialect with distinct political, economic and religious organisation occupying particular geographical distribution. However such characterisation of tribes is an oversimplified view specially so in the context of various tribals assimilation and acculrisation.

A number of tribal groups are recognised by the government and they are the scheduled tribes. There are instances where some tribal communities wanted to identify themselves with the dominant group, the Hindus, in a particular period and at a different period, wanted to assert their tribal identity.

Approaches to tribal related issues have not been a uniform one. The British adopted the assimilation and segregation method simultaneously. These approaches were followed in the early period of post-independence period.

India has 427 "Scheduled" Tribes, each unique in its own right. Constituting about 7 per cent of the country's population, they ostensibly are a major segment of the Indian social tabric. The district self-conceptualisation of tribals in the context of natural, social and historical process is referred to as tribal consciousness', mutual knowledge in distinguishing groups, self from the other. A tribe is regarded as self-sufficient, unstratified, and culturally homogenous, in a universal perspective. When taking into account the dynamics of persistence and change in tribal identities, one notices a significant shift from the earlier view of tribe as a simplistic social formation in the evolutionary scheme to the new approach of teaching tribe as a district to social formation with elements of perpetuity in diverse technological contexts.

The political commitment to uplift the tribals through the positive discrimination policy of the government has geared the tribes to assert their identity.

Voget has also noted a situation, reformative naturalism, which he has defined as a relatively conscious attempt on the part of a subordinate group to attain a personal and social integration through selective rejection, modification and synthesis of both traditional and alien cultural components.

Various boundary maintaining mechanisms by smaller community has also been noted elsewhere when there is a change of absorption of a minor group within a major or dominant cultural milieu. This process is obviously aimed at maintaining self-identity or group solidarity which usually takes place at a much later stage after the initial contact or exposure with the dominant culture.

Different tribal movements can be said to centre around the problem of their identity whether tribal community wanted to identify itself with the dominant wider Hindu social system or wanted to maintain group solidarity and identity by preserving its traditional culture. In the latter process there may even by a conscious symbolic revival of typical traditional tribal culture, demand for a separate state, etc. Rise of tribal consciousness, tribal regionalism, frontier tribalism, etc. gained currency after the movements in North East Frontier areas. Tribal regionalism, political in nature, has been said to be a struggle for identity against alienation from basic sources, viz., land, forests, and aspiration for preservation of traditional culture. Of late, the movement in Tripura led by TUJS and Bodoland in Assam, Jharkhand, Gorkhaland movements have transcended that stage of aspiration limited in culture. The newly emerged elites in these regions prefer to have a share in the power structure.

The regional leaders who improvise or manipulate identity symbols to mobilise group sentiment, could rarely assess the likely responses of the political authorities and the dominant social groups. As the movement proceeds and identity assertions tend to transform the concerned ethic to a political conflict group, the leadership and the group have to adopt modern skills and mobilise resources. In the process, they become participants in modernization and get involved in the democratic power game. In both Gorkhaland and Jharkhand, such democratization has been evident. The Gorkhaland agitation gained momentum on issues such as Indo-Nepal treaty, inclusion of Nepalese language in the eighth schedule of Indian Constitution and other sundry economic factors. The main thrust was on assertion of Indian Nepalese identity through citizenship demand. In the Gorkhaland Accord (1988) enacting the establishment of Gorkha Hill Development Council, both the main issues remained untouched. The identity problem was said to have been solved by putting the word "Gorkha' in the Council. According to Bajni Kothan, ethnicity is a response to the excesses of the modern western project of shaping the whole of humanity around three pivots of world capitalism the state system, world culture based on modern technology, world information order and universalising education system. The non-party political movement at the grass root levels, and awakening of the ordinary people would form the new process, the establishment of 'human governance'. Together with social movements and citizens' action ethnicity provides security and democracy able to translate into real security and democracy for all, including the most marginalised, even though these could be a far dream for all the tribal population in this country.

Gender Justice Struggle

Towards the beginning of 1930's a shift took place in the nature of demands being made by the leaders of the women's movement. The leaders now clearly articulated their claims; for gender equality instead of just pleas for women's upliftment. However the principle of gender equality did not fit very well with the reformist perspective of the rationalist elite. There was a contradiction between the equal rights perspective of woman leaders and the paternal attitude of national leaders and this contradiction was bound to influence the political processes.

With the achievement of independence in 1947, the women leaders were confronted with the opportunity to safeguard the rights and position of women in the new political system. Addressing the issues of inequality in the personal laws meant addressing the issue of male domination in their family. Asking for equal rights within these structures thus meant to threat to 'stable' family.

Safeguards for Women

The constitution of India accepted the principle of equality and hence at first sight, the constitution of India seems to negate discriminations based on sex. However a careful scrutiny of its provisions reveals its endorsement of subordinate and dependent position of women. The retention of personal laws based on the principles of gender inequality and subordination of women and the decision to postpone the enactment of a civil code based on equal rights for men and women, also negated the principles of justice and equality enshrined in the Preamble and Article 14-15 of the Constitution. The right to Freedom of Religion embodied in article 25 to 28 as interpreted and legislated in the form of Personal laws deny equality to women in personal, economic, sexual, social educational and cultural level. Similarly the work women do all day and night for the family is not recognised as economic exploitation.

Struggle : Women did not gain complete legal equality mainly due to resistance encountered from two quarters. One was the resistance that came from Hindu Orthodox opinion which was completely unwilling to grant equal rights to women in family & marriage. Another justification was on the basis of not offending the religious communities. The pre-occupation of political leaders to achieve the goals of national unity and national consensus led them to postpone any decision which was likely to jeopardize these goals. In the process, the political leadership continued to succumb to the pressures of religious and patriarchal forces.

Movements of Women

The mid 1970's witnessed the emergence of a number of women's organisations forming loosely a women's movement. The gender specific research with the help of facts and figures brought to light the structural constraint that women experienced. These works documented the amount of domestic work that women performed and questioned previously held distinction between "productive" and "unproductive" work, thereby raising the issue of women's unpaid labour at home. Thus women's work was made visible and socially and economically valuable leading to a new conceptualisation of women's problems.

Two of the most important rights gained by women as a result of Hindu Law Reform were :

(a) To hold property as absolute owners

(b) Recognise daughters as heirs of father's property at par with sons.

The struggle for gender justice however shall continue until a uniform civil code is formulated. Till this is done women shall continue to suffer due to the unequal provisions in their religion which still governs the Indian legal system.

10

Social Relevance

(Socio-Economic Dimensions of the Nationalist Movement, the communal Question and the Demand for Partition, Backward Caste Movement, Trade Union and Peasant Movements, Civil Rights Movements)

Rise of Communalism

The communal issue was far from being a new element in Indian politics in 1945. Some authorities have looked on the failure of Congress to form coalition ministries in 1937 as the turning point in the relations between the two communities. Others go back to 1928, when the All Parties' Conference rejected separate electorates. Some see Jinnah's departure from the Congress in 1921 as the point of no return; others go back to the birth of the Muslim League in 1906. But whatever date is accepted as marking the political breakwater, it is certain that the communal problem goes back much further, to a time when there was no political life as such in India.

Throughout the six centuries between the establishment of the Delhi Sultanate in 1192 and the British occupation of Delhi in 1803, the Muslims had been the political and cultural leaders of the country. During this long period, the relations between the ruling minority and the Hindu population were generally amicable. This was due as much to mutual influence and harmony as to what might be called a policy of peaceful co-existence. Occasionally a fanatical ruler like Aurangzeb upset the prevailing stability; but Muslim emperors who employed Hindus in high positions were perhaps more the rule than the exception.

However, with the establishment of British rule, the cancer of communalism developed. To a large extent, the roots of communalism lay in British policies. But there were other factors too, the most unfortunate of which was the unwitting contribution of the growth of nationalism itself.

Causes of Growth : Communalism was mainly the result of the peculiar development of the Indian social economy under the British rule, the uneven economic and cultural development of different communities, and the action of the strategy both of the British government and the vested interests within those communities.

1. *Socio-economic Factors :* The political awakening of the Muslim masses was canalized into the incorrect communal channel due to a number of reasons. The professional classes and the bourgeoisie developed within the Muslim community later than in the Hindu community. The former found the latter already firmly established in government services, as also in key positions in trade, industry, and finance. They needed the support of the masses of their community in their struggle with the Hindu rivals for jobs and industrial and trade interests. They misdescribed this struggle between the sections of the same classes as communal, as those between the Hindu community and the Muslim community. They began to gather the support of the politically awakened Muslim masses among whom national consciousness increasingly developed as a

result of the growing nationalist movement in the country, as also due to their poverty under the existing system. The upper elements of the Muslim community, composed of the landlords and sections of the bourgeoisie and the professional classes, tried to give this growing national and class awakening of the Muslim masses a deformed communal form. This was done with a view to securing their support to serve their sectional interests as also to prevent a united mass movement of the poor strata of all communities against the vested interests.

The economic backwardness of the country also contributed to the rise of communalism. Due to the lack of modern industrial development, unemployment was an acute problem in India, especially for the educated. Many thought of such shortsighted and short-term remedies as communal and religious and later caste and provincial reservations in an attempt to get a larger share of the existing limited employment opportunities. In this situation, Hindu and Muslim communal leaders, caste leaders and the officials following the policy of 'divide and rule' were able to achieve some success.

Modern political consciousness was late in developing among the Muslims. As nationalism spread among the Hindus and Parsees of the lower middle class, it failed to grow equally rapidly among the Muslims of the same class. During the first half of the nineteenth century, Hindus became the first community in India to accept Western learning, and consequently were the first to advance in the employment of the Company. During this period India's Muslims, who not long before had been masters of the subcontinent, suffered an eclipse. Denied British patronage, and relatively uninterested in British education, they slipped ever deeper into political and economic stagnation.

2. *Divide and Rule Policy* : The Wahabi Movement, and the Great Revolt of 1875 - which the British blamed

> principally on the Muslims-confirmed the foreigners in their pro-Hindu tendency. The post-Mutiny period was politically and culturally perhaps the darkest period in the history of the Indian Muslims. The British government did not trust the Indian Muslims and adopted a policy of disfavouring them. The strategy of political counterpoise which Britain employed throughout the period of her rule in India was to maintain her paramountcy. Lord Elphinstone, soon after the suppression of the rising, remarked, "Divide at impera (divide and rule) was the old Roman motto, and it should be ours."

The Muslims were mostly kept out of the ranks of the army. This had a serious effect on the economic position of the upper class muslims who had hitherto mainly taken to the military profession. The British government introduced English education in India for administrative and other purposes which reduced the importance of the Arabic and the Persian, leading to impoverishment among the Muslim intelligentsia. Their deep resentment against the new policy of the British government made them stay aloof from the new education while the Hindus were joining the new educational institutions and evolving a new English knowing intelligentsia. This resulted not only in the cultural backwardness of the Muslims but also in their exclusion from the administrative posts, the legal, the medical, and other professions. With the assimilation of the new education, the new Hindu educated class imbibed western ideas of democracy and freedom and became the pioneers and leaders of the Indian nationalist movement.

However, in the 1870's there was a perceptible shift in British policy. With the rise of the nationalist movement, the British statesmen grew apprehensive about the safety and stability of their Empire in India. To check the growth of a united national feeling in the country, they decided to follow more actively, the policy of 'Divide the Rule' and to divide the people along religious lines and to encourage communal and separatist tendencies in Indian politics. For this purpose, they decided to come out as 'champions' of the Muslims and to win over to their side Muslim zamindars, landlords, and the newly educated.

One of the first steps the British took to rally the Muslims was to patronize the Muhammadan Anglo-Oriental College of Sayyid Ahmed Khan. This institution provided the impulse for the Aligarh Movements, which not only fostered a muslim cultural renaissance, but also encouraged the sense of muslim separatism.

At every stage of the history of British rule in India, examples of the strategy of 'divide and rule' may be found. The British government introduced the communal principle in the constitutional machinery of the Indian state. After the Mutiny, the princes and the zamindars had served as a counterpoise. Minto found in the rising muslim professional classes a counterpoise against the militant nationalists composed mainly of the Hindu professional classes and the middle classes of the Indian National Congress. In the twentieth century alone there were the Partition of Bengal, the engineering of the Muslim deputation, the wrecking of the Unity Conference of 1932, and many other acts reflecting what a retiring British Secretary of State called a predominant bias in British officialism in India in favour of the Muslim community, partly on the ground of closer sympathy, but more largely as a makeweight against Hindu nationalism.

3. *Sayyid Ahmed Khan towards Communalism* : Sir Sayyid Ahmed Khan was the first Muslim leader to organize a movement for uniting the Muslims and instilling into them a desire for the western education and culture. He worked for the establishment of good relations between the British government and the Indian Muslims.

With the financial aid of the muslims middle classes and the support of the government, he founded the Muhammadan

Anglo-Oriental College at Aligarh, which was subsequently transformed into a University. The Muslim middle classes enthusiastically responded to the Aligarh Movement.

In his early life, Sayyid Ahmed Khan took a broad minded view of communal relations. Unconsciously echoing Emperor Akbar, he said that Hindus and Muslims were the two eyes of India. Injure the one and you injure the other'. But in his concern for the betterment of his community, Sir Sayyid was easily persuaded that democratic institutions would result in the permanent subservience of the minority community. Therefore he discouraged muslims from joining the Indian National Congress, and looked on the British administration as the protector of muslim interests.

The British did nothing to discourage this view. Mr. Beck, Principal of the Muhammadan Anglo-Oriental College, aroused muslim fears by writing in 1893 that the objective of the Congress is to transfer the political control of the country from the British to the Hindus'. In 1889 Beck organized muslim opposition to a parliamentary bill that would have introduced representative institutions in India. His successor, Mr Archbold, was behind the muslim deputation of the 1906 that resulted in the inclusion of separate electorates in the Councils Act of 1909.

4. *Misuse of Indian History Writing* : British writers of Indian history served the imperial cause by initiating, developing and emphasising the Hindu-Muslim approach in their study of Indian history and development of Indian culture. For example, the ancient period of Indian history was described as Hindu period and the medieval period labelled as Muslim period of Indian history, implying that religion was the guiding force behind politics during the whole of the medieval period. In fact the muslim masses were as poor, if not more, as the Hindu masses and were thoroughly oppressed and exploited by the Muslim rulers and

their Hindu collaborators. The base of rule was political and economic then as it has always been. The communal approach to Indian history fostered divisive communal tendencies in Indian politics in the last quarter of the 19th century and first half of the 20th century.

5. *Negative Aspects of Socio-religious Reform Movements* : The religious reform and revivalist movements of the 19th century contained some paradoxical aspects. These movements were launched to purge Hinduism and Islam of irrational and obscurantist tendencies. The Wahabi crusade against all non-Muslims and its aim of establishing Dar-ul Islam (the world of Islam) was as odious to Hindus as Dayananda's slogan or Aryanisation of Indra and his Shuddhi (Conversion of non-Hindus to Hinduism) were unpalatable to Muslims.
6. *Parallel Nationalism* : The militant nationalists of the early 20th century in their search of 'national heroes' referred to Maharana Pratap, Shivaji and Guru Gobind Singh as national heroes and implied that the Muslim rulers like Akbar, Shahjahan and Aurangzeb were 'foreigners'. Tilak, Lajpat Rai, Aurobindo and later Gandhi were strong believers in Hindu-Muslim unity, but in their writings and speeches they often employed a language, imagery and symbolism, perhaps unintentionally, derived exclusively from Hindu sources (e.g. the slogan of Ram Rajya popularised by Gandhi had a religious tinge and created a reaction in the Muslim mind). The Ganapati festival and Shivaji festival started by Tilak also added to the fears of Hindu domination through nationalism in Muslim minds.

In the Khilafat issue, Muslims fought imperialism on the ground that it threatened the Caliph and the holy places. While this approach admittedly made its adherents and supporters anti-imperialist and encouraged the nationalist trend among urban Muslims, in the long run it too proved harmful as it encouraged the habit of looking at political questions from a religious view-point.

The Lucknow Pact marked an important step forward in Hindu-Muslim unity. Unfortunately, it was based on the notion of bringing together the educated Hindus and Muslims as separate entities; in other words without secularisation of their political outlook which would make them realise that in policies they had no separate interests as Hindus or Muslims. The Lucknow Pact, therefore, left the way open to the future resurgence of communalism in Indian politics.

7. *Role of Hindu Mahesabha :* British imperial policies in India provided a congenial climate for the emergence, growth and popularity of communal organisations. A communal organisation, though primarily community, also indirectly promoted British imperial interests apart from serving the personal ambition of an opportunistic leadership. The Hindu Mahasabha never gained that popularity with the Hindu masses as the Muslim League with the Muslims in India. All the same, against the Muslim League's demand for Pakistan, it raised the slogan of Akhand Hindustan. The Hindu Mahasbha's propaganda of a Hindu race, Hindu culture, Hindu civilisation and Hindu Rashtra in India hardened the Muslim League's attitude and made it more suspicious and more determined to demand Pakistan.

Crystallization of Communal Politics : The absence of a central political organisation to safeguard the Muslim interests against the preponderance of the Congress was keenly felt by the Muslim leaders. The Aga Khan, who had been associated with the Congress Moderates since 1892, shook off their influence when he visited Aligarh in 1906. He led a Muslim delegation to the Viceroy in Simla, in August 1906 and asked the members of the delegation to form a permanent committee. Nawab Salimullah of Dacca took the initiative and proposed a scheme of a central Mohammedan Association to look after the interests of the Muslims. Immediately after the conclusion of the session of the Mohammedan Educational Conference, the scheme was accepted on 30th December, 1906 and a political association-All India Muslim League-was established. A committee with Nawab Mohsinul-Mulk and Nawab Waqar-ul-Mulk as joint secretaries was appointed to frame a draft constitution of the League. The Committee framed the rules and regulations which were accepted at a meeting held at Karachi on 29th December, 1907.

The League had the following objectives: (1) to promote amongst the Muslims of India loyalty towards the British Government (2) to protect and advance the political and other rights of the Muslims of India and to represent their needs, aspiration to the Government, and (3) to prevent the rise among the Muslims of India any feeling of hostility towards other communities without prejudice to the other objects of the League. Zaka Ullah, the Secretary of the League, frankly confessed that the aims and objects of the two organisations-the Muslim League and the Indian National Congress-were irreconciliable. With the foundation of the Muslim League, the cleavage between the Hindus and the Muslims deepened.

The Muslim League supported the partition of Bengal and demanded special safeguards for the Muslims in government services. Later, with the help of Lord Minto, the Viceroy, it put forward and secured the acceptance of the demand for separate electorates.

Demand of Separate Electorates : When in 1906, Morley announced in the House of Commons that the Viceroy, Lord Minto, was about to appoint a small committee to consider the question of extending the representative element in the Legislative Council, the Muslims took the opportunity of negotiating, in advance, with the Government. A Muslim deputation pleaded that the Muslims were a distinct community who did not like the idea of placing their interests at the mercy of an unsympathetic majority of Hindus. They enunciated two clear points of policy. First, in all elections, whether for the legislative councils or for local bodies, the Muslims must be separately represented and their representatives separately elected by purely Muslim electors. Secondly, their representation must not only be commensurate with their numerical strength, but also with their political importance and the value of the contribution which they made to the defence of the Empire.

The Government of India took two full years to evolve its scheme of representation embodying the principle of separate electorate for the Muslims. The Secretary of State, Lord Morley did not approve the plan of separate electorate. But the Muslim League and their leaders in England tried to persuade Morley to accept the principle of communal representation. The Government of India supported the Muslim demands and the reluctant Secretary of State ultimately gave in.

The Act of 1909 embodied in substance the concessions virtually promised by Minto to the Muslims. Thus, the Government recognised the theory of two nations of two religions which was preached by Sayyid Ahmed. It constituted the chief problem of Indian Politics the problem which ultimately led to the creation of Pakistan.

Communalism Reaches Point of No Return. The collapse of the Non-Cooperation Movement in the mid-twenties marked the end of joint political action by Hindus and Muslims. The Muslim League, which had been over-shadowed by the Khilafat Committee, again became prominent. Its leader Mohammed Ali Jinnah, promoted Muslim interests at the negotiations in India and England that followed the coming of the Simon Commission in 1927. He became increasingly embittered at what he considered Hindu obstinacy, and eventually this man, who once called himself an Indian first and a Muslim second, became a fervent opponent of the Congress.

Idea of Pakistan : While politicians were arguing over the details of the safeguards to be written into India's future constitution, Muslims outside the political arena began to formulate more ambitious demands. In 1930, the great poet-Sir Muhammad Iqbal, addressing the Allahabad session of Muslim League, declared that 'the formation of a consolidated North-West Indian Muslim State appears to me to be the final destiny of Muslims in that region'. Iqbal did not specify that this state would be independent of India. This element was introduced only later, when his idea was taken up and expanded by some young Muslims studying in England, Chaudhury Rahmat Ali, the leader of these students, proposed in pamphlets of 1933 and 1935 the creation of a separate Muslim nation in north-west India. It would be called 'Pakistan', from the first letters of Punjab, Afghan Province (NWEP), Kashmir and Sind, and the last three letters of Baluchistan. When Rahmat Ali's idea was presented to Muslim delegates of the Joint Select Committee, they condemned it as an impractical 'student's scheme'. But as relations between Hindus and Muslims degenerated, the idea caught on.

After the League's defeat in the 1937 elections, Jinnah turned to the muslim masses. They were not, he claimed, a minority community in India: they were really an entirely separate nation. As for the Congress governments, they were nothing but Hindu governments out to oppress members of the Muslim nation. Such were Jinnah's contentions.

The Muslim League hoped to form coalition ministries with the Congress in some provinces. The Congress, consistent with its principles and policies and being proud of its non-communal outlook and policies of liberation of the country and amelioration of the condition of the masses advised Muslim League members to sign the Congress pledge and become its members, they desired to accept responsibilities of office. Jinnah interpreted these moves of the Congress as a calculated policy against the Muslim League and concluded that the Muslims could expect neither justice nor fairplay from the Congress ministries. The Muslim League observed a 'Day of Deliverance' and thanksgiving when the Congress ministries resigned in October 1939 over the war issue.

Resolution for Pakistan : The stage now was set for the fatal demand. It came on 24th March 1940, at the Muslim League's annual session at Lahore. A resolution was passed calling for the grouping of 'geographically contiguous units' in areas where Muslims predominated, such as north-western and eastern India, which would form 'Independent States in which the constituent units shall be autonomous and sovereign'. The language was vague, and deliberate so. The Lahore resolution asked for 'adequate, effective and mandatory safeguards' for Muslims in areas of the country where they were in a minority.

After this, Pakistan became the cornerstone of the League and the demand was deliberately fostered by the British.

At the time of the Lahore resolution, the League was strong precisely in areas where Muslims were in a minority. In provinces where they predominated the North-West Frontier, Punjab, Baluchistan, Sind, Bengal-they had no use for the excessive demands of the League. In these provinces ministries had been elected that were responsive to the needs of the local population-Muslim, Hindu or Sikh. They did not want to have anything to do with Pakistan. The whole idea was 'undesirable even from the Muslim point of view', as Sir Sikandar Hyat Khan, Unionist Premier of the Punjab, said in 1941. Later, however, the League grew in strength in the Muslim majority provinces.

Increasing communal pressure, aggravated by the clamour raised by Hindu communalist groups, drove moderate Muslims into Jinnah's camp. The resignation of the Congress ministries in 1937, the imprisonment of the Congress High Command in 1942, and the hostility of the government after the Quit India Movement, prepared the way for the establishment of League-dominate ministries in Bengal, Assam, Sind and NWFP. The Unionist coalition was weakened by the death of Sir Sikandar in 1942, and Punjab eventually entered the League's sphere of influence. Encouraged by its growing strength, the League adopted a new slogan in 1943: 'Divide and Quit'. It was a sad alteration of Gandhi's intrepid battle-cry of the year before.

Towards Separate Pakistan : The August Offer of 1940 gave the plan of setting up a constitution-making body after the War but assured the minorities that the British Government would not agree to any system of government whose authority was directly denied by large powerful elements in India's national life. The Muslim League welcomed this part of the August Offer.

Cripps proposals contained within themselves provisions which could divide India into hundreds of independent pieces.

After the failure of the Cripps Mission in 1942, Chakravarti Rajagopalachari, the Congress leader of Madras, concluded that the only way to break the communal deadlock was to accept the League's demand for separate state. At this instance, a resolution accepting Pakistan in principle was adopted by the Madras legislature and submitted to the AICC. The resolution was opposed by Congress President Azad, disapproved of by Gandhi, and unpopular with the Congress rank-and-file. In exchange for the League's endorsing 'the Indian demand for independence', and pledging cooperation 'with the Congress into the formation of a provisional interim Government', it in effect accepted the Lahore's Resolution.

Jinnah turned down Rajagopalachari's formula. He would not be content, he said, with the 'maimed, multilated and moth-eaten Pakistan' it offered. He now wanted six full provinces, including even Assam, where Hindus predominated. As for the franchise, Jinnah said that Muslims alone should be entitled to vote for partition. The Hindu population in the disputed areas did not count. After making these proposals, which were intended more to improve his bargaining position than to be taken seriously, Jinnah offered to discuss the matter with Gandhi. Gandhi accepted Jinnah's offer, and the two met in September 1944, but no agreement could be arrived at. Gandhi would not accept the idea that India's Muslims constituted a separate nation. The two leaders parted, saying they would meet again, but they never did.

The Muslim League scuttled an attempt by Sir Tej Bahadur Sapru to set up a Conciliation Committee, and threw a spanner in the works when Bhulabhai Desai and Liaqat Ali Khan tried to work out a settlement.

It now was obvious that if the deadlock was ever to be broken, the initiative would have to come from the British Government. In (June 1945 the Viceroy put forward the Wavell Plan, and summoned the Simla Conference.

The Congress proposed to include two Congress Muslims out of its quota, but Jinnah insisted that all Muslim members of the Council must be nominated by the League. Lord Wavell announced the breakdown of the conference, giving the general impression that Jinnah had been given the veto to obstruct all constitutional advancement in India. From this point onward the communal question dominated the struggle for freedom. Indeed, the attainment of freedom was already certain; the conflict now was between those who struggled to achieve a united and secular Indian state, and those whose rigid sectarianism stood in the way of this accomplishment.

The Simla Conference marked 'a breakwater in Indian political history', wrote Maulana Abul Kalam Azad. It was, he said, 'the first time that negotiations failed, not on the basic political issue between Indian and Britain, but on the communal issue dividing different Indian groups'.

Partition, a Reality : In the elections of 1945, the Muslim League captured an overwhelming majority of Muslim seats in all the provinces except the N.W.F.P The Cabinet Mission rejected the demand for Pakistan and suggested instead a Central Government in charge of Foreign Affairs, Defence and

Communications. It, however, conceded the Muslim League's demand half-way by arranging provinces in three groups, viz., one in the north-west, one in the north-east, and one consisting of the rest of the country.

Direct Action Plan

The Muslim League withdrew its acceptance of the Cabinet Mission plan and observed 16th August, 1946 as 'Direct Action Day'. Direct Action was not directed for wresting Pakistan from the hands of the unwilling British Government but was directed against the Hindus. There were mass killings and rioting.

The new Viceroy, Lord Mountbatten, realised that the Cabinet Mission plan was unworkable and a partition of India was inevitable and sought to effect the transfer of power without any delay. Mountbatten accepted the plan of V.P. Menon, a high official in the Viceroy's Secretariat, which involved the partition of India into two states, the predominantly non-Muslim areas in the Punjab and Bengal being excluded from Pakistan. On 3rd June, 1947, he announced the British Government's acceptance of the principles of partition.

The Muslim League accepted the plan within a week and the Congress within another week.

The June 3rd Plan was given legal effect by the Indian Independence Act, 1947. The Act created two independent Dominions. India had won her freedom, but the price had been partition.

Movements of Backward Castes

A number of circumstances in the 19th and 20th centuries created class consciousness among the lower castes who took upon themselves to struggle for caste equality. The British policy of "Divide and Rule", the growth of Western system of education, the introduction of a common Indian Penal Code (1861) and Code of Criminal Procedure (1872), the extension of the railway network all led to the growth of national consciousness and the modern political thought based on equality. Various lower caste movements were organised in Southern and Western India.

Revolt Against Social Leadership

In South India, the lower caste movements were a direct revolt against the Brahmanical domination in the Madras Presidency. The lower caste leaders propagated that the Dravidians were the original inhabitants of India while the Aryans were the immigrants into India and they had brought the evil institution of the caste system with them.

Justice Party : The first Non-Brahmanical organisation called South Indian Liberal Federation later known as the Justice Party was organised by Shri P. Theagacaya and Dr. T.M. Nair in 1917.

In 1937, Ramaswamy Naicker was elected the President of the Justice Party. He was a crusader for social equality and fought against the evil of untouchability. He denounced Hinduism as an instrument of Brahmanical control, the laws of Manu as inhuman and the Puranas as fairy tales. He condemned religion as superstition and opposed imposition of Hindi on the Dravidians. He tarred caste name boards on hotels, cut off the holy thread of Brahmins, beated the deities with chappals and broke off idols.

DMK: C.N. Annadurai, Ramaswamy Naicker's follower and friend, carried further the Dravidian movement. He came from a weaker community of Kansheepuram. In 1944, the Justice Party was renamed Dravida Kazhagam (Dravidian Federation). In September 1949, the party split and under Anna's leadership Dravida Munnetra Kazhagam (Dravidian Progressive Federation) came into existence.

SNDP: In Kulala, Shri Narayana Guru, the leader of the Ezhava Caste, established the SNDP. Shri Narayana and his associates launched a two point programme for the upliftment of the Ezhavas.

Firstly, to give up the practice of untouchability with respect to caste below their castes. Secondly, he built a number of temples which were open to all castes. He simplified rituals regarding marriage, religious worships and funerals. He achieved considerable success in transforming the untouchable groups into a backward class. He gave a new slogan—"One religion, one caste and one god for mankind."

Satya Sholdhak Samaj : In Western India, Jyotirao Govindrao Phule (1827-90) struggled for the lower castes. He was born at Poona in 1827, in a Mali Caste (gardener). Some incidents of Brahmanical arrogance changed the outlook of Jyotiba. He believed that the Brahmin under the pretext of religion tyrannized other castes and turned them into their slaves.

In 1873, Jyotiba started the Satya Shodhak Samaj (Truth Seeking Society) with the aim of securing social justice for the weaker sections of the society. He opened a number of schools and orphanges for the children and women belonging to all castes.

Dr. Ambedkar's Role : Bhim Rao Ambedkar was born on April 14th, 1891, in a Mahar Caste at Mohar. He started an organisation in Bombay called 'Bahishkrit Hitkarni Sabha', in July 1924, for the moral and material progress of the untouchable. He resorted to methods of agitation and launched Satyagraha to establish civic rights of the untouchables to enter the Hindu temples arid draw water from public wells.

In 1930, Ambedkar entered national politics. He demanded separate electorates for the untouchables. In April 1942, he founded the Scheduled Caste Federation.

Movement of Trade Unions

The Indian Working class suffered from all forms of exploitation—low wages, long working hours, unhygienic conditions in factories, employment of child labour and absence of all amenities—from which the labour force suffered in the early stages of industrialisation and capitalism in England and the West and the evils of imperialism.

The colonial situation gave a destructive touch to Indian Working Class movement. They had to face an imperialist political rule and economic exploitation at the hands of both foreign and native capitalist classes. Under these circumstances, the Indian Working Class Movement became inter-twined with the political struggle for national emancipation.

The first ever demand for regulation of the condition of workers in factories in India came from the Lancashire textile capitalist lobby; apprehending the emergence of a competitive rival in the Indian textile industry under conditions of cheap and unregulated labour, they demanded the appointment of a commission for investigations into factory condition. The first commission was appointed in 1875. But the First Factory Act was passed by 1881. The Act prohibited the employment of children under the age of 7, limited the number of working hours for children below the age of 12 years and provided that dangerous machinery should be fenced. Again in 1891, the Factory Act was passed under extraneous pressure from British textile industry, which limited the working day to 11 hours with an interval of 11/2 hours for women labour, increased the minimum and maximum ages of children from 7 and 12 to 9 and 14 years. In 1900, the Indian Working Class for the first time demonstrated the emergence of political consciousness. The Bombay workers went on a political six-day strike over the conviction and imprisonment of Lokmanya Tilak in 1908. In 1909 and 1911, Factory Acts were passed for the benefit of jute industry workers.

In 1900, the Indian Working class for the first time demonstrated the emergence of political consciousness in them. The Bombay workers went on a political six-day strike over the conviction and imprisonment of Lokmanya Tilak in 1908.

After the First World War, prices soared, industrialists made unprecedented profit but the workers were paid miserably low wages. The average dividend paid by the jute mills during 1915-24 was 14% (42% in 1919) while the average wage of the worker in the industry was only 12 p.a.

Gandhiji mobilised both the workers and the peasants for the national cause. The workers were brought into a national Trade Union and drawn into the vortex of the struggle for independence.

The Russian Revolution and the formation of the Comintern gave an open call to the workers of the world to combine and dispossess the capitalists and institute a Proletarian Revolution. The setting up of the League of Nations' International Labour Organisation (ILO) gave an international complexion to the labour problem. On 31st October 1920 a trade union on national basis, the All India Trade Union Congress was founded with the initiative of national leaders. By 1927 the number of trade unions affiliated to the AITUC increased to 57 with a total membership of 1,50,555. Earlier the AITUC was influenced by social democratic ideas of the British Labour Party Moderates like N.M. Joshi influenced it saying that the political activities of labour organisations should not go beyond agitation for the amelioration of their economic grievances.

Gandhian philosophy of non-violence, trust and class-collaboration also greatly influenced it, for strikes were employed rarely. In 1926, Trade Union got recognition as legal association under the Trade Union Act. Conditions were laid down for registration and regulation of trade union activities, securing their immunity, both civil and criminal, from prosecution for legitimate activity, both civil and criminal from prosecution for legitimate activities but some restrictions were put on the political activity.

The rise of communist movement in India lent a militant and revolutionary content to the trade Union Movement. The Indian Communists urged them to fight overthrow capitalism and imperialism and organise and Trade Union movement 'on class basis and purge it of all alien basis.' During 1926-27, the

AITUC was divided in two groups called the 'reforming' or the 'Geneva-Amsterdam' group and the 'revolutionary' or the Moscovite group'. The former wanted to affiliate AITUS to the International Federation of Trade Union (IFTU) with the headquarters at Amsterda and the latter desiring affiliation with the Red Labour Union (RITU) organised from Moscow. During 1928, the country witnessed unprecedented unrest. The total number of strikes was 203 involving about 5, 06, 851 people and the loss of 3, 16, 47, 404 working days. The Communist viewpoint prevailed on the question of AITUC affiliation to an international labour body and it became affiliated to the Pan Pacific Secretariat and to the Third International at Moscow. In protest, the moderate group withdrew from AITUC and formed the All India Trade Union Federation.

In order to put a curb on the increasing strength and activities of the Trade Union Movement, a Public Safety Bill was introduced in the Legislative Assembly in 1928 but could not get majority support and had to be issued in the form of an ordinance in 1929. The Trade Disputes Act, 1929 provided for the compulsory appointment of Courts of Enquiry and Conciliation Boards for settling industrial disputes, made strikes illegal in public utility services unless each individual worker planning to go on strike gave an advance notice of one month to the Administration and above all forbade trade union activities of coercive or purely political nature and even sympathetic strikes.

In March 1929, the Government of Lord Irwin arrested the principle leaders of the working class movement and brought them to Meerut for trial on charge of conspiring to deprive the king of his sovereignty of India. The trial lasted for more than three years and Muzaffar Ahmed, Dange, Joglekar, Spratt, Bradley, Usnani and other were convicted to various terms of transportation or rigorous imprisonment. This received much world-wide publicity, but at the same time it dealt a heavy blow to the working class movement and weakened the political role of the working class.

During 1930-34, when the Non-Cooperation Movement was in progress, the Government arrested large number of people, victimized them through repression, legislation and appointment of commissions.

Now the Union leaders started making attempts to unify the different trade union movements. During 1935-36, the AITUC, the Red Trade Union Congress and the National Federation of Trade Unions worked towards unity and was formally united by April 1938.

By 1938, the number of trade unions increased to 296. The Congress ministries in six provinces supported the workers demands. The most successful strike during this period was the Kanpur workers strike which continued for 55 days and involved 10,000 workers.

During this time some beneficial legislations like the Bombay Industrial Disputes Act (1938), the Bombay Shop Assistants Act (1939), the C.P. Maternity Act (1939) and the Bengal Maternity Act (1939) were enacted.

The Second World War again led to the rise in prices and lagging behind of wages. This resulted in many strikes in 1940. In September 1940, the AITUC adopted a resolution disavowing any sympathy for imperialism or fascism.

A communist turned Radical Democratic leader, M.N. Roy formed a Pro-Government Union called the Indian Federation of labour after breaking away from AITUC. The section of the AITUC under the communist influence also showed a pro-Government stance after the Soviet Union joined the war on the side of the Allied Powers. During the Quit India Movement in 1942, the nationalist wing of the AITUC suffered the most.

Communists controlled the AITUC for a long period. In 1944, the national leaders led by Sardar Vallabhbhai Patel organised the Indian National Trade Union Congress.

Movements of Peasants

Under the British rule the ownership of land was conferred on the Zamindars who tried to extort as much as they could from the peasants. The excessive state land revenue demand and exactions of the zamindars drove the peasants into the clutches of the money lender. They were badly exploited.

Important Protests, Revolts and Rebellions

In the 19th century peasant uprisings were in the form of protests, revolts and rebellions primarily aimed at loosening the bonds of feudal exploitation. They protested against enhancement of rent, evictions, and usurious practices of money leaders. Their demands included occupancy rights, commotion of produce rent into money rent etc.

(i) *The Rebellion of Santhale :* The Santhals originally belonged to Manbhum, Barabhum, Hazaribagh, Birbhums, Midnapur and Bankura areas. They left their ancestral homes due to the oppressive demands of the zamindars after the Permanent Settlement of Bengal in 1793 and they settled in the plains along the Rajmahal hills. When the Santhals cleared the lands and raised crops on them, the zamindars from the adjoining areas claimed those lands and started extorting money from the Santhals peasants. The money lenders' also started oppressive measures. The zamindars were invested with the powers of ownership of lands which peasants had customarily considered and cultivated as their own. The moneylender had power to get peasants imprisoned for future to repay debts. The self-respecting Santhal peasants could not reconcile themselves to the preposterous rights conferred by the British government on the zamindars to distrain their properties including their draught cattle and grain crops. The Santhal peasants revolted against the unjust order imposed on them by the British Government, Indian zamindars and money lenders.

In June 1855, under the leadership of two brothers, Sidhu and Kanhu, the Santhals announced their intention to take possession of the country and set up a government between Bhagalpur and Rajmahal. The Company began military operations against the rebels and the rebels took shelter in the thick jungles and carried on their struggle. A British force under Major Burrough suffered a humiliating defeat. In February 1956, the rebel leaders were arrested and the rebellion suppressed with great brutality. The government tried pacification by creation of a separate district of Santhals parganas.

(ii) *Peasant in the 1857 Revolt* : In the Revolt of 1857, the peasants of most of Oudh and Western U.P. forgot their oppressions by the local zamindars and joined hands with them against the British Government. They played a heroic part in the revolt and achieved victories. But they had to pay a heavy price for their patriotism. After the Revolt was crushed, the lands of peasants were treated as the property of the zamindars and they were reduced form the status of proprietors to that of tenants-at-will of their own former lands. The peasants of Meerut division were made to pay some additional cesses as a punitive imposed for participation in the revolt.

(iii) *Bengal Indigo Cultivators' Strike, 1860* : The indigo agitation in Bengal in 1859-60, was the greatest peasant movements of modern era. The revolt was directed against British planters who oppressed the poor peasants by forcing them to produce indigo at uneconomic rates and resorting to illegal beatings and detention. In April 1860 all the cultivators of Barasat sub-division and in the districts of Pabna and Nadia resorted to strikes. They refused to sow any indigo. The strike spread to Jessore, Khulna, Rajshahi, Dacca, Malda, Dinajphe, and other piaces in Bengal.

The Government received a set back in face of such solid unity and in apprehension of further agrarian uprising ordered a notification to be issued enjoining on the police to protect the *ryot* (peasant) in the possession of his lands, on which he was at liberty to sow any crop he liked, without interference on the part of the planter or anyone else. The planter could move the civil court for breach of contract. An Indigo Commission was also appointed in 1860. Its recommendations were embodied in Act IV of 1862. Gradually, the indigo planters of Bengal moved to Bihar and Uttar Pradesh. The indigo peasants of Bihar revolted on a large scale in Darbhanga and Champaran in 1866-68. the peasants of Jessore in Bengal revolted in 1883 and 1889-90.

(iv) *East Bengal Agrarian Unrest (1872-76)* : During the 1870s agrarian unrest broke out in East Bengal. The all-powerful zamindars of Bengal were notorious for the oppression of their tenants and they ejected, harassed and illegally seized the property, including crops and to prevent the peasants from acquiring occupancy rights. From 1872 to 1876 they united in no rent unions and attacked zamindars and their agents in different parts of East Bengal. Peasant resistance collapsed only when the Government intervened and took strong action against them nevertheless, peasant unrest broke out time and again in the succeeding years. Ultimately, the Government had to undertake legislation to protect the peasants from the worst aspects of the Zamindari system.

(v) *Satyagraha in Champaran (1917-18)* : The European Planters of Champaran district in the north western part of Bihar practised illegal and inhuman methods of indigo cultivation. They under the Tinkathia system compelled the peasants to grow indigo on 3/20 part of their land and send the same to the British planters at prices fixed by them.

Gandhiji along with Rajendra Prasad enquired into the condition of peasants in the district and instigated them to employ the method of open, disciplined, non-violent non-coperation or *satyagraha.* The Government arrested Gandhiji for instigating the peasants. Later on, the Government appointed an Enquiry Committee with Mahatma Gandhi as a member which resulted in the Champaran Agrarian Act which freed the tenants from the special imposts levied by the indigo planters.

(vi) *Satyagraha in Kaira (1918) :* In the Kaira(Kheda) district of Gujarat crop failures and drought brought misery to the peasants in 1918. The Government officials insisted on collecting the full land revenue. At the instance of Gandhiji, the peasants launched a *Satyagraha* and refused to pay the land revenue which resulted in their imprisonment. Ultimately, in June 1918, the Government was forced to surrender and a settlement was made with the peasants and their demands conceded.

(vii) *Rebellion by Moplahs (1921) :* The Moplah formed a majority of the population in the Eranad and Walluvanad Talukas and they followed the Khilafat leaders. These Moplahs or Muslims worked as agrarian tenants of Hindu landlords.

The Moplah rebellion of 1921 stemmed from their grievances of continued landlord oppression and British Government's anti-khilafat policies. Both the Congress and Khilafat parties had begun to organise a movement for tenancy reforms which was strongly opposed by the big landlords of Malabar.

The immediate provocation for the revolt was provided by E.F. Thomas, the District magistrate of Eranad Talika, who on 20th August 1921 raided a mosque at

Tirurangadim in a bid to arrest Ali Musahar who was declared as their Raja by the Muslims. Soon the rebellion spread to Walluvanad and Ponnani Taliks and they sacked the police stations, looted the government treasuries and destroyed the records of debts and mortgages in the courts and registries. For six months there was no British rule throughout the region, for the rebels had killed some European officers.

Later on, the government sent a strong contingent to deal with the rebellion which lent communal colour to it. The rebels killed about 500 Hindus, sacked about 100 temples and forcibly converted 2,500 Hindus to Islam. By the end of the year 1921 the government crushed the rebellion resulting in the killing of about 10,000 Muslims. The leaders of the rebels were shot, hundreds of their followers were hanged or deported to the Andamans and 61 prisoners died of suffocation.

The ruthless crushing of Moplah rebellion so greatly demoralised the community that thereafter they dared not take part in any peasant revolt or national political activity till the British rule lasted in India.

(viii) *Revolts of Chauri-Chaura (1922)* : In Chauri Chaura village in Gorakhpur district of Uttar Pradesh some of the peasants and volunteers started vigorous picketing of foreign cloth and liquor shops in the bazaar against the oppressive government policies.

On February 1st, 1922, the local police officer visited the bazaar with police force and beat some of the volunteers and peasants engaged in the picketing of the shops. As a result, a large number of people from the surrounding villages came to Chauri-Chaura on February 4th, 1922 and marched in a big crowd to the police station. There was a scuffle and the police constables opened fire and killed a few persons. All the constables at the police station were over-powered and both the police station and the placement in it were set on fire.

(ix) *Vizag Revolt (1923)* : The Vizag tribes waged a two year war against the British Government under their leader, Sri Rama Razu. Their demand was the free use of forest land and produce and ultimately they demanded the establishment for the whole of the area. The British Government took strong action against the rebels and killed thousands of them along with their leaders. This revolution was also called the Rampa rebellion. The Rampa rebellion under the leadership of Shri Rama Razu in the hilly areas of the Rampa sub-division of the agency tracts in the modern Andhra Pradesh between 1922 and 1924, cost heavily for the British Raj in terms of men, resources, military equipments and strategy. Rampa rebellion was a political struggle in which Sri Rama Razu organised the tribal people in Vizag Agency against British rulers. The Rampa armed rebellion was the reaction to the atrocities committed by the British police officials on the poor and innocent tribals inhabiting agency tracts.

(x) *Peasant Movements between 1921-30* : Peasants launched a number of Satyagraha campaigns against unjust laws and imposts during this period. In 1921 a struggle was launched against land tax in Bardoli, Pedanadipadu and Duddukuru. In .1921, 1931-34 struggles were launched against Karnataka Forest Laws in 1921 and 1931-33 against the rent exactions in Uttar Pradesh and Bihar. In 1931, the anti-resettlement campaigns were launched in Godavari and Krishna Deltas and a number of peasant struggles against the" landlords of Venkatagiri. In 1939, Tsadumu and Munagala were organised in the south and land satyagraha was launched in Bihar. In 1939 the anti zamindari fight took place in Bengal and Andhra and canal duties struggle took place in Punjab and Bengal. In 1937-42, the jute prices struggle and the debt relief agitation took place in Bengal.

(xi) *Bardoli Satyagraha in Bardoli (1929-30) :* Sardar Patel with the help of Mahatma Gandhi organised the Bardoli peasants against the resettlement enhancements proposed by the government. The peasants braved all risks like the loss of their cattle and ancestral lands and eviction from their villages and ultimately won in 1929.

Again in 1930 the peasant rose in revolt, refused to pay taxes faced the auction sales and the eventual loss of almost all of their lands but refused to submit to the government. However all their lands were returned to them when the Congress came to power in 1937-39.

(xii) *First Time Kisan Sabhas :* The kisan leaders became aware of the inner contradictions in Congress agrarian policy. The Congress was virtually indifferent to inter-agrarian relations between landlords on the one hand and tenants, cultivators and agricultural labour on the other hand and between the rich farmer and share croppers or landless labours. The propaganda of the communists and other left parties created class consciousness among the peasants that led to the formation of Kisan Sabhas.

In the 1920s Kisan Sabhas were organised in Bengal, Punjab and UP. The Andhra Provincial Ryots Association was formed in 1928. On April 11th, 1936, the first All India Kisan Sabha was formed at Lucknow. Its objective was to secure complete freedom from economic exploitation and achievement of full economic and political power for peasants and workers and all exploited classes.

The All Indians Kisan Sabha also demanded a moratorium on debts, abolition of land revenue and rent, licensing of money lenders, minimum wages, for agricultural workers, fair prices for sugarcane and commercial crops, irrigation facilities, abolition of zamindari and the vesting of land in the tiller of the soil. The Kisan Sabha launched various agitations like:-

(i) Anti-settlement agitation against zamindar's *zulum* in Andhra Pradesh.

(ii) Struggles against zamindar's exploitation in Bihar and U.P.

(iii) In 1936 an agitation against Bakshat in Bihar was started. Bakshat was zamindar's special land which Was cultivated by tenants on condition that a certain portion of the produce will be given by them to the land-owner as rent. The zamindars sought to bring more and more land under this category in a bid to prevent tenants from claiming occupancy rights. Tenants were evicted on a large scale on one pretext or the other.

Movement for Civil Rights

Definition of Civil Rights : Those basic privileges which were extended to all the citizens irrespective of distinctions of caste, creed, religion or sex can be classified as Civil Rights. This is indispensable for the development of an individual. Some of the major Civil Rights will now be studied.

Right to Life : Security of one's life is perhaps the most important guaranteed by the state without security of life enjoying other rights is not possible. Thus state makes elaborate arrangement in this respect. The human life is considered very precious. So in countries like Holland, Switzerland capital punishment has been abolished and attempt to suicide is considered punishable.

Right to Liberty : The mere existence of life without the freedom to move would equate humans with plants. Thus to enjoy and fully utilize the right to life, right to liberty enables the citizens to freely exercise their inner faculties without obstacles.

Right to Education : Every individual has the right to acquire basic education. As Laski said that all the citizens have the right to such an education which will make him fit for the task of citizenship. Education is also necessary to earn a livelihood.

Right to Property : This implies absolute right to enjoy one's property. However the desire to acquire more property has been the main source of corruption in Indian politics.

Right to Religion : In modern democratic nations people have been given complete freedom to pursue their own religion. The state neither forces its citizens to adopt a particular religion nor discriminates on the basis of religion. However the state has the power to regulate the activities of those religious institutions which spread communalism and threaten national integrity.

Right to Express : Democracy implies the freedom to express. Every individual can openly discuss about his thoughts, views through the various forms of expression like newspaper, electronic media, processions. The ideal example of this type of civil right granted to an individual and also exercised by people is in Hude Park of London. Here on Sundays everyone can freely talk about their views. However this right is also provided within specific limits. It cannot be used to spread anti-patriotic sentiments.

Right to Equality : This means that the state recognizes that all men are born equal and hence will be treated equal. There shall be no discrimination on the basis of birth, race, sex, religion, community. All shall be given equal opportunities. However the State believes that some people are below the line of equality. Thus to encourage them, state follows protective discrimination. In India the scheduled castes and scheduled tribes, handicapped have reserved seats in all spheres of life.

(1) Civil rights are those rights which are legally protected as fundamental rights enjoyed by everyone respective of her status.

(2) These can be divided into two categories : Basic human right for fair treatment of an individual and political rights, which are vital for a healthy society. This includes all those rights which are taken for granted in liberal democracy.

In the late 1950's, a mass movement broke out in United States of America. It began as a non-violent protest action against the policy of racial segregation in southern region. It was the first major breakthrough regarding the equal rights legislation since post-Civil War.

Since 1787, the negroes of America were denied all types of constitutional guarantee. In 1865 in the 13th, 14th, 15th constitutional amendments for the first time these black Americans were promised fundamental citizenship right. By 1900 eighteen states of U.S.A. had legislated a public policy against racial discrimination. But opposite happened down South. New laws eroded the franchise and reinforced segregational practise.

During the II World War another progressive step was taken. All discriminations in the defence industry were banned. After the war, the armed forces were desegregated. In 1954, in a decisive judgement, the Supreme Court announced that the separate educational facilities were unequal and hence unconstitutional.

This historic decision sparked off a mass movement on the part of the blacks to end segregation and inequality, still practised by many southern whites. On 5th December 1955, a black women, Mrs. Rosa Parks refused to move to the negro section of a bus in Montgomery. She was arrested which was marked by one day boycott to show their sympathetic in her favours. The guidance of Rev. Dr. Martin Lurther King, Jr, succeeded in transforming a spontaneous racial protest into a massive resistance movement. Picketting and boycotting spread rapidly consequently the bus company was forced to desegregate its facilities followed by desegregation in the departmental stores, super-markets, libraries and theatres.

By September 1961, 70,000 students had participated, 36, 000 arrested and more than 100 cities in 20 states affected. The movement reached its climax in August 1963 with the great march to Washington D.C., to protest racial discrimination.

Impact of the Movement

(1) Strong civil rights platform was adopted by both the Democratic and Republican parties.

(2) By encouraging this movement John F. Kennedy won elections but few steps were taken towards actual implantation.

(3) In 1964 a civil rights bill was passed, forbidding discrimination at public places and even threatened to withhold federal funds from those who still persisted in maintaining segregation.

(4) This united the widely disparate elements of the black community.

Bibliography

Aided, M. F. and Ruhela, S. P. : *The Preferred Future Development in Somalia*, Vikas Publishing House, New Delhi, 1999.

Andrew Kernohan : *Liberalism, Equality, and Cultural Oppression*, Cambridge, New York, 1998.

Anne Phillips : *Democracy and Difference*, Oxford, New York, 1993.

Avnon, D. : *Nationalism and its Practice*, Routledge, London, 1999.

Bela, Balassa, and Jesdijk, Ardy Stont : *Economic Integration among Developing Countries*, IBRD, Washington D.C., 1974.

Bennet, Lee : *International Organisations*, Prentice Hall, New Jersey, 1985.

Bose, P. : *Communism and Communist Systems : Some Reflections*, Deep & Deep Publications, New Delhi, 1995.

Brain Urquhart : *A Global Affair : An Inside Look at the United Nations*, Jones & Janello, New York, 1998.

Chand Attar : *Democracy's in Asia*, Goodwill Publishers, London, 1993.

Chandra, P. : *International Politics*, Vikas Publishing House, New Delhi, 1996.

Chaurasia, R. S. : *History of Western Political Thought*, Atlantic Publishers, New Delhi, 2001.

Chowdhary, R. : *Ideology & Politics of Ruling Parties in India*, Deep & Deep Publications, New Delhi, 1991.

Claude Lefort : *Democracy and Political Theory*, Minnesota Publishers, 1988.

David Shambaugh : *The Modern Chinese State*, Cambridge, New York, 2000.

Diwan, P., Diwan, P. : *Amending Powers and Constitutional Amendments*, Deep & Deep Publications, New Delhi, 1997.

Donald J. Puchala : *Theory and History in International Relation*, Routledge, London, 2003.

Edwards, G. C. : *Government in America : People and Policy*, Longman, New York, 2001.

Fiorina, M. P. : *The New American Democracy*, Allyn & Bacon, London, 1998.

Fischer Mary Ellen : *Establishing Democracies*, Oxford, New York, 1996.

Fred W. Friendly & Martha J. H. Ellitt : *The Constitution that Delicate Balance : Landmark Cases that Shaped the Constitutions*, Oxford, New York, 1984.

George C. Herring : *America's Longest War : The United States and Vietnam, 1950-1975* McGraw Hill Publishers, 1996.

Ghosh, B. N. : *Political Economy of Development and Underdevelopment*, Deep & Deep Publications, New Delhi, 1996.

Gopalakrishnan, R. : *Socio-Political Framework in North-East India*, Vikas Publishing House, New Delhi, 1987.

—— : *Foundations of Political System and Sociological Aspects*, Deep & Deep Publications, New Delhi, 1997.

Gupta, D. C. : *Indian Government and Politics*, Vikas Publishing House, New Delhi, 1989.

Gupta, U. N. : *Indian Parliamentary Democracy*, Atlantic Publishers, New Delhi, 2003.

——: *Comparative Governments*, Atlantic Publishers, New Delhi, 2000.

Jim Shultz : *The Democracy Owners' Manual : A Practical Guide to Changing the World*,Oxford, New York, 2002.

John Dunn : *Contemporary Crisis of the Nation State*, Blackwell, London, 1995.

Kush, Satyendra : *Encyclopaedic Dictionary of Political Science*, Sarup & Sons, New Delhi, 2003.

Mukherjee, S. and Ramaswamy, S. : *Great Western Politics Thinkers*, Deep & Deep Publications, New Delhi, 2000.

Narasaiah, M. L. : *Gender Inequity and Poverty*, Discovery Publishing House, New Delhi, 2004.

Narasimhan, C. V. : *The United Nations*, Vikas Publishing House, New Delhi, 1995.

Nolla, Eduardo : *Liberty Equality Democracy*, MacMillan, London, 1992.

Pillai, K. G. : *Political Philosophy of Rammanohar Lohia*, Deep & Deep Publications, New Delhi, 1994.

Prasad, Bimal : *India's Foreign Policy in a Challenging World*, Vikas Publishing House, New Delhi, 2000.

Prasad, Ravi D. M. : *Changeology : A New Discipline*, Deep & Deep Publications, New Delhi, 2004.

Richard Hofferbert : *Parties and Democracy : Party Structure and Party Performance in Old and New Democracies*, Blackwell, London, 1998.

Sims, R. L. : *Political History of Modern Japan*, Vikas Publishing House, New Delhi, 1995.

Singh, Naunihal : *Strategy of International Business*, South Asian Publishers, New Delhi, 1986.

Talbot, Phillip : *South Asia in the World Today*, University of Chicago Press, Chicago, 1989.

Thiagarajan, J. : *Governance and the Electoral Process*, Vikas Publishing House, New Delhi, 1995.

Varma, S. P. : *Modern Political Theory*, Vikas Publishing House, New Delhi, 1997.

Wickramasinghe, N. : *Ethnic Politics in Colonial Sri Lanka*, Vikas Publishing House, New Delhi, 1997.

Wolf Mendi : *Japan's Asia Policy : Regional Security and Global Interests*, Routledge, London, 1995.

Index

O

P

Q

R

□□□